Nᴇᴡ Dɪᴍᴇɴsɪᴏɴs *of*
Eᴄᴏɴᴏᴍɪᴄ
Gʟᴏʙᴀʟɪᴢᴀᴛɪᴏɴ
Surge of Outward Foreign Direct Investment from Asia

New Dimensions *of*
ECONOMIC
GLOBALIZATION

Surge of Outward Foreign Direct Investment from Asia

Editors

Ramkishen S. Rajan
George Mason University, USA

Rajiv Kumar
Indian Council for Research on International Economic Relations, India

Nicola Virgill
George Mason University, USA

World Scientific

NEW JERSEY · LONDON · SINGAPORE · BEIJING · SHANGHAI · HONG KONG · TAIPEI · CHENNAI

Published by

World Scientific Publishing Co. Pte. Ltd.

5 Toh Tuck Link, Singapore 596224

USA office: 27 Warren Street, Suite 401-402, Hackensack, NJ 07601

UK office: 57 Shelton Street, Covent Garden, London WC2H 9HE

British Library Cataloguing-in-Publication Data
A catalogue record for this book is available from the British Library.

NEW DIMENSIONS OF ECONOMIC GLOBALIZATION
Surge of Outward Foreign Direct Investment from Asia

ISBN-13 978-981-279-310-2
ISBN-10 981-279-310-0

Typeset by Stallion Press
Email: enquiries@stallionpress.com

Printed in Singapore.

Preface

This volume focuses on the issue of outward foreign direct investment (OFDI) from developing Asia in general, and South–South FDI more specifically.

The chapters in this volume were initially presented at an international workshop held on 25–26 April 2007 at the Indian council for Research on International Economic Relations (ICRIER) in New Delhi to discuss the interim results. Of the 11 papers presented at the workshop, 9 were selected after appropriate review and editing. The unifying introductory chapter written by the editors provides and overall frame for the volume.

The volume is rather unique in the sense of the country coverage. It focuses on China, India, and South–East Asia, rather than just having a sub regional-specific focus. The chapters in this volume tackle important policy issues and use rigorous empirical analysis to address the issues. The volume has been written in a manner that is accessible to policymakers, students, and business/financial journalists interested in contemporary issues in Asia economic development in general, and in the emergence of outward FDI flows from developing Asia in particular.

The authors would like to acknowledge generous financial support by international Development Research Center (IDRC), Canada, Radha Chawla and other colleagues at ICRIER for valuable academic support and logistics assistance.

The authors would also like to acknowledge Ms Sandhya and her colleagues at World Scientific Publishing Company (Singapore) for their highly professional and personable editorial services.

Rajiv Kumar (New Delhi, India)

Ramkishen S. Rajan and Nicola Virgill (Virginia, USA)

Contents

Section I

Introduction and Overview

Chapter 1

Overview: Explaining the New Surge of Outward Foreign Direct Investment (FDI) from Asia

Ramkishen S. Rajan, Rajiv Kumar and Nicola Virgill

1. Introduction

There has been a dramatic expansion of foreign direct investment (FDI) across the globe over the last 30 years. Indeed, between 1970 and 2005, total world outward foreign direct investment (OFDI) flows have increased from US$ 14 billion to almost US$ 1,215 billion (UNCTAD, 2007). The data reveal that much of this OFDI has occurred through cross-border merger and acquisition (M&A) activity rather than entirely new (greenfield) investments, and that the majority of this OFDI has been directed into the services sector (UNCTAD, 2006, p. 105). While the lion's share of OFDI flows and stocks still originate from developed economies, since the late 1980s, developing economies have also emerged as important sources of OFDI. Developing economies have seen their share of OFDI increasing from 3 percent of global OFDI over the period 1978–1980 to 12.3 percent of total OFDI during the period 2003–2005 (UNCTAD, 2006, p. 7).

The increasing, but somewhat volatile volumes of Asian OFDI flows (see Table 1) have given rise to some important questions for policymakers: Why has this trend emerged and what are the implications for the region and individual countries of this trend? What is the magnitude of these flows, and can they be expected to persist or even accelerate over time? In which countries are these investments most

3

Table 1: Direct investment abroad (FDI Outward Flows) for Asia and selected Asian countries. (US Dollars at current prices in millions).

Economy/Region	1980	1990	1995	2000	2002	2004	2005	2006
Japan	2,385	48,024	22,630	31,558	32,281	30,951	45,781	50,266
Developing Asia	1,146	10,948	44,678	82,230	35,427	87,461	77,747	117,067
East Asia	150	9,574	33,558	71,973	27,555	62,924	49,836	74,099
China	—	830	2,000	916	2,518	5,498	12,261	16,130
Hong Kong, China	82	2,448	25,000	59,352	17,463	45,716	27,201	43,459
Republic of Korea	26	1,052	3,552	4,999	2,617	4,658	4,298	7,129
Taiwan Province of China	42	5,243	2,983	6,701	4,886	7,145	6,028	7,399
South Asia	4	9	126	524	1,723	2,247	2,579	9,820
India	4	6	119	509	1,679	2,179	2,495	9,676
South–East Asia	394	2,328	11,627	8,225	4,681	14,212	11,918	19,095
Indonesia	6	(11)	1,319	150	182	3,408	3,065	3,418
Malaysia	201	129	2,488	2,026	1,905	2,061	2,972	6,041
Singapore	98	2,034	6,787	5,915	2,329	8,074	5,034	8,626
Thailand	3	154	887	(22)	171	76	552	790

Source: UNCTAD (2007).

concentrated in and what are the policy actions required, if any, to ensure that positive impacts of intra-Asian ODFI flows can be maximized for the region? How do these rising intra-Asian FDI flows compare with investments by Asian multinationals to the rest of the world? Should governments in developing countries like China and India, with large domestic investment needs, promote the outward expansion of multinationals from their countries? What is the distinction between FDI flows in the North and the South? And what are the challenges faced by emerging market multinationals and future prospects of intra-Asian FDI flows.

This volume attempts to provide answers to some of these questions using a combination of statistics, survey analysis, and firm-specific evidence. This chapter provides a broad overview of the key issues involved in understanding the rationale underlying the rise in Asian OFDI and its magnitudes. This is achieved not by attempting to summarize the main findings of each chapter, but instead by trying to weave together the country case studies provided in the subsequent chapters to understand the rationale for the emergence Asian OFDI.

2. Data Limitations and Issues

Before proceeding it should be emphasized — as highlighted by various chapters in this volume — that there are a host of problems when analyzing FDI data, especially in the case of developing economies. In **Chapter 3, Rabin Hattari and Ramkishen S. Rajan** highlight that FDI outflow and inflow data between country pairs in many cases do not match and indeed, some types of information have only begun to be recorded by some countries. UNCTAD (2006) notes "the divergence in trends in FDI inflows and outflows reflects differences in the way countries compile FDI data" (p. 5). In **Chapter 2, Dilek Aykut** find that the recording of OFDI flows in some countries is a recent occurrence and that some countries' do not include all the relevant components of OFDI. In other countries, FDI statistics are limited to the transactions of larger companies. In **Chapter 5, Cheng and Stough** note in those cases where the data on OFDI is collected by the approving authority, the data will under-represent the volumes of

OFDI as it would necessarily exclude those projects which may not require approval. Conversely, however, not all approvals are always translated into actual inflows.

Another important issue in examining OFDI data is determining the true country of origin. Low, Ramstetter and Yeung (1996) point out that there are two possible ways to account for OFDI. The first is by the "country of capital source" and the second is "by country of ownership" (pp. 2–3). According to the authors, the latter takes into consideration investments which are funneled through offshore centers as "it makes little sense to attribute such investments to the tax havens themselves" (p. 3). Such distinctions are particularly relevant in the case of accounting for OFDI between China, Hong Kong and Macau.[1]

3. The Intra-Asian OFDI Phenomenon

There has been a rise in the importance of South–South FDI flows as well as realignment in terms of the sources of OFDI.

UNCTAD (2006), for example, states that:

> Data on FDI outflows from developing countries to the increasing dynamism of this group of countries as sources of FDI... The increasing importance of FDI from developing countries reflects stronger ownership advantages of developing-country firms, related somewhat to growing importance of their home countries in the world economy (UNCTAD, 2006, p. 6).

Asian economies have generally replaced Latin America and the Caribbean as OFDI developing-country leaders (UNCTAD, 2006, p. 112). For example, Singapore, Hong Kong and Malaysia have been among the developing economies with the largest M&A deals between 1987 and 2005 (UNCTAD, 2006, p. 111). In **Chapter 2, Aykut** finds that while global M&A transactions have been driven by

---

[1] In **Chapter 3, Hattari and Rajan** also highlight the importance of offshore financial centres as sources and hosts of Asian FDI.

actual and expected stock price increases, the response in Asia has generally been more subdued because of lower levels of privatization deals. However, this is changing.

Traditionally, investments have flowed into developing Asia from Western economies and Japan. In **Chapter 4, Daisuke Hiratsuka** discusses the extent of and rationale for Japan's FDI to the rest of Asia. Increasingly, emerging Asian economies are also becoming important sources of FDI. In fact, after 1995, ODFI flows from developing Asian economies to all regions generally surpassed outflows from Japan (see Table 1). Certainly, Hong Kong and China have emerged as leading sources of foreign investment in terms of OFDI volumes. Other Asian economies, specifically, Taiwan, Singapore and Malaysia have also gained in importance particularly in the aftermath of the Asian crisis. OFDI flows from each of these three countries were over US$1 billion in 2005.

In **Chapter 3, Hattari and Rajan** explain that the largest sources of FDI throughout the region have expectedly come from the pre-crisis Asian Tigers (Hong Kong, Singapore, Taiwan and Korea) and in recent years, emerging economies such as India and China have become increasingly important. Having described the OFDI boom in East Asia since 1997, the authors examine the determinants of intra-Asian FDI flows using an augmented gravity model which they apply to a panel data set. They find that proximity, both cultural and geographical, in addition to the usual economic determinants (i.e. market size, economic growth) and institutional variables played an important role in determining where countries invested. This is broadly consistent with other studies of the determinants of OFDI in both developed and developing economies (see UNCTAD, 2006; Sethi *et al.*, 2003).

It is clear from the evidence presented in papers that the Asian OFDI experience has been extremely varied. The various country-specific chapters in this volume have identified four major factors that explain recent trends in Asian OFDI. First, there have been "Push factors" related to conditions in local economies and markets which have become saturated, or have become increasingly unstable due to policy changes or economic shocks. As a result, investments are pushed out from these countries. Second, a significant portion of OFDI flows have been driven by governments through their "national champion" strategies. Indeed, many governments in Asia have explicitly pursued OFDI as a development strategy. Third, a large part of the intra-Asian FDI flows is affected by the "Greater China" effect — that is FDI flows between mainland China, Hong Kong, Taiwan and the Chinese diaspora throughout Asia. Finally, in more recent times, OFDI has been spurred by more traditional FDI motives and facilitated by FDI liberalization policies promoted throughout Asia and many other developing countries. It should be noted, however, that these four drivers are not mutually exclusive and OFDI from many Asian economies is actually a result of a combination of more than one factor.

3.1. *Push Factors (Exhausted Markets)*

One of the key motivators for the increase in Asian OFDI emanated from Asian economies where local investment opportunities were exhausted or became less attractive due to poor domestic investment policies and crisis events. As a result, OFDI flowed to relatively more attractive destinations. For instance, in **Chapter 4, Hiratsuka** finds that Japan's low population growth rates and maturing markets have resulted in the increased importance to Japanese corporations of profits from their overseas operations.

In **Chapter 7, Nathalie Aminian, K.C. Fung and Chelsea Lin** find that overseas investment decisions by Taiwanese firms have been motivated by both a desire to achieve lower costs of production by locating production in China and also by push factors such as the declining political stability in Taiwan that is perceived to adversely affect prospects in domestic markets. Sutter (2002) also points to growing political and economic pressures within Taiwan which facilitated the flow of OFDI to China (pp. 527 and 532).

Even in the case of Singapore, discussed in **Chapter 8** by **Goldstein and Pananond,** the authors note that the country's small markets and leveling business prospects (features of an exhausted market) have facilitated the push for investment abroad.

In **Chapter 9, Mohamed Ariff and Gregore Lopez** find that the key drivers for the increasing levels of Malaysian OFDI have been the structural and institutional changes in the economy. The increasingly liberalized capital and investment policy regimes have permitted the overseas expansion of efficiency, market and resource-seeking Malaysian firms. In addition, the cyclical economic factors that have seen a relative slow-down of economic activity and the resulted exhaustion of the local market have also pushed investment abroad. While OFDI collapsed to its 1980s levels in the immediate aftermath of the Asian financial crisis— since 2001, Malaysian OFDI has generally been on an upward trend. Malaysian OFDI was largely channeled to Labuan, an Asian offshore financial center to disguise the actual identity of firms taking this route. However, substantial investments were also made in Singapore, Indonesia, Hong Kong and China. Interestingly, the services sector made up the largest share of OFDI while Malaysian government-linked companies and majority-owned Malaysian private companies were the key participants in OFDI in Malaysia.

In **Chapter 10, Reza Siregar and Anton Gunawan** emphasize that the domestic investment environment matters and can create an incentive for local businesses to invest overseas. While Indonesia's OFDI is considerably smaller than some of the more prominent Asian economies, the surge of OFDI in recent years provides an important opportunity for analysis. Using economic and financial risk rating and an investment profile indicators from the International Country Risk Guide (ICRG) database, the authors find that deterioration in the investment climate and, in particular, the increase in investment risk, has contributed to the rise of OFDI in Indonesia. The authors also point to high start-up costs and changes in labor laws which have raised costs and worsened the investment environment. This has induced domestic Indonesian enterprises to invest abroad. Indeed the authors find that as Indonesian firms strengthened their financial positions, they opted to invest overseas rather than expanding operations locally.

3.2. *National Champion Strategy*

For another group of Asian countries, governments consciously pursued a "national champion" strategy to allow their firms to gain market share, achieve lower production costs and improve access to resources and raw materials. Countries like China and India, for example, have promoted "national champions" with aggressive investment agendas. These strategies were facilitated by the adoption of liberal policy developments and as UNCTAD (2006) points out "Asia and Africa were the leading regions in terms of introducing further sectoral liberalization." (pp. 23–24).

Cai (1999) acknowledges the important role of the Chinese government in facilitating Chinese OFDI in support of its development strategy and states:

> It was after the Chinese government initiated its open-door policy at the end of the 1970s that Chinese outward FDI began to develop...[Those] early outward FDI activities were mainly conducted by centrally controlled state-owned enterprises, that is, various long-established specialized foreign trade corporates (FTCs) and newly created foreign oriented corporations (FBOCs) (p. 859).[2]

As recently as 2000, Deng (2006) finds that China had pursued a "Go Global" policy which encouraged its state-owned enterprises to undertake strategic overseas investments (p. 72). Similarly, Wu and Chen (2001) also noted that the initial Chinese OFDI surge was led by "state-owned enterprises, with an emphasis on labour collaboration and contracting" (p. 1237).

In the case of Singapore, Low, Ramstetter and Yeung (1996) note:

> Government-linked companies dominate[d] outward FDI by locally controlled firms in Singapore. Another difference [between Singapore and Hong Kong] is the relatively conspicuous role the government play[ed] in Singapore's economy, in particular, the government's active promotion of the development of corporate regionalization strategies and outward FDI in recent years (p. 10).

Indeed, in **Chapter 8, Goldstein and Pananond** also point to the significance of Singapore's state-owned company in explaining the

---

[2] Buckley *et al.* (2005) also acknowledge that China's "Open Door" policy and the introduction of Special Economic Zones also facilitated the inflow of FDI into China (pp. 4 and 7).

increase in Singaporean OFDI. However, while these government-linked companies were prominent, OFDI was also driven by market factors such as the need to secure lower costs of production and improve competitiveness, avoid trade quotas and to reduce vulnerability. Therefore, we see that in some Asian economies, governments played an important role in promoting OFDI through their state-owed or linked enterprises.

3.3. *The "Greater China" Effect*

A third rationale for the large increase in intra-Asian OFDI relates specifically to investment within and between *Greater China* (i.e. mainland China, Hong Kong and Taiwan and the Chinese diaspora throughout Asia). China is Asia's largest recipient of inward FDI (Kim and Mah, 2006, p. 896; UNCTAD, 2006). In their discussion of the development strategies of India and China, Huang and Khanna (2003) note that one core difference between the two emerging economies is that inward FDI for China was the engine of economic growth, "serv[ing] as a substitute for domestic entrepreneurship" (p. 75). For China, in particular, the business environment was so complicated for and disadvantageous to local firms that entrepreneurs decided to "roundtrip" through Greater China to take advantage of FDI incentives within mainland China offered to foreign firms (Huang and Khanna, 2003, p. 76).[3] Low, Ramstetter and Yeung (1996) further observe:

> The observation of significant Chinese FDI in Hong Kong is consistent with the often heard assertion that much of what the Chinese

---

[3] Kim and Mah (2006) find that "Beijing still has many problems in its FDI regime, including frequent changes in economic policies, arbitrary official interpretations of FDI regulations, disputes with investment partners in joint ventures, difficulties in securing raw materials for production, and low productivity because of insufficient social overhead capital." (p. 894). Wu and Chen (2001) also state that "since equity markets remain relatively small in size, and are subject to discretionary administrative intervention in China, offshore investments can offer protection against domestic inflation and exchange rate depreciation. China's enterprises have the incentive to set up subsidiaries overseas to achieve a more balanced portfolio, and to evade foreign exchange and other restrictions with which they are saddled at home...In other words, for Chinese enterprises, overseas development is a further possible destination for capital flight" (p. 1251).

record as FDI from Hong Kong is in fact investment originating in local Chinese firms, but circulated through Hong Kong in order to benefit from the incentives offered to foreign investors (p. 7).

In **Chapter 7, Aminian, Fung and Lin** explore the outward FDI experiences of Hong Kong and Taiwan. In particular, they examine the increasing flows to China from these two countries after the Asian financial crisis. Indeed, based on UNCTAD's Outward FDI Performance Index, Hong Kong is an "exceptional exporter" of FDI compared to its size in the world economy with a large share of its FDI channeled into services. Hong Kong, with its more flexible business environment is providing an important entryway into China. Some of these investments also appear to be funneled through special purpose offshore vehicles in the British Virgin Islands and the Cayman Islands.

Additionally, **Aminian, Fung and Lin** point out that a large portion of the investment flows were actually "round tipped" to China via Hong Kong. This is consistent with findings by Low, Ramstetter and Yeung (1996) that Hong Kong has been used both as a "springboard for investment by foreign-controlled companies in South–East Asia as well as in China" (p. 8) and "also as a regional center of decision making and control in its own right" (p. 22). Such investments, which are eventually intended for China and Hong Kong, "may have been preferentially diverted...in the few years prior to WTO accession" (Buckley *et al.*, 2005, p. 14).

Chang (1995) also points out that a large share of China's foreign investment is actually "overseas Chinese...living outside of mainland China" (p. 957) and that "as Hong Kong's economy matured and China undertook economic reforms in the late 1970's, Hong Kong's labor-intensive manufacturing began transferring their production to the mainland to take advantage of its cheap land and labor" (p. 961). Huang and Khanna (2003) offer that "China has a large and wealthy diaspora that has long been eager to help the motherland, and its money has been warmly received" (p. 75). Indeed, in some Chinese towns these investments were quite substantial.

In **Chapter 10, Siregar and Gunawan** find that ethnic Chinese Indonesians were the major source of OFDI in Indonesia. Similar forces explain increasing Taiwanese investments in China (Chang 1995, p. 962). The author notes that a significant part of FDI flows to China from Hong Kong, Japan, the United States, and South–East Asia may actually be "the activities of Taiwanese firms in disguise" " with much of this investment attracted to the Guangdong region and the Shenzhen special economic zone (pp. 962–963). Buckley *et al.* (2005) point out that firms from Hong Kong and Taiwan, "enjoy transaction cost-related ownership advantages in these places [Fujian and Guangdong provinces] relative to other investor nationalities because of geographic proximity, cultural convergence and familial ties" (p.11).

In **Chapter 4, Hiratsuka** also shows that Japanese FDI began to flow into China as China's business and investment climate began to improve in the early 1990's. However, Japan eventually instituted a "China plus one" policy such that Japanese firms also chose one ASEAN country in addition to China when choosing hosts for their OFDI.

While there has been a great deal of attention paid to Chinese FDI inflows, it is important to realize that China is also an important investor throughout Greater China. Cai (1999) points out that the bulk of China's OFDI was channeled to neighboring, culturally-similar countries as investments in the services and natural resources sectors (pp. 864–865). Furthermore, Cai (1999) acknowledges the large flows from China to Hong Kong (p. 858). Wu and Chen (2001) also note that "the main reason for the heavy investment in Asia was the big push by Chinese capital into Hong Kong and Macao" (p. 1245).

In **Chapter 5, Cheng and Stough** define three distinct periods of Chinese ideology towards OFDI. They find that between 1978 and 1986 there was strong opposition towards outward investments by Chinese firms; though by 1987 with the introduction of the Chinese Special Economic Zones (SEZs) this bias against OFDI began to change beginning with state corporations. However, political acceptance of an OFDI development strategy came during the period 1992 to 2000 as demonstrated by important policy changes which relaxed investment requirements. By 2001, the Chinese government had launched its "go global" strategy aimed at encouraging those Chinese firms which were able to compete effectively to invest abroad. **Cheng and Stough** point out that not only have Chinese OFDI volumes and the list of recipient countries grown over the last few years, but also the average size of the projects have increased — suggesting growing confidence in their OFDI activities.

3.4. *Traditional FDI Motives Facilitated by Liberalization of Policy Regimes*

The final OFDI motivation explored in this volume reflects the more traditional economic rationale for OFDI. China, for example, has emerged as an important source of OFDI, notwithstanding its late liberalization measures. Deng (2007) finds that Chinese OFDI has been directed mainly to Hong Kong and Western, high income, industrialized countries for strategic reasons (p. 72). While earlier Chinese OFDI may have been driven by changes in government policies, economic and strategic motivations increasingly now drive the process.

Wu and Chen (2001) also highlight the change in motivation from political to economic ones in Chinese OFDI after 1986 when OFDI became to be driven by (a) Chinese firms' comparative advantage, (b) the desire for better returns and (c) the need to acquire resources (p. 1239). Specifically, more recent Chinese OFDI was motivated by new markets, the potential for greater trade, the existence of export quotas, the search for resources and raw materials, and technology and skills transfer (Cai, 1999, pp. 867–871). Deng (2007) finds that Chinese OFDI has been led by the country's desire to acquire "strategic resources" in addition to the traditional motivations of investments for new markets and natural resources (p. 74). Deng (2007) notes:

> It is evident that Chinese firms invest overseas because they wish to acquire knowledge and learn new skills and capabilities in order to enhance their competitive advantages and build global brands. The asset-seeking investments tend to be conducted [mainly in industrialized countries] by strong Chinese firms, which have special

resource endowments but may need additional resources to be competitive in particular markets (p. 77).[4]

Similar conclusions were reached by **Goldstein and Pananond in Chapter 8.** They find that while the majority of Thai OFDI is resource or market-seeking, a small but significant number of Thai MNCs are seeking strategic investments overseas.

Conversely, China also remains an attractive FDI destination because of its low labor costs and "technological capability in several sectors, notably in electronics due in part to its economic isolation in recent decades and to the spillover effects of FDI" (Buckley *et al.*, 2005, p. 19). Policy changes in China also led to large FDI inflows (Buckley *et al.*, 2005, p. 9). Guar (2003), for example, offers that OFDI reform within India may result in "many attractive investment opportunities to Indian companies" within ASEAN (p. 287).

In their analysis of the effects of Korean OFDI on trade, Seo and Suh (2006) find that as Korea liberalized its FDI policies, "labor-intensive manufacturing industries mostly relocated to developing countries, particularly ASEAN countries were China, while most Korean FDI conducted in industrialized countries were capital-intensive manufacturing" (p. 160). Seo and Suh (2006) divide OFDI motivations into two categories: "factor seeking" and "market" or "strategic asset seeking" (p. 163). Kim and Mah (2006) show that in response to policy changes in South Korea which made overseas investments by South Korean firms easier, South Korean OFDI flows to both developed regions and to developing Asia increased dramatically after 1987 (pp. 884–885). While initially these investments were concentrated in petroleum and chemical industries (31 percent in 1980), by 2000, electronic and communications equipment (31 percent) and textiles and apparel industries (12 percent) were the largest uses of Korean OFDI (Kim and Mah, 2006, p. 887). Kim and Mah (2006) also point out that Korea's OFDI strategies shifted from resource seeking to

---

[4] This finding is consistent with Helpman, Melitz and Yeaple's (2004) study of the US market where it is offered that "only the most productive [firms] engage in FDI" (p. 300).

production-base seeking FDI, in later years, to augment Korea's export activities (p. 887). Again, Korea's OFDI activities within China and other developing Asian economies, although driven by cost efficiencies, were facilitated by liberalizing policy changes within the recipient countries (Kim and Mah, 2006, pp. 890 and 893).

India's OFDI surge has emerged from the strength of its *home-grown* enterprises responding to improvements in India's business environment and building on the country's "intellectual capital" (Arunachalam, 2003, p. 81). Huang and Khanna (2003) opine:

> India has managed to spawn a number of companies that now compete internationally with the best that Europe and the United States have to offer. Moreover, many of these firms are in the most cutting-edge, knowledge-based industries-software giants Infosys and Wipro and pharmaceutical and biotechnology powerhouses Ranbaxy and Dr. Reddy's Labs, to name a few (p. 75).

In **Chapter 6**, **Nagesh Kumar** shows that as India liberalized its capital flows beginning in the early 1990s, Indian firms responded by expanding abroad, first in manufacturing and then increasingly into the services sector. Indeed, many of these firms were seeking strategic acquisitions and access to important marketing networks. **Kumar** examines various factors which affect the likelihood of Indian firms undertaking OFDI and finds that R&D investments and exporting activity among other factors increases the probability of Indian firms undertaking investments abroad. The search for the latest technology and access to large developed economy markets is likely to result in increasing investment activity by Indian and Asian firms to finance acquisitions abroad.

4. Concluding Remarks

The surge of intra-Asian OFDI continues to remain strong but the question remains if these are sustainable long-term trends. This will expectedly depend on future strength of the four structural drivers identified in this volume. Push factors related to mature markets, raising labor costs in some of the more developed Asian economics and to a lesser extent, bouts of political and economic instability, are likely to continue to affect production costs. China, therefore is likely to remain an attractive destination for Asian OFDI because as Buckley *et al.* (2005) point out: "The unevenness of China's development means that the underdeveloped northern and western provinces will continue to offer many equivalent benefits to foreign investors, certainly in respect of labor, should manufacturing costs rise in the coast provinces after [WTO] accession" (p. 20). This will also hold for India, where the working population is set to increase for the next four decades. Many Asian economies appear to be continuing or expanding their "go global" strategies and are actively promoting outward investments for various reasons. As Asian economies continue to improve their business environments, intra-Asian FDI flows are likely to continue to grow rapidly. The remaining chapters in this volume explore country-specific rationale underlying the rise in Asian OFDI.

References

Buckley, P, J Clegg, A Cross and H Tan (2005). China's inward foreign direct investment success: Southeast Asia in the shadow of the dragon. *Multinational Business Review*, 13, 3–30.

Cai, KG (1999). Outward foreign direct investment: A novel dimension of China's integration into the regional and global Economy. *The China Quarterly*, 160, 856–880.

Chang, MH (1995). Greater China and the Chinese "Global Tribe". *Asian Survey*, 35, 955–967.

Deng, P (2006). Investing for strategic resources and its rationale: The case of outward FDI from Chinese companies. *Business Horizons*, 50, 71–81.

Feenstra, R (1998). *Facts and Fallacies about Foreign Direct Investment*. Davis, California: Institute of Governmental Affairs, University of California, Davis.

Gaur, S (2003). Framework agreement on comprehensive economic co-operation between India and ASEAN: First step towards economic integration. *ASEAN Economic Bulletin*, 20, 283–291.

Globerman, S and D Shapiro (2005). Assessing international mergers and acquisitions as a mode of foreign direct investment. In Eden, L and W Dobson (eds.) *Governance, Multinationals and Growth*, pp. 68–99. London: Edwin Elgar.

Helpman, E, MJ Melitz and SR Yeaple (2004). Export versus FDI with heterogeneous firms. *The American Economic Review*, 94, 300–316.

Huang, Y and T Khanna (2003). Can India Overtake China? *Foreign Policy*, 137, 74–81.

International Monetary Fund (IMF) (2003). *Foreign Direct Investment Trends and Statistics.* Washington DC: The International Monetary Fund.

Kim, EM and JS Mah (2006). Patterns of South Korea's foreign direct investment Flows into China. *Asian Survey,* 46, 881–897.

Kim, WC and V Terpstra (1984). Intraregional foreign direct investment in the Asian Pacific region. *Asia Pacific Journal of Management,* 2, 1–9.

Low, I, ED Ramstetter and HW-C Yeung (1996). Accounting for outward direct investment from Hong Kong and Singapore: Who controls what? NBER *Working Paper* No. 5858.

Rajan, RS (2005). Financing development in the Asia-Pacific Region: Trends and linkages. *The Role of Trade and Investment Policies in the Implementation of the Monterrey Consensus: Regional Perspectives,* Studies in Trade and Investment No. 55, pp. 21–65.

Seo, JS, C-S Suh (2006). An analysis of home country trade effects of outward foreign direct investment: The Korean Experience with ASEAN, 1987–2002. *ASEAN Economic Bulletin,* 23, 160–170.

Sethi, D, SE Guisinger, SE Phelan and DM Berg (2003). Trends in foreign direct investment flows: A theoretical and empirical analysis. *Journal of International Business Studies,* 34, 315–326.

Sutter, KM (2002). Business dynamism across the Taiwan Strait. *Asian Survey,* 42, 522–540.

UNCTAD (2006). *World Investment Report 2006: FDI from Developing and Transition Economies: Implications for Development.* New York: United Nations.

UNCTAD (2007). *Foreign Direct Investment Online* 2007 [accessed 16 November 2007]. Available from http://www.unctad.org/Templates/Page.asp?intItemID= 1923&lang=1.

Wu, H-L and C-H Chen (2001). An assessment of outward foreign direct investment from China's transitional economy. *Europe-Asia Studies,* 53, 1235–1254.

Chapter 2

Emerging FDI Trends in Developing Asia*

Dilek Aykut

1. Introduction

Global FDI flows have expanded rapidly over the last two decades. Technological progress in transport, communications, and data processing coupled with policy reforms, has fueled the growth of cross-border production networks in which multinational corporations (MNCs) break down their production of final goods into stages and organize their production across countries to achieve the lowest cost of production. The remarkable progress in information and telecommunication (IT) technologies has boosted the value-added of the services sector in the world economy and has enhanced the globalization process by enabling companies to better manage and control geographically dispersed businesses.

The last two decades have also marked considerable progress in terms of the liberalization of FDI and trade policies in developing countries.[1] As many impediments including restrictions on the forms of investment and the degree of foreign ownership have been gradually eased, FDI flows in developing countries have surged. In addition, several changes have emerged in terms of modes of investment, recipient industries, and the investor base. Mergers and

---

* The opinions expressed and arguments employed are the author's sole responsibility and do not reflect the views of the Board of Executive Directors of the World Bank Group or the governments they represent. Comments by Amitendu Palit at the ICRIER workshop are appreciated. The usual disclaimer applies.
[1] The developing country definition used in the paper is the UN definition, which is slightly different from that of the World Bank. In addition to the list of developing countries defined by the World Bank, the UN includes newly industrialising economies (NIEs) such as Hong Kong, China, Taiwan Province of China (POC), and Singapore.

Acquisitions (M&As) as a form of FDI and external financing have become more prominent in many developing countries that have gone through a wave of large privatizations. Spurred by this wave, the sectoral distribution of FDI in many developing countries has shifted toward services. In the process, firms in developing economies have amassed sufficient capital, knowledge and know-how to invest abroad on their own and claim the status of emerging multinationals (EMNCs).

This chapter highlights these emerging FDI trends and policy issues. In doing so, it tries to gain a better understanding of how they apply to Asian developing economies, which account for almost 50 percent of FDI flow to all developing countries. Almost all Asian economies have become home for large EMNCs, there are significant differences in terms of drivers, internationalization patterns, and ownership structures among them.

The chapter is organized as follows. Section 2 examines the increased role of M&A as a form of FDI. Section 3 analyzes the shift toward services in FDI flows. Section 4 discusses EMNCs from developing countries. Section 5 concludes with some policy implications.

2. The Increased Role of M&A as a Form of FDI

The importance of M&A activity as a form of FDI increased in the 1990s. Global M&A activity rose more than five-fold between 1995 and 2000 (after increasing by only 24 percent in the first half of the 1990s) to a peak of US$1.1 trillion in 2000, before dropping by some 45 percent in 2001 with the decline in stock markets and the global economic slowdown. Reflecting the recent favorable economic conditions, global cross-border M&As reached yet another peak of US$1.3 billion in 2006. The M&A activity has been driven in part by rapid increases in the stock prices of some major corporations and in part by expectations (during the boom) that continuing productivity increases would fuel continued rises in stock prices (World Bank, 2006). The bulk of the cross-border M&A transactions continues to be in the service sectors (more than half in finance, transport, storage,

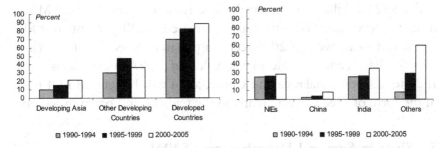

Figure 1:   The ratio of cross-border M&A sales to FDI flows, 1990–2005.

Note: See Footnote 1.

Source: Author's calculations based on UNCTAD M&A data.

and communications alone). Extensive privatization of state-owned assets during the late 1990s also attracted FDI in the form of M&As in a number of developing countries particularly in Latin America and Eastern Europe.

In Asian developing countries, M&As have been less significant compared to developed and other developing countries, as indicated by the relatively lower ratios of cross-border M&A sales to FDI flows (Figure 1). One reason for this has been the limited privatization-related FDI generated in many Asian developing countries. The region accounted for only 17 percent of the US$140 billion total foreign exchange raised through privatization deals in developing countries during 1990–1999 (World Bank, 2000).[2] This said, the importance of M&A activity has increased since the late 1990s. Following the Asian crisis of 1997–1998, the acquisition of distressed banking and corporate assets surged in several Asian economies, particularly in Thailand and Malaysia. This, in part, contributed to a doubling in the value of cross-border M&A activity in Asia in 1998 relative to 1996. During the last few years, cross-border M&As and privatization deals have picked up again in Asian countries. The value of M&A sales almost doubled, both in newly industrialising economies (NIEs) — Hong Kong, China, Republic of Korea, Taiwan Province of China, and Singapore — as well as other developing countries, reaching US$23.2

---

[2] Excluding Hong Kong, China, Taiwan POC and Singapore.

and US$21.7 billion, respectively. The region's share in total M&A deals to developing countries also increased to 30 percent in 2005 compared to an average 20 percent in previous years. The front-runners in the recent increase in the value of M&A transactions were Indonesia, India, Malaysia and China, all of which received FDI flow in the form of M&As, particularly in the telecom and banking sectors.

3. Shift in Sectoral Distribution of FDI

Starting in the late 1980s and early 1990s there has been a shift of global FDI flows into the services sector as most countries — developed and developing — have opened up their services sectors to foreign investment, and FDI flows into these sectors surged (World Bank, 2004; UNCTAD, 2005). Spurred by the surge in privatization and M&A deals, FDI flows in services rose to overtake FDI in manufacturing. By 2004, services accounted for more than half of the FDI stock in developing countries (Figure 2).

3.1. *Trends in Services FDI*

The shift to services has taken place in almost all regions and income groups except Africa (Figure 2). Boosted by mega privatization deals, services FDI surged in Latin American and Eastern European countries particularly into infrastructure (especially transportation, storage, and communication), financial intermediation, and insurance sectors. Between 1999 and 2002 during the climax of developing countries' privatizations and mega M&A deals era, in Latin America, for example, the total FDI to the services sector — mainly in infrastructure and financial sectors — in Brazil and Mexico was US$67 and US$36 billion, respectively. During the same time, Eastern European countries led by Czech Republic, Hungary, and Poland received almost US$40 billion in the infrastructure and financial sectors. In recent years, the Eastern European countries have once again become the main recipients of privatizations and M&A deals, but this time newcomers such as Romania, Bulgaria, and Turkey were also major recipients. Africa,

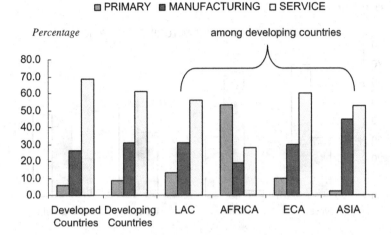

□ PRIMARY ■ MANUFACTURING □ SERVICE

Figure 2: Sectoral composition of FDI stock in regions in 2004.

Note: Estimated by accumulating available FDI flows by sector. Data taken from country sources. Data definitions may vary according to the country's classification system. ECA = Europe and Central Asia; LAC = Latin America and Caribbean.

Source: Author's calculations based on data collected from U.N. ECLAC based on country sources for Latin American countries; China Statistical Yearbook (various years); ASEAN, Foreign Equity Investment in Singapore Report (2004), and country resources for other Asian countries; OECD, UNCTAD, and country sources for Eastern Europe and Central Asia and developed countries. FDI flows to Africa were approximated by the outflows of the continent's major investors including France, Netherlands, the United Kingdom, and the United States.

on the other hand, continues to receive a higher portion of its FDI in resource-related sectors despite the increased role of services sector FDI in North African countries such as Egypt and Tunisia (World Bank, 2004).

For Asian developing countries, the role of the services sector has been significant on aggregate, though its importance varies among countries (Figure 3). While FDI in the sector has been dominant in most NIEs, particularly in Hong Kong and Singapore, FDI in manufacturing is still the leading sector in countries such as China, Taiwan, Malaysia, Thailand, and Vietnam. As Singapore and Hong Kong have positioned themselves as financial and trade centers in Asia, services sector FDI reached US$174 billion and

Percentage

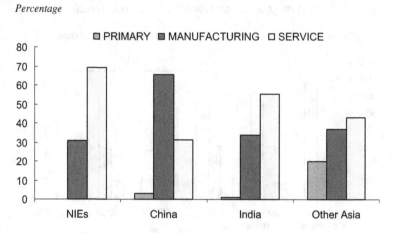

Figure 3:   Sectoral composition of FDI stock in Asia in 2004.

Note: Estimated by accumulating available FDI flows by sector. Data taken from country sources. Data definitions may vary according to the country's classification system.

Source: Author's calculations based on data collected from China Statistical Yearbook (various years); ASEAN, Foreign Equity Investment in Singapore Report (2004), Reserve Bank of India and country resources for other Asian countries.

US$100 billion, respectively, or 64 percent and 96 percent of their respective FDI stocks. In Singapore, financial services — foreign investment holding companies — attracted US$98 billion of FDI flows or 36 percent of the country's FDI stock (Foreign Equity Investment in Singapore Report, 2004). In Hong Kong and China, FDI in investment holdings, real estate and various business services accounted for two-thirds of the FDI stock valued at US$300 billion in 2005, and the rest was in commerce and financial services (Census and Statistics Department of the Hong Kong Special Administrative Region of the People's Republic of China, 2005). Similarly, FDI in services accounted for more than half of FDI stock in India but most of it remains concentrated in infrastructure industries. Highly publicized investment in business services — outsourcing — has been increasing in recent years but only accounts for about 10 percent of inward FDI stock (McKinsey, 2004). In Pakistan, increased FDI in the infrastructure and financial sectors through large M&A deals led the shift toward services.

On the other hand, manufacturing continues to be the dominant sector in other Asian developing countries such as China, Malaysia, Taiwan, and Thailand, even while services FDI has increased over the years. In China, the manufacturing sector received an aggregate of US$240 billion FDI between 1997 and 2004, accounting for 66 percent of the FDI flows. Among services FDI, real estate sector is the main sector, receiving more than 10 percent of all FDI received during 1997–2004. Some portion of this FDI is due to accounting standards that some of the real estate expenses of foreign individuals and companies in China are counted as FDI (Tse, 2001; Zhang, 1999). The rest is increasing real estate purchases by non-residents (UNCTAD, 2006).

FDI flows into the financial sector in China are also on the rise. Since China joined the World Trade Organization (WTO) in 2001, foreign banks have been positioning themselves in the Chinese market. Foreign banks can enter the market in one of the two ways: they may either invest in a domestic bank and hold a minority share (less than 25 percent), or they can establish fully owned branches. To gain immediate access to a large branch network, many foreign banks are increasing their holdings in domestic banks and have invested an estimated US$17 billion since 2001.

Similar to China, FDI in services is still limited in Malaysia, accounting for only 10 percent of the FDI flows during 1999–2004. The shares of the primary and manufacturing sectors were 33 percent and 57 percent, respectively. The approval data between 1996 and 2000 also confirms the dominance of the manufacturing sector. During this period, electrical and electronics and the petroleum and petroleum products industries received 41 percent and 18 percent of the approvals, respectively. Similar to Malaysia, Taiwanese electronics industry received US$16 billion, which was more than half of the country's FDI flows during 1951–2002. With US$8 billion FDI stock, banking and insurance sectors were listed as the second largest sector in Taiwan. Interestingly, FDI sectoral composition is almost divided equally between manufacturing (mostly electronic appliances) and services with manufacturing in Thailand. Most of the services FDI flows to Thailand have been in financial services where majority foreign ownership of banks, finance firms, brokerage firms, and insurance agencies became possible for the first time in 1997.

3.2. *Factors Affecting Services Sector FDI and Policy Implications*

Conventionally defined, the service sector includes electricity, gas, water, transport, communication, construction, wholesale and retail trade and repairs, hotels and restaurants, transport, storage and communications, finance and insurance, real estate, renting, and business services, public administration, defense, education, health, social services, social and personal service activities, and recreational, cultural, and sporting activities. Unlike the primary and manufacturing sectors, where output is tradable, services are mostly non-tradable and require close proximity between producers and consumers (i.e., location-bound).[3] Hence, most of the products in the services sector are usually produced to serve domestic markets. Among the factors that expanded the share of services in global economic activity were income growth in developing countries and changes investment and trade policies toward the sector, as well as the overall investment climate toward services. We consider each of the factors in turn below.

(a) *Income Growth*

The shift in FDI toward the services sector came in tandem with significant developments in the services sector during the 1990s, which boosted its share of world GDP to almost 75 percent in 2005 from 60 percent in 1990. The sectoral composition of FDI, in fact, mirrors that of GDP in most developing and developed countries (Table 1). As the demand for services rose with income level, FDI grew to meet demand. In Africa, however, service-sector FDI has lagged behind the sector's share in GDP for various reasons.

---

[3] Not all the services are non-tradable or require physical proximity, however. For example, some information technology services (software programming, database, and customer support etc.) and business process services (call centers etc.) are not location-bound and can be provided without proximity to customers. These exceptions notwithstanding, services are conventionally portrayed as intangible, invisible and perishable, requiring simultaneous production and consumption (World Bank, 2002).

Table 1: Average share of services in FDI flows and in GDP (percent).

Services share in	FDI	GDP
Asia		
NIEs	69	65
China	31	41
India	55	52
Other Asian Countries	43	45
Europe and Central Asia	65	60
Latin America and the Caribbean	65	59
África	29	52
Memo ítem		
High-Income OECD	69	72

Note: Estimated by accumulating available FDI flows by sector. Data taken from country sources. Data definitions may vary according to the country's classification system.

Source: Author's calculations based on data World Development Indicators (World Bank) and data collected from U.N. ECLAC based on country sources for Latin American countries; China Statistical Yearbook (various years); ASEAN, Foreign Equity Investment in Singapore Report (2004), and country resources for other Asian countries; OECD, UNCTAD, and country sources for Eastern Europe and Central Asia and developed countries. FDI flows to Africa were approximated by the outflows of the continent's major investors including France, Netherlands, the United Kingdom, and the United States.

(b) *Investment and Trade Policy*

A major factor that has led to the rise in FDI in services has been the progress in these countries' investment and trade policies, opening up the services sector to foreign participation, and provoking a significant shift in the composition of FDI toward services. In developed and developing countries alike, services have been liberalized much later than manufactures (Figure 4). Governments' policies with respect to FDI in services have been influenced by considerations of national security and independence, consumer protection, and ensuring the provision of public goods.[4] Because of the monopolistic structure of

---

[4] Some services sectors are labor intensive, and governments are concerned that foreign participation in the sector may harm the domestic skilled workers. In fact, 32 countries (mostly African and Latin American) have included domestic labor requirements for FDI policies in their GATS schedules (Markusen *et al.*, 2000).

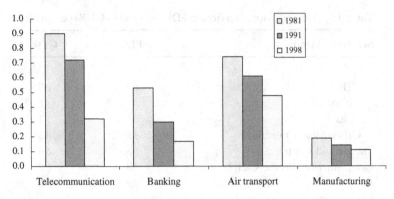

Figure 4: Indices of FDI restrictions over time in selected sectors, 1981–1998 (OECD average).

Note: The indicator is calculated based on limits of foreign ownership, restrictions on foreign personnel and operational freedom, and screening requirements. It ranges from 0 (least restrictive) to 1 (most restrictive).

Source: Golun (2003).

many service markets, designing the necessary regulatory systems has been difficult and costly (World Bank, 2002).

In many developing countries, impediments, including restrictions on the forms of investment and the level of foreign ownership, have been gradually eased during the last decade through unilateral liberalization policies, bilateral and regional investment agreements, and commitments under the WTO and the General Agreement on Trade in Services (GATS). In the case of many Asian developing countries, more liberal FDI policies were implemented following the Asian crisis of 1997 to attract more FDI. Many affected countries such as South Korea, Thailand, and Indonesia have progressed in opening up more services sectors for FDI. In China, progress in liberalization has come through WTO accession.

Such impediments still exist and they seem to be higher in Asian developing countries compared to other regions (Figure 5). These impediments include limitations on foreign ownership, screening or notification procedures, management restrictions, and operational restrictions (UNCTAD, 2006). Particularly, in the case of transmission, distribution, and supply of electricity, many Asian countries (Korea,

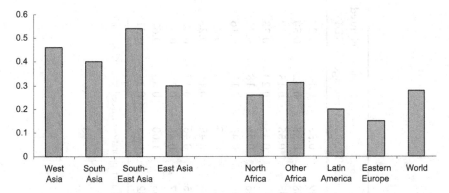

Figure 5:   Indices of FDI restrictions (simple averages) in all services, 2004.

Note: The indicator is calculated based on limits of foreign ownership, restrictions on foreign personnel and operational freedom, and screening requirements. It ranges from 0 (least restrictive) to 1 (most restrictive).

Source: UNCTAD (2006).

Indonesia, Malaysia, and Thailand) as well as other developing countries (Mexico, Tunisia, Turkey, and Uruguay among others), foreign participation is prohibited (Table 2). Impediments in several other services sectors continue to be relatively higher to foreign participation in Asian countries. For example, almost all of the Asian countries have higher FDI restriction indices in the infrastructure sectors (communication and transportation) and financial sectors.

(c) *Investment Climate in Case of Services FDI*

Investment climate issues are very important in attracting and sustaining services FDI. Most of the products in the services sector are non-tradable (i.e., location-bound) and usually produced to serve domestic markets. Moreover, infrastructure services such as electricity, gas, transport facilities etc. were assumed to be public goods, with governments being responsible of producing them. Because of this characteristic of the sector, governments have been highly involved in the operations even after these sectors were opened to private investors. Operations in the sector usually require coordination of several units within the government, and are subject to several rules and regulations (Sader, 2000). Therefore,

Table 2:   Indices of FDI restrictions (simple averages) in all services, 2004.

	China	Korea	India	Indonesia	Malaysia	Pakistan	Philippines	Sri Lanka	Thailand	Simple average	Weighted GDP
Business	0.23	0.18	0.60	1.00	0.74	0.51	0.95	0.09	0.53	0.19	0.23
Communication	0.55	0.51	0.45	0.65	0.63	0.48	0.80	0.38	0.58	0.42	0.50
Construction	0.15	0.33	0.35	0.68	0.20	0.10	0.70	0.05	0.55	0.15	0.19
Distribution	0.55	0.18	0.60	0.35	0.70	0.30	0.30	0.45	0.45	0.20	0.28
Education	0.25	0.78	0.15	0.65	0.20	0.50	0.60	0.45	0.45	0.18	0.21
Environment	0.25	0.28	0.15	0.35	0.20	0.30	1.00	0.05	0.45	0.13	0.16
Finance	0.48	0.24	0.58	0.57	0.40	0.40	0.63	0.45	0.65	0.29	0.38
Health	0.55	0.23	0.35	0.65	0.20	0.33	1.00	0.08	0.45	0.18	0.23
Tourism	0.15	0.20	0.13	0.75	0.70	0.30	0.60	0.15	0.45	0.17	0.22
Transport	0.61	0.49	0.47	0.59	0.40	0.30	0.68	0.67	0.45	0.31	0.37
Electricity	0.55	1.00	0.15	1.00	1.00	0.50	0.70	0.65	1.00	0.56	0.67
All Services	0.44	0.30	0.45	0.61	0.54	0.35	0.69	0.32	0.53	0.24	0.31

Note: The indicator is calculated based on limits of foreign ownership, restrictions on foreign personnel and operational freedom, and screening requirements. It ranges from 0 (least restrictive) to 1 (most restrictive).

Source: UNCTAD (2006).

issues like transparency within the government, stability of the regulatory environment, and adequate legal framework are particularly critical.

The other critical factor for MNCs investing in the services sector is the macroeconomic stability of the host country. These companies serve the domestic markets and earn revenues in local currency. Therefore, exchange rate volatility is detrimental to the rates of return. In addition, MNCs usually finance their expansion (at least the initial investment) through borrowing in major international currencies. Any macroeconomic shocks such as sharp exchange rate fluctuations will lead to balance sheet losses and deterioration of company's equity-debt ratio. Thus, countries with better investment climates not only attracted significantly more FDI, but also more FDI into their services sector measured both as a percentage of GDP as well as percentage of total FDI flows (Table 3).

The elevated importance of investment climate in the case of services FDI was highlighted by sudden fall in FDI in Latin America following the crisis in Argentina in 2002. The local currency earnings of service-sector FDI severely affected the foreign firms in the sector, which had financed their expansion using foreign currency debt. More important, the policy changes in Argentina following the almost 200 percent devaluation of the peso between 2001 and 2002 prompted many direct investors in banking and infrastructure to revisit their business strategies toward the region (IMF–World Bank, 2003). Following the crisis, the Argentine government enforced an asymmetric conversion of

Table 3: Better investment climate attracted higher services FDI in selected Economies.

Investment climate	Services FDI as share of total FDI	Services FDI as share of GDP	Total FDI as share of GDP
High	61	3.9	6.4
Average	42	1.5	3.6
Low	34	0.6	1.6

Note: All averages are weighted averages for 1999–2004, and World Bank Country Policy and Institutional Assessment (CPIA) is used for investment climate index for 35 developing countries in Asia, Eastern Europe, Central Asia, and Latin America regions that the data are available.
Source: Author's calculations based on the data from World Development Indicators (various years).

US dollar-based assets and liabilities into pesos (pesification) and a mandatory rescheduling of term deposits. In addition, the government converted US dollar-denominated contracts of private and public utilities into pesos at an exchange rate of 1 peso per US dollar, while not allowing public utility rates to rise (Economist Intelligence Unit, 2002). Following these policies, most foreign companies cut back financial support to their affiliates in the country, postponed new investments, repatriated profits, and paid back inter-company loans. Some companies tried to find new strategic partners, while a few others sold off their assets.[5] As a result, FDI flows to the region's services sector fell by US$20 billion (53 percent) in 2002. The decline was especially sharp in infrastructure (37 percent) and financial services (65 percent).

During the Asian crisis, however, while many Asian developing countries experienced adverse effects, FDI proved to be resilient. In 1997, FDI flows were concentrated in the manufacturing sector in the region as a whole. In fact, the services sector FDI increased significantly after that, since many Asian economies opened up their services sector to recover from the crisis. Now with increasing service FDI flows, the importance of regulatory and institutional environment in attracting and sustaining services FDI has become more significant. Particularly, in the face of economic turbulence, further deterioration of investment climate might hinder the resilience of FDI.

4. Emerging Multinationals from Developing Countries

The late 1980s and 1990s also witnessed the emergence of MNCs from developing countries as FDI investors.[6] Over the last two decades,

---

[5] Banks that left Argentina following the crisis include Canada's Bank of Nova Scotia, France's Credit Agricole, the Italian financial group Intesa Bci, and Korea's Kookmin. In the following years, several utility MNCs from OECD countries also disinvested from the region.

[6] Developing-country MNCs first appeared as a focus of interest about 25 years ago, with the advent of some overseas expansion by companies from a small number of countries (Lecraw, 1977; Lall, 1983; Wells, 1983). The earliest major developing-country sources of FDI in this latter period were a small group of economies, including Argentina, Brazil, Hong Kong, India, Korea, Singapore, and Chinese Taipei. It is only since the 1990s that an increasing number of developing countries, including Chile, China, Egypt, Malaysia, Mexico, Russia, South Africa, Thailand, and Turkey, have become significant sources of FDI.

these EMNCs have become more engaged in cross-border economic activities, and now larger shares of their sales, assets, and operations are outside the borders of their home country. The rise of EMNCs reflects the impact of globalization on developing countries. While the increased openness of home economies to international capital flows and trade and increased globalization of economic activities have increased competition for developing country firms in sales and in access to resources and strategic assets, it has also increased opportunities in other developing and developed countries. As many developing-country governments have eased their policies toward capital outflows, their companies have expanded their operations abroad. In fact, the progress in the liberalization of the services sector has been an important factor for the rise of EMNCs. Privatization of state-owned assets in the infrastructure sector has provided great opportunities for developing-country companies to acquire important assets domestically and expand regionally.

The increase of cross-border assets and the global expansion of operations have put some EMNCs on par with large MNCs from developed countries. In certain sectors, some EMNCs are considered to be major global players. For example, Mexican Cemex (cement) and Brazilian CVRD (mining) are number one and four in their respective industries in the 2006 *Fortune Global 500*. While OFDI from the BRIC countries — Brazil, Russia, India and China — have received more attention (Sauvant, 2005), other developing countries are home to new important global businesses. EMNCs from new source countries such as Lebanon, Peru, or Uganda are now emerging. Sri Lankan firms, for example, are now very important players in export-oriented clothing industry in many countries (in particular Bangladesh, India, and Madagascar).

The internationalization of developing country firms is partially explained by the well-known investment development path (IDP) theory: OFDI is undertaken when the country reaches a certain minimum development (Dunning, 1981). As countries move along the IDP from the initial stage of only receiving inward FDI, domestic firms acquire ownership and other advantages to go abroad and the country reaches the final stage and becomes an important outward investor. This being said, there is some evidence indicating that EMNCs are investing abroad at earlier stages of the IDP (UNCTAD, 2006), mainly because many such firms do not have the luxury of waiting given the fierce competition at home and in the export markets as a result of increased level of globalization. Even in a low-income country, firms (such as business services of Indian Tata Consultancy or Nigerian Telecom) may develop certain comparative advantages vis-à-vis other countries/companies in certain sectors because of large consumer and production bases.

Such comparative advantages for EMNCs range from a patent, recognized brand, production capacity to access to certain resources, knowledge of culture, and language. For example, EMNCs experience some comparative advantages in services sector vis-à-vis Northern MNCs in their regional investments — particularly, in other developing countries (South–South FDI) — because the services sector often requires proximity between producer and consumer and favor language and culture similarities. As a result, Southern telecom giants Mexican América Movil, Egyptian Orascom, and South African MTN compete fiercely with Northern firms in their regions. In manufacturing, specialization in production has brought comparative advantages to many developing country firms. Brazilian bus and coach producer Marcopolo have developed flexible production systems to produce custom-made buses, which they have carried to Portugal and other Latin American countries. Jordanian Hikma's ability to produce low-cost, diverse and high-quality pharmaceuticals enable them to expand in other Arab countries as well as other regions. In the primary sector, Southern firms' access to resources have helped them in terms of access to funding as well as their scale of production while they expand their operations abroad.

Firms may also engage in internationalization by acquiring "strategic" assets (commonly through M&A) such as technology, brands and distribution networks in case of lack or limited comparative advantages (asset augmentation). In an environment with the increased competition in the domestic and foreign markets due to globalization and technological advances that can erode the comparative advantages quickly, developed and developing firms alike use cross-border takeovers as an important strategy (UNC-TAD, 2006). Recent mega deals by Cemex and CRVD as well as Chinese Lenavo's purchase of IBM are great examples for asset-augmenting expansion. Developing country firms expand abroad using combinations of both of these strategies. For example, Egyptian telecom giant Orascom Telecom has become a major regional telecom provider in Africa and the Middle East after investing heavily in the neighboring countries as an asset-exploiting strategy, while its leveraged buy-out of Italian Wind Telecommunications was more of an asset-augmentation strategy.

4.1. *Trends in Outward FDI Flows*

Globalization of operations and complex business strategies made it harder than ever to define and monitor international operations of an MNC. All such limitations are further magnified in the case of FDI outflows from the South. OFDI statistics for non-OECD countries tend to be patchy and relatively unreliable. Some of these countries that have invested abroad (such as Malaysia and Mexico) just started reporting FDI outflows in recent years. Moreover, for several countries, estimates of FDI outflows are considerably smaller than the actual level of flows. Official statistics do not usually include financing and reinvested components of OFDI as well as the capital that is raised abroad (Aykut and Ratha, 2004). Also, in general, these statistics only reflect the large investments while excluding small and medium size transactions. In addition, countries with capital controls, exchange controls or high taxes on investment income provide a substantial incentive for under-reporting by investors. Several country case studies based on company level data highlight the under-reporting (Aykut and Ratha, 2004). For example, Wong and Chan (2003) document the substantial under-reporting of FDI flows from China: the reported numbers reflect only investments with official approval (which is required for initial investments only), and China's State Administration and Foreign

Exchange (SAFE) estimates that unauthorized capital outflows from China between 1997 and 1999 totalled US$53 billion.

Further care is required with Chinese bilateral data with Hong Kong. As FDI enjoys favorable treatment compared to domestic investment, resulting in an incentive to investors to channel funds out of, and subsequently into, an economy in the form of FDI. Because the funds originate in the host economy itself, "round-tripping" inflates actual FDI inflows. Official estimates of this type of FDI are not available, but others have suggested that such flows may account for up to 25 percent of the total inflows (Aykut and Ratha, 2004; Xiao, 2004). The Chinese government has started to address this issue. In November 2005, for example, SAFE promulgated a regulation concerning foreign exchange management related to "round-tripping" investments (UNCTAD, 2007). In addition, as Athukorala (2006) shows, another, perhaps even more important, problem with Chinese FDI data has to do with "over-reporting" of inward FDI, a phenomenon that seems to affect flows from other developing Asian countries more than OECD source countries.

Nevertheless, reported FDI outflows from developing countries rose significantly during the 1990s reaching US$143 billion in 2000 from US$12 billion in 1990. After a fall following the Asian crisis, OFDI from developing countries recovered to US$117 billion in 2005. Till 2005, the value of OFDI stock held by developing countries was US$1.4 billion, accounting 13 percent of world total (Figure 6). The positive trend has continued in recent years and FDI by EMNCs reached yet another peak in 2006 as they have started to acquire major MNCs from developed countries through mega M&A transactions.

Among developing economies, EMNCs in Asia remain by far the largest investors (Figure 6). The NIEs accounted for almost 68 percent of total OFDI in 1992–1999 and 61 percent in 2000–2005. Including China, the five largest economies, all in Asia, accounted for more than two-thirds of the total in 2000–2005. In Hong Kong, firms allocated 53.2 percent of their total investment in 2001–2003 to foreign markets; Singapore channelled 23.3 percent; and Taiwan

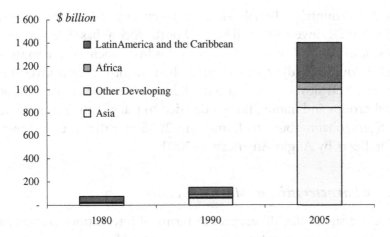

Figure 6: Outward FDI Stocks from developing countries by region, 1985–2005.
Source: UNCTAD World Investment Report (various years).

6.4 percent. For the two latter countries, a large chunk of FDI out-flows went to China. Within Asia, Malaysia, Indonesia, and India are the next group of major outward Asian investors. Reported OFDI of India, which is already found to be almost half of the actual outflows (Pradhan, 2005), increased significantly in the last few years, as Indian EMNCs were very active in cross-border asset acquisitions, particu-larly in developed countries. For example, since 2004, FDI flows from India into the United Kingdom exceeded flows from the United Kingdom to India.

Another country with significant OFDI stocks is Russia, with major investments in former Soviet Union countries. In the Russian case, the Cypriot offshore sector has developed into a landing place for Russian capital, to the extent that Cyprus is currently the biggest direct investor in Russia. Also, the investment flow from (or via) Cyprus to other Eastern European countries is relatively big and a sig-nificant share of these "Cypriot" investments is considered to be of Russian origin. In addition, some portion of the estimated US$245 billion capital flight from Russia during 1992–2002 is believed to be unrecorded FDI outflows (Vahtra and Liuhto, 2004). Several Latin

American countries (Brazil, Mexico, Argentina, and Chile) are other major OFDI investors. Although South Africa has been a major investor in Africa since 1990s, part of this investment is due to significant accounting adjustments rather than major outward investment projects. FDI flows were reduced when many of the country's traditional groups and mining houses decided to transfer their primary listing from Johannesburg to London in 2005 and the reverse takeover of De Beers by Anglo-American in 2001.

4.2.   *Characteristics of Main Investors*

There are significant differences in terms of internationalization patterns and ownership structures among large EMNCs. As summarized in Table 4, these characteristics of major EMNCs vary considerably among regions. In the case of Latin American MNCs, the increasing competition due to liberalization in the 1990s has acted as a main driver and selection mechanism. After significant restructuring, the mostly privately owned survivor firms have become far leaner and meaner and therefore are able to compete on global markets. The car industry and, in particular, the manufacturing of parts and components, provides a nice illustration. Most Brazilian and Mexican companies that had grown under import substitution industrialization (ISI) strategies since the 1950s have been either taken over by OECD-based competitors, or gone bankrupt. Survivors, however, have proven to be reliable suppliers to American and European assemblers, to the point of being asked to follow their customers and invest overseas. Latin American MNCs have operations abroad in fields such as beverages, petrochemicals, petroleum, mining, steel, cement, pulp and paper, textiles and agribusiness, and a little or no presence in technology- or marketing-intensive products like automobiles, electronics, telecommunication equipments, and chemicals.

Internationalization of South African MNCs accelerated after 1990 following the removal of sanctions and liberalization of OFDI. To further strengthen South African investment abroad, the Government adopted policies to encourage its MNCs to go into the rest of Africa after apartheid, and in 2004, it eased foreign exchange

Table 4: Patterns of national and regional development and the internationalization of companies.

Region	Development policies since the 1980s	Characteristics of major MNCs	Competitive advantages
Latin America and the Caribbean	Washington consensus	Private firms, mostly focused on core business (Gerdau → steel; Tenaris → tubes; Embraer → aircraft)	Know how to play the post-privatization regulatory game and have become leaner and meaner as suppliers to Western MNCs to Western MNCs
South Africa	Post-apartheid reconciliation	Unbundled and London-listed conglomerates (Anglo-American, Rembrandt) and state-owned enterprises (Eskom, Transnet)	SA regional players in services, strong in project execution capabilities that can be deployed in pillage economies, and global ones in mining
New Europe	EU convergence	Privatized firms, Turkish conglomerates (Koç, Sabanci)	Regional players in telecoms, electricity and gas, retail
Russia and the CIS	Big bang and crony capitalism	State-owned enterprises (Gazprom) and privatized firms still dependent on Kremlin support (Severstal)	Russian regional players in telecoms and global ones in metals and natural resources

(Continued)

Table 4: (*Continued*)

Region	Development policies since the 1980s	Characteristics of major MNCs	Competitive advantages
NIEs	Export-oriented with strong state	Conglomerates (*chaebols*, Temasek) and contract manufacturers	Innovation capabilities
ASEAN	FDI-driven	Conglomerates (CP Group)	Management of mainland China's insertion into global value chains, *Guanxi*
China	FDI-driven with strong state	Public-private firms, mostly focused on core business (Lenovo → PCs; Haier → appliances; Huawei → telecom equipment)	Leverage on huge domestic market
South Asia	Gradual opening backed by diaspora linkages	Private conglomerates (Tata) and ICT firms (Infosys, Wipro)	Low psychic distance with the US and Commonwealth, engineering skills

Source: Aykut and Goldstein (2006).

restrictions on South African companies' OFDI. More than half of South Africa's FDI outflows are estimated to have gone to other countries in Africa, in other Southern African Development Community (SADC) members and elsewhere. South Africa is actively supporting the Maputo Development Corridor public–private partnership, with Nigeria, Mauritius, and the Democratic Republic of Congo also being other significant FDI recipients. Many South African firms, mostly privately owned, have strong presence in other African countries and outside Africa, in remarkably wide-range of sectors.

Within Asian developing countries, there are major differences among NIEs, China, and South Asian EMNCs. The internationalization of companies from NIEs has taken place in the context of rapid industrial upgrading in the sub-region in the late 1980s. In South Korea, MNCs have evolved from *chaebols* — large privately owned conglomerates supported by government polices — with increased foreign participation in management following the financial crisis. They have a significant global focus rather than regional. Large portion of investments are in manufacturing (automobiles, electronics, petroleum refining) and steel production. EMNCs from Singapore that have invested abroad are transformed from state-owned to GLCs — companies in which the Government owns at least 20 percent stake.[7] Malaysian MNCs, mostly state-owned, operated in oil (Petronas) and infrastructure industries. China, on the other hand, has a mix of private and state-owned outward investors but the role of state-owned companies in overseas investments is still significant — accounting for 43 percent of OFDI stock in 2003 (Giroud, 2005). While state-owned companies invest abroad mainly in resource-related assets, privately owned EMNCs operate in competitive manufacturing sectors such as consumer electronics (Haier), personal computers (Lenovo), and communication technologies. Although India's largest MNC, Oil and Gas Corporation (ONGC), is state-owned, most Indian MNCs are privately owned. Following the liberalization in the mid-1990s, Indian firms have leveraged on their language and engineering skills

---

[7] See Chapter 8 in this volume by Goldstein and Pananond for a more detailed discussion of Singapore-based GLCs.

and have become important global players in several services sectors including software and IT-enabled business services (UNCTAD, 2006). This being said, most of their OFDI stock is still in manufacturing. However, overseas investment related with financial services (for countries with large Indian diasporas), pharmaceuticals and software and IT business services are increasing.[8]

Not all the outward investments are made by large EMNCs, however. Till 2005, in China and India, the number of EMNCs was 3429 and 1700, respectively, and most of them are small and medium-size enterprises (SMEs) with limited cross-border investment. Several country case studies show that SMEs from developing countries contribute a considerable share of overseas investment in developing countries. In India, for example, SMEs accounted for 26 percent of overseas projects (6.7 percent of the value) in manufacturing and 41.1 percent (47.1 percent of the value) in the software industry (Pradhan, 2005).

4.3. *Geographic Distribution*

EMNCs tend to invest regionally and in other developing countries (South–South) where they have acquired a certain familiarity through trade, or ethnic and cultural ties before going global. As a result, there is a significant South–South expansion and regional aspect to EMNCs outflows. For example, supported by government policies, South African investments in other developing countries are almost completely in the southern part of Africa (Goldstein, 2003). Following trade liberalization in Latin America, MNCs from Argentina, Brazil, and Chile expanded their operations mainly in other developing countries in the region (Chudnovsky and Lopez, 2000). Russian investments abroad have primarily been in the countries of the former Soviet Union. Turkey has also been actively investing regionally, particularly in West and Central Asia, and Russia.

---

[8] See Chapter 6 in this volume by Kumar for a more detailed discussion of Indian multinationals investing overseas.

Intra-regional South–South FDI flows are also significant for most of the Asian developing countries. In fact, the internationalization of East Asian EMNCs is closely intertwined with the evolving regional institutional and policy context. Most of these countries are usually part of regional production process making each other preferable investment destination. In addition, the emergence of South–East Asian EMNCs is part of overall internationalization process of "ethnic Chinese" business in Asia (Weidenbaum and Hughes, 1996) and a large number of these companies have become major regional players. On the contrary, while Indian EMNCs invest in the neighboring countries such as Bangladesh and Nepal, they have recently begun to go to the West rather than going to the East and expanding in the rest of Asia. As a result, the United States is the main destination for Indian EMNCs, followed by Russian Federation, Mauritius, and Sudan.

Regional investments are also encouraged by many governments and regional arrangements. For example, Malaysia supports special deals for FDI outflows to countries such as India, the Philippines, Tanzania, and Vietnam (Mirza, 2000). The Thai government actively promotes Thai firms' involvement in infrastructure projects in selected developing countries in the region (UNCTAD, 2005). Some of the regional arrangements offer various incentives for outward investment within the region, including lower tax and tariff rates and easier profit repatriation. Encouraged by cooperation arrangements, ASEAN countries have been the top destination for Thai companies (Mathews, 2006). Some members of the region maintain bilateral investment agreements and double-taxation treaties.

5. Conclusion and Policy Implications

As a result of technological progress and policy reforms both in developed and developing countries, FDI flows have evolved in terms of its mode, the sectors it goes to and in terms of who is investing over the years. Today, for developed and many developing countries alike, the services sector has become the major sector, attracting investment from foreign MNCs. These MNCs are not only from developed countries, but also from developing countries. Developing country MNCs are not necessarily inferior to their developed country competitors in terms of technology, managerial skills and access to capital. On the contrary, some of them are major global players in their fields.

Many Asian economies have not only experienced these changes, but have also been the leading forces behind them. FDI flows in the developing Asian region have shifted toward the services sectors, and services FDI in the region is expected to rise in coming years as impediments to such flows that are prevalent in many Asian economies have continued to ease. The sectoral shift in FDI may have implications in terms of its sustainability and its resilience in the face of economic turbulences. The non-tradability nature of most services sectors' products and their high dependence on countries macro-economic conditions and institutional framework make them more sensitive to sudden macro-economic shocks especially when they are coupled with deterioration in institutional and regulatory framework.

The number of EMNCs from developing Asia has grown rapidly and continues to grow. Increased internationalization of developing-country firms seems to have significant development policy implications particularly in the context of regional South–South FDI. One well-documented important feature of regional South–South FDI flows is its importance for low-income and small economies. Among other destinations, EMNCs tend to invest also in other neighboring developing countries with similar or lower levels of development than their home country. Hence, South–South FDI flows, however small, may be significant to many poor countries. Similar to other regions, for Asian low income countries like Bangladesh, Cambodia, Lao People's Dem. Rep., Myanmar and Nepal, regional South–South FDI accounts for more than 50 percent of FDI inflows. Hence, EMNCs represent an opportunity for receiving more FDI for low-income countries apart.

Also, the enlargement and diversification of the pool of countries' sources of FDI may moderate any decline in FDI flows that may happen due to changing conditions or expectations in some of the source countries. In fact, following the Argentinean default, while

North–South FDI slumped, several assets were bought by Brazilian investors. For example, in May 2002 AmBev, a leading beer and beverages producer, unveiled plans to purchase a one-third share of Argentina's top beer-maker, Quilmes, a deal valued at US$700 million. That was the first major foreign investment since the default. That same year, Petrobras, the oil company, bought a controlling stake in Perez Companc for some US$1.1 billion.

This being said, FDI flows from other developing countries may pose risks as well as benefits. The operational and financial challenges facing developing-country MNCs, coupled sometimes with a deterioration in host-country economic conditions have contributed to several examples of unsuccessful South–South investment deals and transactions, which were followed by disinvestments. In addition, the increased South–South integration could also lead to increased vulnerability of developing countries to an economic crisis. The rise of cross-border flows between developing countries makes it likely that it will become easier for shocks to be transmitted between developing countries.

References

Athukorala, P-C (2006). *Multinational Enterprises in Asian Development*. Cheltenham, UK: Edward Elgar.

Athukorala, P-C and SK Jayasuriya (1988). Parentage and factor proportions: A comparative study of third-world multinationals in Sri Lankan manufacturing. *Oxford Bulletin of Economics and Statistics*, 50(4), 409–423.

Aykut, D and D Ratha (2004). South–South FDI flows: How big are they? *Transnational Corporations*, 13(1), 149–176.

Aykut, D and A Goldstein (2006). Developing country multinationals: South–South investment comes of age. Working Paper # 257, OECD Development Centre.

Census and Statistics Department of the Hong Kong Special Administrative Region of the People's Republic of China (2005). Retrieved from http://www.censtatd.gov.hk/hong_kong_statistics/statistical_tables/index.jsp?charsetID=1&tableID=050.

Chudnovsky, D and A Lopez (2000). A third wave from developing countries: Latin American TNCs in the 1990s, *Transnational Corporations*, 9(2), 31–74.

EIU (Economist Intelligence Unit). *Country Finance* (2002).

Foreign Equity Investment in Singapore Report (2004).

Giroud, A (2005). Chinese outward FDI. Background paper for the UNCTAD Conference *Enhancing the Productive Capacity of Developing Country Firms through Internationalization*.

Goldstein, A (2003). Regional integration, FDI, and competitiveness: The case of SADC, Prepared for Africa Investment Roundtable, 19 November 2003, OECD.

Golun, SS (2003). Measure of restrictions on inward foreign direct investment for OECD countries. OECD Economics Department Working Papers No 357.

International Monetary Fund (2003). *Foreign Direct Investment in Emerging Market Countries.* Washington D.C. (A joint study with the World Bank).

International Monetary Fund–World Bank (2005). FDI Monitoring Working Project — Series of interviews with major investors both from developing and developed countries.

Lall, S (ed.) (1983). *The New Multinationals: The Spread of Third World Enterprises.* Chichester: Wiley.

Lecraw, D (1977). Direct investment by firms from less developed countries. *Oxford Economics Papers,* 29(3), 442–457.

Levy-Yeyati, E, U Panizza and E Stein (2002). The cyclical nature of North-South FDI flow. IADB Research Department, Working paper, No. 479.

Markusen, J, TF Rutherford and D Tarr (2000). Foreign direct investment in services and the domestic market for expertise. NBER Working Paper no 7700.

Mathews, J (2006). *Strategizing, Disequilibrium, and Profit.* Palo Alto, CA: Stanford University Press.

McKinsey (2004). The McKinsey Global Survey of Business Executives. Retrieved from http://www.mckinseyquarterly.com/article_page.aspx?ar=1411&L2=7&L3=10&pagenum=5

Mirza, H (2000). The globalization of multinational enterprise activity and economic development. *Business and East Asian Developing-Country Multinationals,* St.Martin's Press.

Pradhan, JP (2005). *Outward Foreign Direct Investments from India: Recent Trends and Patterns,* Jawaharlal Nehru University, New Delhi: Mimeo, Centre for the Study of Regional Development.

Sader, F (2000). Attracting foreign direct investment into infrastructure: Why is it so difficult? Foreign Investment Advisory Service Occasional Paper no 12, Washington DC: World Bank.

Sauvant, KP (2005). New sources of FDI: The BRICs. *The Journal of World Investment and Trade,* 6(5), 639–711.

Tse, RYC (2001). China's real estate market and the Asian financial crisis. *Emerging Markets Quarterly,* Winter 2001.

UNCTAD (various years). *World Investment Report,* Geneva.

UNCTAD (2005). Internationalization of developing-country enterprises through outward foreign direct investment. Prepared for the Commission on Enterprise, Business Facilitation and Development, Expert Meeting on Enhancing

Productive Capacity of Developing-Country Firms through Internationalization, Geneva, 5–7 December, TD/B/COM.3/EM.26/2.

UNCTAD (2006). Measuring restrictions on FDI in services in developing countries and transition economies. Geneva. Retrieved from http://www.unctad.org/en/docs/iteiia20061_en.pdf.

UNCTAD (2007). Rising FDI into China: The facts behind the numbers. UNCTAD Investment Brief. Number 2 2007. Retrieved from http://www.unctad.org/en/docs/iteiiamisc20075_en.pdf

Weidenbaum, M and S Hughes (1996). *The Bamboo Network: How Expatriate Chinese Entrepreneurs are Creating a New Economic Superpower in Asia*, New York: Free Press.

Wells, LT Jr (1983). *Third World Multinationals: The Rise of Foreign Investment from Developing Countries.* Cambridge, Mass.: The M.I.T. Press.

World Bank (2000). *Global Economic Prospects*, Washington, DC

World Bank (2002). *Global Economic Prospects*, Washington, DC

World Bank (2004). *Global Development Finance*, Washington, DC

World Bank (2006). *Global Development Finance*, Washington, DC.

World Bank. World Development Indicators (various years). Washington D.C.

Wong, J and S Chan (2003). China's outward direct investment: Expanding worldwide. *China: An International Journal*, 1(2), 273–301.

Xiao, G (2004). People's Republic of China's round-tripping FDI: Scale, causes, and implications, Asia Development Bank Institute Discussion Paper No.7.

Zhang, X (1999). Real estate investment in china legal — review and analysis of foreign investors' participation. *Murdoch University Electronic Journal of Law*, 6(2). Retrieved from http://www.murdoch.edu.au/elaw/issues/v6n2/zhang62_text.html

Chapter 3

Intra-Asian FDI Flows:
Trends, Patterns, and Determinants*

Rabin Hattari and Ramkishen S. Rajan

1. Introduction

According to the UNCTAD (2006), "a number of developing countries have emerged as significant sources of FDI in other developing countries, and their investments are now considered a new and important source of capital and production know-how, especially for host countries in developing regions" (p. 6). The phenomenon of South–South FDI flows, particularly those arising from multinational corporations (MNCs) from China and India, has generated significant interest from policymakers, academia and the popular press in recent times.

Available data from the Word Bank indicates South–South FDI to have increased almost three-fold (from US$14 billion in 1995 to US$47 billion in 2003), and accounts for almost 37 percent of total FDI flows to developing countries, up from 15 percent in 1995 (Table 1). Of the top hundred MNCs from developing economies that have the potential to become global players, 65 are from Mainland China and India (BCG, 2006; also see Aguiar et al., 2006). The Chinese government has stated its intention to help develop 30–50 "national champions" that can "go global" by 2010 (Accenture, 2005; Sauvant, 2005, Wu, 2005). Given this, along with aggressive overseas acquisition plans by cash-rich and highly confident firms from India, Hong Kong, South Korea, and Taiwan, as well as by national holding companies in Singapore (Temasek Holdings) and Malaysia (Khazana National Berhad), outward investments by Asian companies are set to rise further.

---

* Comments by K.C. Fung at the ICRIER workshop are appreciated. The usual disclaimer applies.

Table 1:   Growing importance of South–South FDl, 1995–2003 (USS billions).

	1995	1999	2000	2001	2002	2003e
Total inflows (1)	90.3	163.5	154.7	159.3	135.3	129.6
From high-income OECD (2)	48.1	95.4	93.7	B4.8	55.1	59.4
From high-income non-OECD (3)	28.2	35.0	22.7	24.8	27.2	22.3
South–South FDl (1)-(2)-(3)	14.0	33.1	38.3	49.7	53.0	47.4
South–South FDl (percent)	15.5	20.2	24.8	31.2	39.2	38.6

Notes: The South–South estimates are based on 35 countries that account for 85 percent of total FDl flows to developing countries. The estimates are based on the World Bank's classification of developing countries.
Source: World Bank (2006).

Apart from the usual efficiency-seeking, resource-seeking, and market-seeking investments, OFDI from developing Asia is motivated by a desire to build a global presence and buy brand names, technology, processes, management know-how and marketing and distribution networks. The international expansion of some Asian firms may also have been motivated by a desire to offset or diversify risks at home, for tariff-jumping reasons, geopolitical factors, etc.[1] Policy-makers in many Asian countries like China and India have been particularly keen on promoting an internationalization thrust and have facilitated OFDI via gradual liberalization of rules governing capital account outflows and in many cases, providing a financing mechanism to domestic firms looking to invest abroad.[2]

While Asian companies have become significant foreign direct investors abroad, a large share of outward investments from Asia may have been recycled intra-regionally. According to some rough estimates,

[1] A rather tangential rationale for — or rather, result of — overseas acquisitions and concomitant capital outflows has been an easing of exchange rate pressures on Asian currencies, thus reducing the need for reserve buildup and having to manage its inflationary consequences.
[2] See Chapter 1 for a general overview of determinants of outward FDI from Asia and Chapters 5 and 6 for discussions of outward FDI from China and India more specifically.

intra-Asian FDI flows in 2004 have accounted for about 40 percent of Asia's total FDI inflows in 2004 (Kwan and Cheung, 2006; also see UNCTAD, 2006, Chapter 2). If correct, this share is broadly comparable with the extent of intra-Asian trade flows. However, unlike trade flows there has been little to no detailed examination of FDI flows between Asian economies at a bilateral level.

This chapter uses bilateral FDI flows data to investigate trends and drivers of intra-Asian FDI flows over the period 1997–2005. Eichengreen and Tong (2007), Liu *et al.* (2007) and Sudsawasd and Chaisrisawatsuk (2006) are three of possibly just a handful of papers that examine FDI to Asia using bilateral data. However, these papers only consider FDI from OECD economies as the source country since they use data from the OECD.[3] In contrast, the focus of this chapter is on developing Asian economies as the sources of FDI to other developing Asian economies using data from UNCTAD.

The remainder of the chapter is organized as follows. Section 2 discusses FDI definitions and data sources. Section 3 discusses broad patterns and trends in intra-Asia FDI flows using bilateral net FDI flows over the period 1997–2005. Section 4 employs an augmented gravity model framework to examine the main determinants of intra-Asian FDI flows using bilateral data based on a panel dataset. We examine a range of drivers of FDI flows, from macroeconomic variables, transactional and informational distance (proxied by distance and common official language) to institutional quality. The final section offers a few concluding remarks.

2. Definitions and Data Sources

According to the IMF *Balance of Payments Manual (5th Edition, 1993)*:

> FDI refers to an investment made to acquire lasting interest in enterprises operating outside of the economy of the investor.

---

[3] A selective list of recent papers that use bilateral FDI data from OECD but are not specifically limited to Asia are Bénassy-Quéré *et al.* (2007), Daude and Stein (2004), Head and Ries (2007), Loungani *et al.* (2002). Razin *et al.* (2003), and Stein and Daude (2007).

Further, in cases of FDI, the investor's purpose is to gain an effective voice in the management of the enterprise. The foreign entity or group of associated entities that makes the investment is termed the 'direct investor'. The unincorporated or incorporated enterprise—a branch or subsidiary, respectively, in which direct investment is made—is referred to as a 'direct investment enterprise'.[4]

At an operational level, FDI commonly bears three broad characteristics. First, it refers to a source of external financing rather than necessarily net physical investment or real activity *per se*.[5] Second, as a matter of convention, FDI involves a 10 percent threshold value of ownership. Third, FDI consists of both the initial transaction that creates (or liquidates) investments as well as subsequent transactions between the direct investor and the direct investment enterprises aimed at maintaining, expanding or reducing investments. More specifically, FDI is defined as consisting of three broad aspects, viz. new foreign equity flows (which is the foreign investor's purchases of shares in an enterprise in a foreign country), intra-company debt transactions (which refer to short-term or long-term borrowing and lending of funds including debt securities and trade credits between the parent company and its affiliates) and reinvested earnings (which comprises the investor's share of earnings not distributed as dividends by affiliates or remitted to the home country, but rather reinvested in the host country). New equity flows could either be in the form of M&A of existing local enterprises or Greenfield investments (i.e., establishment of new production facilities).[6]

While this is the most common definition, it is not always adhered to by all countries systematically. In fact, reported OFDI often be underreported as it excludes the financing and reinvested components. For

---

[4] See http://www.unctad.org/Templates/Page.asp?intItemID=3146&lang=1.

[5] *A priori* it is unclear whether FDI over or under-estimates actual real economic activity as this requires consideration of the impact of FDI on existing domestic investment, extent of technology transfer, employment creation, and the like. The impact on FDI on net capital flows is also uncertain, as greater FDI inflows could encourage portfolio and bank flows, while simultaneously, M&A inflows could lead to the previous local owners choosing to invest some of their returns overseas, leading to capital outflows. The nexus between FDI and other sources of financing is explored in Rajan (2005).

[6] Globerman and Shapiro (2005) find many common determinants in both modes of FDI.

emerging economies, the two most comprehensive databases on FDI inflows and outflows are IMF-BoP Manual and UNCTAD (see Duce (2003) for a comparison of the two sources). Neither source divides FDI into M&A versus Greenfield investments.[7] While most M&A statistics are compiled by commercial data sources, they tend to include announced rather than actual financial flows and some of the announced flows may not even include activities considered to be FDI (as defined above). More to the point, announced flows often include funding of capital via equity from local minority share-holders or local/international borrowing (as opposed to funds from the parent or sister companies) and are thus of limited use for the purposes at hand.

UNCTAD by far has the most complete FDI database, and unlike the IMF-BOP data, it compiles data on *bilateral* FDI flows — both inflows and outflows. The UNCTAD data are on a net basis (capital transactions credits less debits between direct investors and their foreign affiliates). The main sources for UNCTAD's FDI flows are national authorities (central banks or statistical office). These data are further complemented by the data obtained from other international organizations such as the IMF, the World Bank (*World Development Indicators*), the Organization for Economic Co-operation and Development (OECD), the Economic Commission for Europe (ECE) and the Economic Commission for Latin America and the Caribbean (ECLAC), and UNCTAD's own estimates.[8]

---

[7] See UNCTAD (2006, pp. 15–21) for a discussion of Greenfield versus M&As. Cross-border M&A have been experiencing a surge in recent years. UNCTAD reports that in 2005 both the value and the number of cross-border M&A rose to US$ 716 billion and to 6134 which are increases of 88 percent and 20 percent, respectively. Bloomberg, Thomson Financial, Dealogic and OCO Consulting's LOCO Database record all M&A deals that are reported by news and media in their database. The UNCTAD M&A database is drawn from Thomson Financial.

[8] The process of data collection for UNCTAD FDI/TNC databank is complicated and requires using data from different databases or own estimation. For instance, UNCTAD uses data from the World Bank's *World Development Indicators* for economies that lack data from national official sources or the IMF or for which available data do not cover the entire period. For developing countries in which their FDI flows data are unavailable in either IMF or World Bank, UNCTAD employed regional cooperation databases, such as ECLAC, and ECE, to fill in the missing data. For OECD countries, data on the FDI outflows from OECD database are used as proxy for FDI inflows. For those economies for which data were not available from either of the above-mentioned sources or only partial data were available, UNCTAD uses its own estimates.

3. The Extent of Intra-Asian FDI Flows: Trends and Patterns

One could analyze FDI data on either *stocks* (i.e., International Investment Positions) or *flows* (i.e., financial account transactions) data. While much empirical analysis to date has been undertaken using the former, changes in stocks could arise either because of net new flows or because of valuation changes and other adjustments (such write-offs, reclassifications etc). To abstract from these valuation and other changes we consider only data on flows of OFDI (net decreases in assets or when a foreign country invests in the country in question) and inward FDI (net increases in liabilities or when the home country invests abroad).

Our focus is on selected South, South–East Asia and East Asian developing economies. The economies included in our sample are Bangladesh, Cambodia, China (Mainland), Hong Kong, India, Indonesia, Malaysia, Pakistan, the Philippines, Singapore, Taiwan, Thailand, South Korea, and Vietnam. Thus, apart from excluding West Asia and some smaller Asian economies in South, South–East and East Asia, we exclude Japan but follow UNCTAD in defining the NIEs like Hong Kong, Singapore, South Korea, and Taiwan as "developing".

3.1. *Aggregate Inflows to and Outflows from Developing Asia*

Table 2 reveals relative shares of global FDI inflows and outflows. As is apparent, the Triad (the EU, Japan, and the United States) continue to dominate both as sources and hosts of FDI in terms of both stocks and flows. However, it is interesting to note that in 2003–2005 the Triad's share of FDI flows declined to a low of below 60 percent compared to about 80 percent on average between 1978 and 1990, while that to developing economies rose to a corresponding high of 40 percent, over half of which was destined to Asia. The share of FDI outflows from developing economies which were negligible until the mid-1980s, rose to about 15 percent of world outflows in 2005. According to the UNCTAD (2006), the stock of

Table 2: Distribution of FDI by region and selected countries, 1980–2005 (In percent)

Region	Inward Stock				Outward Stock			
	1980	1990	2000	2005	1980	1990	2000	2005
Developed Economies	75.6	79.3	68.5	70.3	87.3	91.7	86.2	86.9
European Union	42.5	42.9	37.6	44.4	37.2	45.2	47.1	51.3
Japan	0.6	0.6	0.9	1.0	3.4	11.2	4.3	3.6
United States	14.8	22.1	21.7	16.0	37.7	24.0	20.3	19.2
Developing Economies	24.4	20.7	30.3	27.2	12.7	8.3	13.5	11.9
Africa	6.9	3.3	2.6	2.6	1.3	1.1	0.7	0.5
Latin America and the Caribbean	7.1	6.6	9.3	9.3	6.5	3.4	3.3	3.2
Asia	10.5	10.8	18.4	15.4	2.9	3.8	9.5	8.2
West Asia	1.4	2.2	1.1	1.5	0.3	0.4	0.2	0.3
South, East, and South–East Asia	8.8	8.5	17.2	13.8	2.5	3.4	9.3	7.6
South–East Europe and CIS	—	0.01	1.2	2.5	—	0.01	0.3	1.2
World	100.0	100.0	100.0	100.0	100.0	100.0	100.0	100.0

(*Continued*)

Table 2: (*Continued*)

Region	Inflow				Outflow			
	1978–1980	1988–1990	1998–2000	2003–2005	1978–1980	1988–1990	1998–2000	2003–2005
Developed Economies	79.7	82.5	77.3	59.4	97.0	93.1	90.4	85.8
European Union	39.1	40.3	46.0	40.7	44.8	50.6	64.4	54.6
Japan	0.4	0.04	0.8	0.8	4.9	19.7	2.6	4.9
United States	23.8	31.5	24.0	12.5	39.7	13.6	15.9	15.7
Developing Economies	20.3	17.5	21.7	35.9	3.0	6.9	9.4	12.3
Africa	2.0	1.9	1.0	3.0	1.0	0.4	0.2	0.2
Latin America and the Caribbean	13.0	5.0	9.7	11.5	1.1	1.0	4.1	3.5
Asia	5.3	10.5	11.0	21.4	0.9	5.6	5.1	8.6
West Asia	–1.6	0.3	0.3	3.0	0.3	0.5	0.1	1.0
South, East and South–East Asia	6.7	10.0	10.7	18.4	0.6	5.1	5.0	7.7
South–East Europe and CIS	0.0	0.02	0.9	4.7	—	0.01	0.2	1.8
World	100.0	100.0	99.9	100.0	100.0	100.0	100.0	100.0

Source: UNCTAD FDI/TNC database.

OFDI from developing economies rose from around US$70 billion in 1980 to about US$150 billion in 1990 and to more than US$1 trillion in 2005.

Table 3 focuses specifically on FDI inflows and outflows of selected Asian developing economies between 1990 and 2005. During 1990–1996, FDI inflows to Asia grew at an average annual rate of just over US$50 billion, while outflows grew at a rate of US$30 billion during the same period. Buoyant global economic conditions and the liberalization of most of the Asian economies in the early 1990s led to an influx of inflows to the region. In contrast, during 1997–2005 average annual FDI growth in outflows from Asia outpaced inflows to Asia (US$22 billion on average compared with US$50 billion annually). Further, FDI outflows and inflows for most countries during the sub-periods 1990–1996 and 1997–2005 appear to have been positively correlated, with the exceptions of Korea (first sub-period), the Philippines (second sub-period), and Bangladesh (entire period). The correlations in Greater China (Mainland plus Hong Kong) and India are particularly high, suggesting that periods of economic liberalization have been characterized by simultaneous rises in both FDI inflows as well as outflows (Table 4).

Interestingly, the two countries with the highest magnitudes of inflows and outflows are Mainland China and Hong Kong. In both of our sample periods (1990–1996 and 1997–2005), Mainland China has been the single largest host of FDI, contributing between 38 percent and 40 percent of inflows to developing Asia during the last 15 years. More specifically, for the period 1990–1996, the average FDI inflows to Mainland China was around US$20 billion, while for the second sub-period, 1997–2005, the average FDI inflows to Mainland China crossed US$50 billion. With regard to outflows, Hong Kong is clearly the single largest source of FDI outflows from Asia. FDI outflows from Hong Kong averaged just under US$15 billion annually in the first sub-period and over US$25 billion in the second sub-period.[9]

---

[9] Chen and Lin (2006) discuss patterns and determinants of FDI outflows from Hong Kong and Mainland China. Also see Chapters 5 and 7 of this volume.

Table 3: FDI inflows and outflows of selected Asian Economies (in billions of U.S. dollars)

Country	1990–1996	1997–2005	1997	1998	1999	2000	2001	2002	2003	2004	2005
Inflows											
World	248.30	816.23	489.71	712.03	1,099.92	1,409.57	832.25	617.73	557.87	710.75	916.28
Asia (excluding Japan)	51.31	114.56	100.40	91.06	108.66	143.83	103.99	88.61	93.72	137.02	163.72
New Industrial Asia	9.18	21.55	18.64	12.60	29.13	30.06	23.62	11.83	14.72	24.45	28.91
Korea	2.34	5.75	2.64	5.07	9.63	8.65	3.87	3.04	3.89	7.73	7.20
Singapore	5.89	13.60	13.75	7.31	16.58	16.48	15.65	7.34	10.38	14.82	20.08
Taiwan POC	0.95	2.21	2.25	0.22	2.93	4.93	4.11	1.45	0.45	1.90	1.63
China	25.00	76.40	56.63	60.23	64.90	102.64	70.65	62.42	67.13	94.66	108.30
China: Mainland	20.43	50.88	45.26	45.46	40.32	40.71	46.88	52.74	53.51	60.63	72.41
Hong Kong SAR	4.57	25.52	11.37	14.76	24.58	61.92	23.78	9.68	13.62	34.03	35.90
ASEAN-4	8.48	8.50	16.13	11.72	9.37	4.83	1.66	5.84	4.32	8.62	14.05
Indonesia	2.71	0.19	4.68	−0.24	−1.87	−4.55	−2.98	0.15	−0.60	1.90	5.26
Malaysia	3.62	3.50	6.32	2.71	3.90	3.79	0.55	3.20	2.47	4.62	3.97
Philippines	0.92	1.17	1.25	1.75	1.25	2.24	0.20	1.54	0.49	0.69	1.13
Thailand	1.23	3.63	3.88	7.49	6.09	3.35	3.89	0.95	1.95	1.41	3.69
South Asia	2.44	5.90	5.34	3.87	3.21	4.65	6.38	6.97	5.70	7.29	9.75
India	1.38	4.42	3.62	2.63	2.17	3.59	5.47	5.63	4.59	5.47	6.60
Pakistan	0.34	0.79	0.71	0.51	0.53	0.31	0.38	0.82	0.53	1.12	2.18
Sri Lanka	0.09	0.23	0.43	0.15	0.20	0.17	0.17	0.20	0.23	0.23	0.27
Bangladesh	0.63	0.47	0.58	0.58	0.31	0.58	0.35	0.33	0.35	0.46	0.69

(Continued)

Table 3: (*Continued*)

Country	1990–1996	1997–2005	1997	1998	1999	2000	2001	2002	2003	2004	2005
Outflows											
World	269.72	776.31	483.14	694.40	1,108.17	1,244.47	764.20	539.54	561.10	813.07	778.73
Asia (excluding Japan)	29.14	50.05	51.23	31.69	39.87	80.69	48.35	33.76	21.15	76.11	67.63
New Industrial Asia	8.92	16.87	20.60	10.74	16.62	17.62	28.07	9.79	12.25	20.32	15.86
Korea	2.25	3.98	4.45	4.74	4.20	5.00	2.42	2.62	3.43	4.66	4.31
Singapore	3.62	7.40	10.90	2.16	8.00	5.92	20.17	2.29	3.14	8.51	5.52
Taiwan POC	3.05	5.49	5.24	3.84	4.42	6.70	5.48	4.89	5.68	7.15	6.03
China	17.21	29.22	26.97	19.62	21.14	60.27	18.23	19.98	5.34	47.52	43.87
China: Mainland	2.32	3.36	2.56	2.63	1.77	0.92	6.89	2.52	-0.15	1.81	11.31
Hong Kong SAR	14.89	25.85	24.41	16.98	19.37	59.35	11.35	17.46	5.49	45.72	32.56
ASEAN-4	2.94	2.96	3.57	1.20	1.98	2.28	0.60	2.26	2.17	6.17	6.44
Indonesia	0.91	0.80	0.18	0.04	0.07	0.15	0.13	0.18	0.01	3.41	3.07
Malaysia	1.44	1.73	2.68	0.86	1.42	2.03	0.27	1.90	1.37	2.06	2.97
Philippines	0.16	0.17	0.14	0.16	0.13	0.13	-0.14	0.07	0.30	0.58	0.16
Thailand	0.43	0.26	0.58	0.13	0.35	-0.02	0.35	0.11	0.49	0.13	0.25
South Asia	0.07	1.00	0.10	0.11	0.13	0.52	1.45	1.72	1.38	2.09	1.46
India	0.07	0.95	0.11	0.05	0.08	0.51	1.40	1.68	1.33	2.02	1.36
Pakistan	0.00	0.03	-0.02	0.05	0.02	0.01	0.03	0.03	0.02	0.06	0.04
Sri Lanka	0.00	0.01	0.01	0.01	0.02	0.00	0.00	0.01	0.03	0.01	0.04
Bangladesh	0.00	0.01	0.00	0.00	0.00	0.00	0.02	0.00	0.01	0.01	0.01

Sources: UNCTAD FDI/TNC database.

Table 4:   Correlations between inflows and outflows to and from Asia.

Country	1990–1996	1997–1905
Asia	1.0	0.9
New Industrial Asia	0.9	0.5
Korea	−0.4	0.6
Singapore	0.9	0.5
Taiwan POC	0.1	0.4
China	1.0	0.8
China: Mainland	0.2	0.6
Hong Kong SAR	0.9	0.9
ASEAN-4	0.8	0.5
Indonesia	0.1	0.6
Malaysia	0.9	0.8
Philippines	0.7	−0.1
Thailand	0.8	0.1
South Asia	0.4	0.8
India	0.8	0.9
Pakistan	0.4	0.4
Sri Lanka	0.8	0.1
Bangladesh	−0.4	−0.1

Sources: Authors calculation.

As will be noted below, a large part of outflows from Hong Kong is bound for Mainland China, some of which is due to round-tripping from the Mainland to begin with. This round-tripping significantly inflates the amount of OFDI from the Mainland which itself experienced a spurt between 1990 and 2005 (UNCTAD, 2006, p. 12).[10]

Referring to Table 3 on flows and Table 5 on stocks, the significant difference between outflows from Hong Kong with the rest of our sample countries is apparent. Hong Kong's outflows are at an altogether different level than any other regional economy. Excluding Hong Kong from the analysis, the picture is more even across our sample countries. It is apparent that the three NIEs of Singapore, South Korea, and Taiwan have consistently remained among the top developing economy

---

[10] Estimates put round-tripping at between 25 percent and 50 percent of total FDI flows from Hong Kong, SAR to Mainland China (UNCTAD, 2006, p. 12).

Table 5: Top 20 developing and transition economies in terms of stocks of outward FDI, 1980, 1990, 2000, and 2005 (in Millions of US dollars).

Rank	Economy	1980	Rank	Economy	1990	Rank	Economy	2000	Rank	Economy	2005
1	Brazil	38545	1	Brazil	41044	1	Hong Kong SAR	388380	1	Hong Kong SAR	470458
2	Taiwan	13009	2	Taiwan	30356	2	Taiwan	66655	2	British Virgin Islands	123167
3	Argentina	5970	3	South Africa	15004	3	British Virgin Islands	64483	3	Russian Federation	120417
4	South Africa	5541	4	Hong Kong SAR	11920	4	Singapore	56766	4	Singapore	110932
5	Mexico	1632	5	Singapore	7808	5	Brazil	51946	5	Taiwan	97293
6	Kuwait	1046	6	Argentina	6057	6	South Africa	32319	6	Brazil	71556
7	Libyan Arab Jamahiriya	870	7	China	4455	7	China	27768	7	China	46311
8	Panama	811	8	Panama	4188	8	South Korea	26833	8	Malaysia	44480
9	Bermuda	727	9	Kuwait	3662	9	Malaysia	22874	9	South Africa	38503
10	Singapore	623	10	Mexico	2672	10	Argentina	21141	10	South Korea	36478
11	Bahrain	598	11	Malaysia	2671	11	Cayman Islands	20553	11	Cayman Islands	33747
12	Botswana	440	12	South Korea	2301	12	Russian Federation	20141	12	Mexico	28040

(Continued)

Table 5: *(Continued)*

Rank	Economy	1980	Rank	Economy	1990	Rank	Economy	2000	Rank	Economy	2005
13	Bahamas	285	13	Saudi Arabia	1873	13	Bermuda	14942	13	Argentina	22633
14	Saudi Arabia	239	14	Bermuda	1550	14	Chile	11154	14	Chile	21286
15	Malaysia	197	15	Libyan Arab Jamahiriya	1321	15	Mexico	8273	15	Indonesia	13735
16	Uruguay	171	16	Venezuela	1221	16	Venezuela	7676	16	Panama	12891
17	Philippines	171	17	Nigeria	1,207	17	Indonesia	6940	17	Venezuela	10665
18	Hong Kong SAR	148	18	Turkey	1157	18	Nigeria	4132	18	United Arab Emirates	10087
19	Colombia	136	19	British Virgin Islands	875	19	Panama	4004	19	India	9569
20	Paraguay	129	20	Bahrain	719	20	Turkey	3668	20	Colombia	8876
Memo											
25	India	78	23	India	124	23	Thailand	2203	26	Thailand	3947
39	Thailand	13	26	Thailand	418	25	India	1859	31	Philippines	2039
43	Indonesia	6	28	Indonesia	86	28	Philippines	1597			

Source: UNCTAD, Foreign Direct Investment, www.unctad.org/fdistatistics.

sources of FDI over the last two decades. Malaysia (a near-NIE) is also notable for the size of their OFDI flows, particularly since the 1990s.[11] Indonesia remains an important source of FDI, while more aggressive internationalization strategies by Indian companies have seen it rise in the rankings from 39 in 1990 to top 20 by 2005.[12] These seven economies constitute the bulk of OFDI from Asia.

3.2. *Intraregional Asian FDI Flows: A First Look*

Having considered broad country aggregate outflows and inflows to and from Asia, we analyze bilateral FDI between Asian economies. This exercise is far from straightforward. UNCTAD data on inflows and outflows do not match exactly (also see UNCTAD (2006), Chapter 3). It is apparent that UNCTAD FDI outflows data from source countries are incomplete for many countries (Table 6). While some source countries have relatively complete outflows data, others either have incomplete data or no data at all. Different reporting practices of FDI data create bilateral discrepancies between FDI flows reported by home and host countries, and the differences can be quite large. For example, data on FDI flows to China, as reported by the Chinese authorities and by the investing countries' authorities, differ by roughly US$30 billion in 2001, US$8 billion in 2001, and US$2 billion in 2002.[13] Faced with these concerns, we draw inferences on FDI outflows by examining FDI inflow data reported in the host economies as they are more complete and are available for all developing Asian economies under consideration. In other words, we focus on the *sources of inflows* rather than *host of outflows*.

---

[11] While there is not necessarily a one-to-one link between nationality of MNCs and FDI outflows, it is instructive to note that the handful of firms from developing economies that made the top 100 list were from Hong Kong, Taiwan, Mainland China, Singapore, Korea, and Malaysia. MNCs from the first four economies (i.e., Greater China and Singapore) constituted 60 percent of the top 100 MNCs from developing economies (UNCTAD, Chapter 1).

[12] Anecdotal evidence suggests that Indian companies have been particularly aggressive in investing overseas in 2006–2007. Also see Chapter 6 of this volume. Hiratsuka (2006) discusses outward investments by ASEAN corporates.

[13] Apart from round-tripping and trans-shipping issues (discussed later in this section), part of the data inconsistencies between inflows and outflows arise because many countries do not include retained earnings or loans when considering FDI outflows.

Table 6:   Average of intra-Asian bilateral FDI outward flows (In millions of U.S. dollars, unless otherwise noted).

	(1997–2000)			Host region 1/ (2001–2005)		
	Asia 2/	in percent of Asia	in percent of World	Asia 2/	in percent of Asia	in percent of World
Source countries						
Newly Industrialized Asia	11024.1	28.8	1.2	9621.1	27.6	1.4
Korea	650.4	1.7	0.1	253.1	0.7	0.0
Singapore	6997.9	18.3	0.8	5331.7	15.3	0.8
Taiwan POC	3375.7	8.8	0.4	4036.3	11.6	0.6
ASEAN-4	1027.3	2.7	0.1	1089.5	3.1	0.2
Indonesia	257.6	0.7	0.0	189.5	0.5	0.0
Malaysia	334.3	0.9	0.0	415.6	1.2	0.1
Philippines	180.3	0.5	0.0	267.2	0.8	0.0
Thailand	255.0	0.7	0.0	217.2	0.6	0.0
China	20179.9	68.3	2.8	24018.0	69.0	3.5
Mainland China	7334.6	19.1	0.8	5576.2	16.0	0.8
Hong Kong SAR	18845.3	49.2	2.0	18441.8	53.0	2.7
India	43.8	0.1	0.0	34.8	0.1	0.0

(Continued)

Table 6: *(Continued)*

| | Host region 1/ | | | | | |
| | (1997–2000) | | | (2001–2005) | | |
	Asia 2/	in percent of Asia	in percent of World	Asia 2/	in percent of Asia	in percent of World
Low income Asia	20.2	0.1	0.0	37.4	0.1	0.0
Bangladesh	0.2	0.0	0.0	0.5	0.0	0.0
Cambodia	0.5	0.0	0.0	3.1	0.0	0.0
Lao PDR	2.6	0.0	0.0	-0.5	0.0	0.0
Myanmar	4.7	0.0	0.0	2.1	0.0	0.0
Sri Lanka	2.7	0.0	0.0	0.2	0.0	0.0
Vietnam	9.5	0.0	0.0	31.9	0.1	0.0
Other Asia	26.4	0.1	0.0	17.4	0.0	0.0
Pakistan	1.4	0.0	0.0	6.2	0.0	0.0
Brunei Darussalam	25.1	0.1	0.0	11.1	0.0	0.0
Developing Asia 3/	27297.6	71.2	2.9	25197.0	72.4	3.7
Asia 2/	38321.7	100.0	4.1	34818.1	100.0	5.1

Source: UNCTAD FDI/TNC database.
1. Asia data is based on FDI inflow data in host economy; world data is based on FDI outflow from source economy.
2. Asia consists of Newly Industrialized Asia, ASEAN-4, China, India, Low Income Asia, and Other Asia.
3. Developing Asia consists of ASEAN-4, China, India, Low Income Asia, and Other Asia.

To keep the analysis manageable, we examine data for the averages of 1997–2000, and 2001–2005 rather than on an annual basis.[14]

FDI inflows between Asian countries accounts for about one-third of all FDI inflows to the region (Table 7 and Figure 1), and is particularly pronounced between and within East Asian economies and South–East Asian economies. This is apparent from Table 8 which highlights that the bilateral flows between East Asian countries are the highest in Asia with an average of US$28 billion for the period of 1997–2005. According to Table 9, the average of FDI flows from Hong Kong to China and vice versa from 1997 to 2005 has been around US$24 billion and accounts for almost 40 percent of intra-Asia. Apart from Hong Kong–China–Taiwan flows, bilateral flows between East and South–East Asia are also significant. Almost three-fifths of flows from East Asia to South–East Asia have been destined for the relatively higher-income South–East economies, viz. Singapore, Malaysia, Philippines, and Thailand. Singapore has attracted about half of all East Asian FDI destined for South–East Asia. The city state has also been a major investor to China. Malaysia and Thailand have also invested in China.

Consideration of intra-Asian bilateral flows highlights a few other important characteristics of intra-Asian FDI flows (Tables 8 and 9). First, the leading investors from the region have stayed the same between 1997 and 2006, with Hong Kong as the leading investor, followed by Singapore, Taiwan, Korea, China, and Malaysia, in that order. The importance of China as a source of capital is noteworthy in that there has been a great deal of debate on whether China has diverted extra-regional FDI from the rest of South–East and East Asia (for instance, see Chantasasawat *et al.* (2004), Eichengreen and Tong (2007), Liu *et al.* (2007), Mercereau (2005), and Sudsawasd and Chaisrisawatsuk (2006).[15]

While Hong Kong's FDI to the Mainland has remained stable between the two sub-periods, that from the Mainland to Hong Kong has

---

[14] It is instructive to note that the top destinations of FDI using inflows data to the host economy and outflows data from the source economy have stayed roughly the same during the period under consideration.

[15] This said, the bulk of FDI flows from China have been to Hong Kong. However, there is evidence of growing investments by China into South–East Asia.

Table 7:   Average intra-Asian bilateral FDI outward flows 1/ (In millions of US dollars).

	Host region					
	(1997–2000)			(2001–2005)		
	East Asia 2/	South–East Asia 3/	South Asia 4/	East Asia 2/	South–East Asia 3/	South Asia 4/
Source region						
East Asia 2/	28453.6	1550.9	201.6	27293.6	937.0	76.8
South–East Asia 3/	6328.7	1652.2	86.6	3622.3	2735.5	111.1
South Asia 4/	0.0	42.8	5.2	0.0	27.1	14.6
Rest of the World	42812.3	21490.0	3732.2	48678.6	21036.2	3823.2

Notes:

1. Based on FDI inflow data in host economy.
2. East Asia consists of China, Hong Kong SAR, Korea, and Taiwan POC.
3. South–East Asia consists of Brunei Darussalam, Cambodia, Lao PDR, Malaysia, Myanmar, Singapore, Philippines, Thailand, and Vietnam.
4. South Asia consists of Bangladesh, India, Sri Lanka, and Pakistan.

Source: UNCTAD FDI/TNC database.

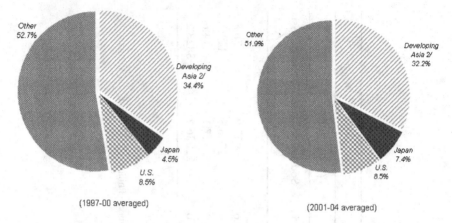

(1997-00 averaged)   (2001-04 averaged)

Figure 1:   Source of FDI Inflows to Asia.

Source: UNCTAD.

1. Definition of Asia follows UNCTAD's definition which includes East, South, and South–East Asia and excludes Japan.

2. Developing Asia consists of Bangladesh, Brunei Darussalam, Cambodia, Hong Kong SAR, India, Indonesia, Korea, Lao PDR, Mainland China, Malaysia, Myanmar, Pakistan, Philippines, Singapore, Sri Lanka, Taiwan POC, Thailand, and Vietnam.

declined. Second, intra South–East Asia investment accounted for 6.7 percent of cumulative FDI flows in Asia between 1997 and 2005. Comparing the two sample periods, intra South–East Asia's investment share of cumulative FDI flows in Asia increased between the two periods from 4.3 percent to 7.8 percent, with Singapore as the leading investor in both periods. Singapore's investments to its ASEAN neighbors, Malaysia and Thailand, have increased in the second sub-period, while the city state's investments to China and especially Hong Kong have declined. Third, FDI between East Asia and South Asia remains low and stagnant.[16]

It is important to note that the data analyzed above exclude the offshore financial centers (OFCs) such as the British Virgin Islands, Bermuda, Cayman Islands, Mauritius, and Western Samoa as sources

---

[16] Recent interest expressed by Japanese, Korean and Taiwanese firms in the booming Indian economy may alter this, though that remains to be seen. There appears to be some desire to diversify export market platforms from China although it is unclear whether this will lead to a shift of some FDI from Korea, Japan, and Taiwan to India or to developing South–East Asian economies such as Indonesia, Thailand, Vietnam, Philippines, Malaysia, etc.

Table 8: Top 50 bilateral flows between Asian countries 1/ (In million of US dollars)

Source	Host	Average		In percent to Asia	
		(1997–2000)	(2001–2005)	(1997–2000)	(2001–2005)
Hong Kong SAR	China	17,750.8	17,819.1	46.2	50.7
China	Hong Kong SAR	7,266.9	5,459.4	18.9	15.5
Singapore	China	2,706.3	2,136.7	7.0	6.1
Singapore	Hong Kong SAR	2,835.3	353.1	7.4	1.0
Singapore	Malaysia	844.1	1,133.8	2.2	3.2
Singapore	Thailand	441.7	1,381.9	1.1	3.9
Malaysia	China	290.8	316.7	0.8	0.9
Hong Kong SAR	Malaysia	272.3	296.5	0.7	0.8
Hong Kong SAR	Thailand	360.1	160.8	0.9	0.5
Korea	Hong Kong SAR	313.0	155.7	0.8	0.4
Thailand	China	185.8	183.7	0.5	0.5
Philippines	China	135.9	212.2	0.4	0.6
Hong Kong SAR	Singapore	250.1	81.9	0.7	0.2
Malaysia	Hong Kong SAR	62.0	147.2	0.2	0.4
Singapore	Philippines	88.9	76.1	0.2	0.2
Hong Kong SAR	Korea	79.2	51.5	0.2	0.1

(*Continued*)

Table 8:   (*Continued*)

Source	Host	Average		In percent to Asia	
		(1997–2000)	(2001–2005)	(1997–2000)	(2001–2005)
Thailand	Hong Kong SAR	-3.1	110.7	0.0	0.3
Hong Kong SAR	Philippines	50.0	54.4	0.1	0.2
Singapore	India	22.0	67.6	0.1	0.2
China	Singapore	-17.3	99.9	0.0	0.3
China	Philippines	71.8	-0.1	0.2	0.0
India	Singapore	36.8	24.9	0.1	0.1
Philippines	Thailand	4.9	48.4	0.0	0.1
China	Cambodia	18.3	33.4	0.0	0.1
Malaysia	Cambodia	24.9	16.7	0.1	0.0
Malaysia	Thailand	19.4	21.2	0.1	0.1
Singapore	Cambodia	19.6	12.9	0.1	0.0
Thailand	Cambodia	19.1	13.4	0.0	0.0
Philippines	Malaysia	6.3	18.7	0.0	0.1
Malaysia	Bangladesh	5.1	19.4	0.0	0.1
Philippines	Singapore	37.5	-15.6	0.1	0.0
Thailand	Malaysia	10.2	11.1	0.0	0.0

(*Continued*)

Table 8: (*Continued*)

Source	Host	Average (1997–2000)	Average (2001–2005)	In percent to Asia (1997–2000)	In percent to Asia (2001–2005)
Malaysia	Lao PDR	17.4	0.9	0.0	0.0
Thailand	Lao PDR	15.2	1.9	0.0	0.0
China	Malaysia	11.5	5.1	0.0	0.0
Pakistan	Bangladesh	1.3	10.7	0.0	0.0
China	Thailand	0.4	10.8	0.0	0.0
China	Lao PDR	3.9	6.6	0.0	0.0
Malaysia	Philippines	6.5	2.4	0.0	0.0
Singapore	Myanmar	0.0	8.7	0.0	0.0
Thailand	Myanmar	0.0	5.6	0.0	0.0
Myanmar	Singapore	4.1	1.1	0.0	0.0
China	Myanmar	0.0	4.7	0.0	0.0
Thailand	Philippines	3.0	0.8	0.0	0.0
Singapore	Lao PDR	1.0	2.3	0.0	0.0
Cambodia	Thailand	0.6	2.7	0.0	0.0
China	Bangladesh	1.2	1.0	0.0	0.0
Lao PDR	Thailand	2.3	-0.4	0.0	0.0

Source: UNCTAD FDI database
1/Based on FDI inflow data in host economy.

of FDI. Insofar as at least some part of inflows from the OFCs involve FDI that originated from other Asian economies, and the inflows are not destined back to originating country (i.e., trans-shipping as opposed to round-tripping), we are undercounting the size of intra-Asian FDI flows. For instance, the British Virgin Islands has consistently been the second largest source of FDI into China, surpassed only by Hong Kong, with the Cayman Islands and Western Samoa also being among the top 10 in 2006.[17] Similarly, investments from other sources may have been re-routed to India via Mauritius which has consistently been the top source of FDI to India.[18]

4. Determinants of FDI Outflows from Asia

The previous section has highlighted the extent of FDI outflows from developing countries and more specifically, the intensification of intraregional FDI flows. But what explains the rise of intraregional FDI flows in Asia? This section undertakes a simple empirical investigation of some of the possible determinants of FDI outflows from Asia to the rest of the region over the period 1997–2004.[19] Is a gravity model framework that is commonly used to rationalize OFDI flows from OECD economies applicable as a tool to understand intra-Asian FDI flows?

4.1. *The Model*

The aim of this section is to develop a relatively parsimonious model which includes commonly used determinants as well as focus on specific bilateral variables. To this end, we follow the basic gravity type

---

[17] http://www.uschina.org/info/forecast/2007/foreign-investment.html#table4. In the literature, OFCs have mainly been discussed in the context of bank flows and portfolio flows. For instance, see Dixon (2001), Rose and Spiegel (2006), and Zoromé (2007).

[18] Mauritius has low corporate tax and has signed a liberal Double taxation agreement (DTA) with India. As such, the extent of actual extent of flows of FDI between India and East and South–East Asia may be understated. This is especially so as many companies from abroad and in India use Singapore as a regional headquarters, particularly following the signing of a bilateral Comprehensive Economic Cooperation Agreement (CECA). This said, Pardhan (2005) has argued that outward investments from Indian MNCs since the mid-1990s have been more global in nature.

[19] While we have FDI data until 2005, some of the independent variables are truncated at 2004.

framework which postulates that market size and distance are important determinants in the choice of location of direct investment's
source countries. The theoretical basis for a gravity model of FDI has
recently been proposed by Head and Ries (2007). The model has
been used in a host of papers with some variations.[20]

The basic specification of our estimated model is outlined below

$$\ln(\text{FDI}_{ijt}) = \beta_0 + \beta_1 \ln(\text{GDP}_{jt}) + \beta_2 \ln(\text{GDP}_{it}) + \beta_3 \ln(\text{COST}_{ij})$$
$$+ \beta_4 X_{ijt} + \mu_{ij} + \lambda_t + \nu_{ijt} \qquad (1)$$

where: FDI_{ijt} is the FDI outflow from source country (i) to host
country (j) in time (t); GDP_{it} and GDP_{jt} are nominal GDPs for
the source country (i) and the host country (j) in time (t); COST_{ij} is
a vector of transaction cost between host and source countries; for
our study we used geographical distance between host and source
countries, a dummy variable equals to one if the two countries share
a border; a dummy variable equals to one if the two countries have a
common language; and share a common border; X_{ijt} is a vector of
control variables influencing FDI outflows; μ_{ij} denotes the unobservable country-pair individual effects; λ_t denotes the unobservable time
effects (we use year dummies); and ν_{ijt} is a nuisance term.

The set of control variables includes: the real exchange rate of
i with respect to j (with depreciation or appreciation constructed by
taking log difference of end-month exchange rates); an index of the
corruption level in country j; an index of investment profile in country j; a binary variable equal to 1 if i and j belong to a common free
trade agreement (FTA); and a binary variable equal to 1 if i and
j belong to a common preferential trade agreement (PTA).

We expect the coefficients of the GDP of the source and host
countries to both be positive as they proxy for masses which are

---

[20] The augmented gravity model for FDI is broadly similar — but by no means identical —
to those used in recent papers including Loungani *et al.* (2002). Stein and Daude (2007),
Liu *et al.* (2007). di Giovanni (2005) applies a gravity model to analyze cross-border M&A
transactions while Portes and Rey (2005) and Lee (2006) applies a gravity model for portfolio equity flows.

important in gravity models.[21] As for the control variables, common official language should positively impact bilateral FDI flows. The contiguity dummy should also have a positive sign, while the sign for distance from source to host country should be negative, as a greater distance makes a foreign operation more difficult and expensive to supervise and might therefore discourage FDI.[22] The bilateral real exchange rate which is measured in terms of the host country, ought to have a negative sign as a depreciated real exchange rate in the host country should raise FDI outflows from the source country (due to the wealth effects). However, there are other channels that could lead to ambiguity of the signage (Cushman, 1985). A common trade agreement should have a positive impact on bilateral FDI flows insofar as it is a proxy for lower transaction and information costs.[23]

Anghel (2005), Bénassy-Quéré et al. (2007), and Daude and Stein (2004) have discussed and explored in some detail the importance of institutional variables in determining FDI flows and Hur et al. (2007) have analyzed the importance of institutions in the case of M&A deals. In view of this we include two institutional measures which are subcomponents of Political Risk Index of International Country Risk Group (ICRG) database. The first is a control of corruption index — a higher control of corruption index in country *j* should encourage FDI inflow (Wei, 2000). The impact of investment profile, on the other hand, is more intuitive. Since the index of "investment profile" measures government's attitude toward FDI, a higher investment profile index should encourage FDI flows into that country.[24]

---

[21] In physics, the law of gravity states that the force of gravity between two objects is proportional to the product of the masses of the two objects divided by the square of the distance between them. Most gravity models in bilateral trade and FDI have replaced the force of gravity with the value of bilateral trade or direct investments and the masses with the source and host countries' GDP.

[22] However, if the foreign firm is looking to service the host country's market, a longer distance also makes exporting from source countries more expensive and might therefore make local production more desirable and encourage investment. This argument is not unlike the tariff-jumping one.

[23] There is a growing body of literature examining the links between FDI and regional trade agreements. For instance, see Jaumotte (2004).

[24] Investment Profile is an index made of various subcomponents including contract viability/expropriation, profits repatriation, and payment delays.

4.2. Data, Methodology, and Results

Tables A1 and A2 summarize the data sources to be used and Table A3 offers the summary statistics of the relevant variables. The FDI data are based on the *UNCTAD FDI/TNC* database. Nominal GDP in US dollar, real GDP per capita, exchange rates (average and deflated by consumer price index) are taken from the IMF's *World Economic Outlook* database. Corruption and investment profile indices are taken from International Country Risk Group (ICRG) database. Data on the share of border land and common official language are from the CEPII.[25]

Although we have 14 countries in the sample, not every country receives FDI from others. There are potentially 130 host–source country pairs (10×13) from 1990 to 2004. However, there are many instances of zero bilateral flows and missing variables. Following convention (see Eichengreen and Irwin (1995) and Stein and Daude (2007) we replaced the zero flows with one. This will make them zeros when we take their natural logs in our empirical analysis.

In all of our estimations, we deal with the issue of censored data. The common approach to dealing with censored data is to run a Tobit model (for instance see Bénassy-Quéré *et al.* (2007), Stein and Daude (2007) and Loungani, *et al.* (2002).[26] We follow di Giovanni (2005) by computing a Tobit model using the two-step procedure. First, a probit model is estimated for whether a deal is observed or not conditional on the same right-hand variables as in Equation (1), and the inverse Mills' ratio is constructed from the predicted values of the model. Second, a regression is run to estimate Equation (1) including the inverse Mills ratio as a regressor.[27]

We calculated our model of Equation (1) using pooled cross-section and panel regression and present two specifications in Table 9.

---

[25] http://www.cepii.fr/
[26] Another alternative suggested by Santos Silva and Tenreyo (2006) is to use the Poison pseudo maximum likelihood method. This methodology has been recently applied to FDI by Head and Ries (2007). Coe *et al.* (2007) suggest another log-linear estimation method to deal with this problem.
[27] The standard errors are corrected for heteroskedasticity and we use an estimated parameter of an exogenous variable (the inverse Mills' ratio) in the second stage. See di Giovanni (2005) for details.

The first specification is based on pooled ordinary least squares. Regression (1) imposes that the slopes and intercepts are the same across country-pair, i.e., $\mu_{ij} = 0$. Regression (2) is based on an unrestricted fixed effect model for panel data. The advantage of using fixed effect is to allow for unobserved or mis-specified factors that simultaneously explain FDI flow between two countries.

Table 9:　The determinants of intra-Asia bilateral FDI outflows.

Dependent variable: ln of bilateral FDI outflows	Regression (1)	Regression (2)
ln (GDPi)	0.317	0.889***
	(0.209)	(0.286)
ln (GDPj)	0.465***	0.560***
	(0.058)	(0.213)
Common border	−0.727***	
	(0.231)	
Common language	1.102***	
	(0.182)	
ln distance	−0.551***	
	(0.153)	
Bilateral real exchange rate of i w.r.t. j	−0.027*	−0.107
	(0.016)	(0.069)
Control of Corruption index j	−0.325**	−0.666***
	(0.136)	(0.136)
Investment profile index j	0.102***	0.185***
	(0.038)	(0.036)
Trade agreement between i and j	2.708**	
	(1.129)	
Preferential agreement between i and j	0.660	3.845***
	(1.148)	(1.367)
Observations	1950	1950
Overall R-squared	0.26	0.11
Number of country-pairs		130
Specific effects		

Notes: Robust standard error in parentheses.
* Significant at 10%; ** significant at 5%; *** significant at 1%.
Year dummies, country-pair dummies, inverse Mills' ratio, and constant are not shown.
Source: Author calculations.

In Regression (2), we remove the restriction that the country-pair intercept terms equal zero, although we maintain the restriction that the slope coefficients are constant across country pairs and overtime to address the biasness of pooled regressions. Specifically, we allowed for $\mu_{ij} \neq \mu_{ji}$. Our country-pair fixed effects application is similar to Wall (1999).[28]

Our specifications broadly concur with earlier findings based on cross-sectional data (for instance, Lipsey (1999). Both specifications show that larger countries receive larger volumes of FDI in dollar terms. The impact of distance comes out as significant with correct sign only in Regression (1); longer distance tends to reduce bilateral FDI flows. Common official language comes out with correct sign and significant in Regression (1). The result for common border, on the other hand, is not consistent to our initial assumption. Consistent with Wei (2000), both specifications suggest that lower levels of corruption lead to a higher FDI bilateral flow. Trade agreements between emerging Asian countries have positive effect on bilateral FDI bilateral flows.

5. Conclusion

Intra-Asian investment flows in the region by Japanese MNCs are not something new, having been fuelled partly by the Plaza Accord of 1984–1985. However, an interesting phenomenon in recent times has been the rise of outward investments by many other developing Asian economies. Many governments in Asia have clearly taken a very positive attitude toward OFDI and have taken notable steps to liberalize capital account transactions, foreign ownership policies and foreign exchange policies and related regulations as a means of facilitating the international expansion of firms in their countries. Consequently, intra-Asian FDI flows are no longer a North–South phenomenon but increasingly a South–South one as well, and a substantial portion of FDI from Asia is intraregional in nature. However, much of the discussion surrounding

---

[28] A recent study by Anderson and Marcouiller (2002) suggests that country-pair fixed effect is important. Also see Eichengreen and Tong (2007).

intra-Asian FDI flows has been anecdotal and qualitative in nature (largely based on case studies), and most existing quantitative studies have only considered FDI from OECD sources to Asia.

This chapter has investigated trends, patterns, and drivers of intra-Asian FDI flows using bilateral FDI flows involving 15 developing Asian countries for the period 1990–2005. In other words, the primary contribution of this chapter is that it is one of the first — if not the first — to examine the magnitudes and determinants of FDI flows from developing Asian sources to other developing Asian hosts.

The data indicates around 35 percent of FDI flows to developing Asia between 1990 and 2005 has come from within the region, with over 90 percent of the flows originating from Hong Kong, China, Singapore, and Taiwan. Clearly some of these flows are overstated as they involve recycling or round-tripping of funds (especially between China and Hong Kong). Against this, trans-shipping from offshore financial centers have not been included, implying a degree of under-stating.[29] While the intra-Asian flows are substantial, two issues stand out. First, a large portion of these flows pertains to bilateral flows between Hong Kong and Mainland China. Second, the data do not indicate that intra-Asian flows are necessarily intensifying. Given that developing Asia is investing aggressively overseas, what this suggests is that relatively more investments are being made outside developing Asia.

The chapter finds that an augmented gravity model fits the data fairly well. We find that greater the host country size and higher institution quality in the host country (proxied by lower corruption levels) appears to facilitate bilateral FDI flows within Asia. There also appears to be evidence that a common language, shorter distance, and a bilateral trade agreement all tend to facilitate intra-Asian bilateral FDI flows. These three variables appear to suggest the importance of "transactional distance" and "informational distance" between countries *a la* Loungani *et al.* (2002).[30]

---

[29] See UNCTAD (2006, pp. 3–12), for a brief discussion of round-tripping and trans-shipping in the context of cross-border FDI flows.
[30] Also see Portes and Rey (2005).

Annex

Table A1: Variables included in the dataset.

Variables	Source
FDI Outflows	UNCTAD FDI/TNC database
Nominal GDP in US dollar	World Economic Outlook, IMF
Nominal GDP in local currency	World Economic Outlook, IMF
Consumer price indices	World Economic Outlook, IMF
Nominal Bilateral Exchange Rate	International Financial Statistics, IMF
Nominal Real Exchange Rate	Authors
Nominal Relative Price Indices	Authors
Distance	CEPII
Common Official Language	CEPII
Shared Land Border	CEPII
Control of corruption	ICRG
Investment profile	ICRG
Trade agreements	WTO website

Table A2: Source and host economies in the dataset.

Source	Host
Bangladesh	Bangladesh
China (Mainland)	China (Mainland)
Hong Kong, SAR	Hong Kong, SAR
India	India
Korea	Indonesia
Malaysia	Korea
Pakistan	Malaysia
Philippines	Pakistan
Singapore	Philippines
Thailand	Singapore
	Sri Lanka
	Taiwan, POC
	Thailand
	Vietnam

Table A3: Summary of statistics.

Variable	Units	Observation	Mean	Std. Dev.	Min	Max
Bilateral FDI outflows from i to j	US$ millions	696	5S9.7	2556.0	−1274.8	20677.0
Nominal GDP country i	US$ billions	1950	208.3	279.0	6.5	1931.6
Nominal GDP country j	US$ billions	1950	246.2	319.6	30.5	1931.6
Common border	Dummy, 1 = yes	1950	0.1	0.3	0	1
Common official language	Dummy, 1 = yes	1950	0.3	0.4	0	1
Distance	Kilometers	1950	3003.7	1325.2	315.5	5840.5
Bilateral real exchange rate of i w.r.t. j	Index	1950	180.0	837.0	0.0	10766.0
Corruption index in i	100 = min; 0 = max	1950	3.0	1.1	0.1	5.0
Investment profile index in i	100=min; 0 = max	1950	6.6	1.8	2.0	12.0
Free trade agreements	Dummy, 1 = yes	1950	0.2	0.2	0	1
Prefential trade agreements	Dummy, 1 = yes	1950	0.2	0.4	0	1

References

Accenture (2005). China Spreads its Wings — Chinese Companies go Global Accenture.

Aguiar, M, A Bhattacharya, T Bradtke, P Cotte, P Dertnig, M Meyer, DC Michael and H Sirkin (2006). *The New Global Challengers: How 100 Top Companies from Rapidly Developing Economies Are Changing the World*. The Boston Consulting Group.

Anderson J and D Marcouiller (2002). Insecurity and the pattern of trade: An empirical investigation. *Review of Economics and Statistics*, 84, 342–352.

Anghel, B (2005). *Do Institutions Affect Foreign Direct Investment?* Universidad Autónoma de Barcelona, Mimeo (October 2005).

Bénassy-Quéré, A, M Coupet and T Mayer (2007). Institutional determinants of foreign direct investment. *The World Economy*, 30, 764–782.

Bénassy-Quéré, A, L Fontagné and A Lahrèche-Révil (2005). How does FDI react to corporate taxation? *International Tax and Public Finance*, 12, 583–603.

Boston Consulting Group (BCG) (2006). *The New Global Challengers: How 100 Companies from Rapidly Developing Economies are Changing the World*. The Boston Consulting Group.

Chantasasawat, B, KC Fung, H Iizaka and AKF Siu (2004). Foreign direct investment in China and East Asia. Working Paper No.1135, Hong Kong Institute of Economics and Business Strategy, The University of Hong Kong.

Chen, EKY and P Lin (2006). Mainland China and Hong Kong emerging TNCs from East Asia. Working Paper No.WP31, East Asian Bureau of Economic Research, Australian National University.

Coe, DT, A Subramanian and NT Tamirisa (2007). "The Missing Globalization Puzzle: Evidence of the Declining Importance of Distance", *IMF Staff Papers*, 5, 34–58.

Cushman (1985), Real exchange rate risk, expectations, and the level of direct investment. *Review of Economics and Statistics*, 67, 297–308.

Daude, C and E Stein (2004). *The Quality of Institutions and Foreign Direct Investment*. mimeo, University of Maryland.

di Giovanni, J (2005). What drives capital flows? The case of cross-border activity and financial deepening. *Journal of International Economics*, 65, 127–149.

Dixon, L (2001). Financial flows via offshore financial centres as part of the international financial system. *Financial Stability Review*, June, 105–116.

Duce, M (2003). *Definitions of Foreign Direct Investment (FDI): A Methodological Note*. Banco de Espana, Mimeo.

Eichengreen, B and D Irwin (1995). Trade blocs, currency blocs and the reorientation of trade in the 1930s. *Journal of International Economics*, 38, 1–24.

Eichengreen, B and D Leblang (2006). Democracy and globalization. Working Paper No. 2006, NBER.

Eichengreen, B and H Tong (2007). Is China's FDI coming at the expense of other countries? *Journal of Japanese and International Economics,* 21, 153–172.

Globerman, S and D Shapiro (2005). Assessing international mergers and acquisitions as a mode of foreign direct investment. In *Governance, Multinationals and Growth,* L Eden and W Dobson (eds.), pp.68–99, London: Edwin Elgar.

Head, K and J Ries (2007). FDI as an outcome of the market for corporate control: Theory and evidence. *Journal of International Economics.* (Forthcoming)

Hiratsuka, D (2006). Outward FDI from ASEAN and Intraregional FDI in ASEAN: Trends and Drivers. ASEAN-UNCTAD Annual Seminar on Key Issues of FDI: Outward FDI from Asia Session 1, UNCTAD and ASEAN.

Hur, J, RA Parinduri and YE Riyanto (2007). Cross-border M&A inflows and the quality of institutions: A cross-country panel data analysis. Working Paper No.2007/08, Singapore Centre for Applied and Policy Economics, National University of Singapore.

International Monetary Fund (IMF) (2003). *Foreign Direct Investment Statistics: How Countries Measure FDI 2001,* Washington, DC: IMF.

Jaumotte, F (2004). "Foreign Direct Investment and Regional Trade Agreements: The Market Size Effect Revisited," Working Paper No. WP/04/2006, IMF.

Kwan, N and F Cheung (2006). Asia Focus: Intra-Asia Investment Reinforces Integration. Standard Chartered, June 21.

Lipsey, RE (1999). The Location and Characteristics of U.S. Affiliates in Asia. Working Paper No. 6876, NBER.

Liu, LG, K Chow and U Li (2007). Determinants of foreign direct investment in East Asia: Did China crowd out FDI from her developing East Asian neighbours? *China and the World Economy,* May–June, 70–88.

Loungani, P, A Mody and A Razin (2002). The global disconnect: The role of transactional distance and scale economies in gravity equations. *Scottish Journal of Political Economy,* 18, 526–543.

Lunding, A (2006). Global champions in waiting: Perspectives on China's overseas direct on direct investment. Deutsche Bank Research, August 4.

Mercereau, B (2005). FDI flows to Asia: Did the Dragon crowd out the Tigers? Working Paper No. WP05/189, IMF.

Pardhan, JP (2005). Outward foreign direct investment from India: Recent trends and patterns. Working Paper No. 153, Gujarat Institute of Development Research.

Portes, R and H Rey (2005). The determinants of cross-border equity flows. *Journal of International Economics,* 65, 269–296.

Rajan, RS (2005). Financing development in the Asia-Pacific Region: Trends and linkages. In *The Role of Trade and Investment Policies in the Implementation of the Monterrey Consensus: Regional Perspectives,* Studies in Trade and Investment, Vol. 55, pp. 21–65.

Razin, A, Y Rubinstein, and E Sadka (2003). Which countries export FDI, and how much? Working Paper No.10145, NBER.

Rose, AK and MM Spiegel (2006). *Offshore Financial Centers: Parasites or Symbionts?* Mimeo (April 4).

Santos Silva, JMC and S Tenreyo (2006). The log of gravity. *Review of Economics and Statistics*, 88, 641–658.

Sauvant, KP (2005). New sources of FDI: The BRICs. *The Journal of World Investment and Trade*, 6, 639–711.

Stein, E and C Daude (2007). Longitude matters: Time zones and the location of foreign direct investment. Forthcoming in *Journal of International Economics*.

Sudsawasd, S and S Chaisrisawatsuk (2006). "Tigers and dragons against elephants: Does the rising Chinese and Indian share in trade and foreign direct investment crowd out Thailand and other ASEAN countries?" *Asia-Pacific Trade and Investment Review*, 2, 93–114.

The Economist (2006). The dragon tuck in. June 30.

Tong, SY (2005). Ethnic networks in FDI and the impact of institutional development. *Review of Development Economics*, 9, 563–580.

UNCTAD (2006). *World Investment Report 2006*. UN: New York and Geneva.

UNCTAD (2007). Rising FDI into China: The facts behind the numbers. *Investment Brief No.2*, UNCTAD.

United Nations (2006). *World Investment Report 2006*. UN: New York and Geneva.

Wall, Howard J (1999). Using the gravity model to estimate the costs of protection. *Federal Reserve Bank of St. Louis Review*, January/February), pp. 33–40.

Wei, SJ (2000). How taxing is corruption to international investors? *Review of Economics and Statistics*, 82, 1–11.

World Bank (2006). *Global Development Finance*. New York: Oxford University Press, Chapter 4.

Wu, F (2005). The Globalization of Corporate China. *NBR Analysis*, Vol. 16, The National Bureau of Asian Research, Seattle.

Zoromé, A (2007). Concept of offshore financial centers: In search of an operational definition. Working Paper No. WP/07/87, IMF.

Section II

Asian Giants (Japan, China, and India)

Chapter 4

Japan's Outward FDI in the Era of Globalization*

Daisuke Hiratsuka

1. Introduction

Outward foreign direct investment (OFDI) in Asia by Japanese enterprises has traditionally been a major source of intra-regional FDI in
Asia since the 1980s. However, today, Japan is no longer the leader in
OFDI in Asia. Indeed, Asia's rapidly growing economy has been
accompanied by new economic phenomena such as the increase in
intra-regional trade and intra-regional FDI. The Asian newly indus-
trializing economies (NIEs) of Hong Kong, Korea, Singapore, and
Taiwan have been leaders in the movement of overseas operations,
followed by Malaysia and Thailand. More recently, the large Asian
economies of China and India have emerged as significant sources of
OFDI in Asia. Put differently, intra-regional FDI has not only been a
North–South phenomenon but also a South–South one as well (see
Chapter 3 by Hattari and Rajan). As for ASEAN, much of the
South–South FDI is initially invested close to the home market, and
then tends to expand more widely (Hiratsuka, 2006a). Furthermore,
the phenomenon of South–South FDI flows is taking place not only
by multinational corporations (MNCs) but also by small and
medium-sized enterprises (SMEs) (Hiratsuka, 2006a).

From the viewpoint of Japan, intra-regional FDI in Asia can be
broadly divided into two phases. The first is globalism — where
Japanese firms operated in overseas markets such as the United States

* Comments by Mandira Sarma at the ICRIER workshop are appreciated. The usual disclaimer
applies.

(US), Europe, East Asia, and elsewhere. The second is regionalism — where Japanese firms have operated in the production and distribution networks where parts and components are produced according to the location advantage of particular Asian countries and cities. Such regionalism in FDI has been accelerated by *de jure* integration, or free trade agreements (FTAs) which integrate segmented markets and work to reallocate the location of industry. FTAs, therefore, activate intra-regional FDI. The development of economic integration raises several questions related to intra-regional FDI and/or Japan's FDI: how is Japan's OFDI changing in magnitude and destination in the Asian region? How are SMEs responding to economic integration where economies of scale/increasing returns to scale work strongly? Given the possibility of further economic integration, what roles are Japanese firms expected to play in OFDI in Asia? What policy environment or policy efforts should the Japanese and Asian governments take for deepening regional integration?

This chapter aims to answer those questions with regard to OFDI from Japan, emphasizing trade (transport) costs and production costs in the core-periphery framework (Krugman and Venables, 1995). Section 2 reviews the theoretical frameworks to explain OFDI and their implications for economic integration. Section 3 discusses the new Asia economic landscape in conjunction with changes in trade and investment patterns. Sections 4 and 5 examine the distribution patterns of OFDI from Japan to the world and within Asia in particular, respectively. Section 6 reviews the investment and production strategies of Japanese multinationals and SMEs, respectively. Section 7 concludes with a policy discussion about the role of Japan in investment activity in Asia and the factors affecting Japan's OFDI.

2. What does Determine OFDI?

2.1. *New Economic Geography's Hypothesis*

What determines the distribution of OFDI? There are many theories on the determinants of FDI. International economics have studied MNCs for a long time. However, spatial economics or new economic geography has addressed the subject of FDI as location of industry only recently. In fact, the distribution of OFDI is an issue related to the location of industry across countries. Paul Krugman pioneered the field of the location of industry, in economic integration, across countries from the viewpoint of spatial economics or new economic geography that incorporates concepts of transport (trade or transaction) costs[1] and economies of scale/increasing returns to scale. Krugman (1991) argued that the interaction of market, transport costs, and fixed investment costs determines the location of industry.[2] Krugman's hypothesis regarding the location of industry is based on the gravity framework that economic size (market) and geographical distance (as a proxy of transport costs) play a significant role in determining trade and investment. Geographical distance determines trade and investment since it affects transport costs (broadly defined). Indeed, transport costs matter in determining the location of industry. If the costs to transport a good from one place to another are very high, the industry will locate close to the primary market, because firms wish to have lower transport costs.[3]

2.2. *Agglomeration Forces versus Dispersion Forces*

High transport costs give rise to the "home market effect" where suppliers located near a large market can attain economies of scale and

---

[1] International economists use the term "trade costs", while spatial economists instead use "transport costs". Anderson and Wincoop (2004) define transport costs to include all costs incurred in getting a good to a final user other than the marginal costs of producing the good itself.

[2] The author asked the Managing Director of Soode Johor, a Japanese affiliate, producing parts of hard disc drive, in Johor, Malaysia how he would respond to the growing hard disc drive production in Shenzhen China. At that time, his major customer, Hitachi Global Storage Technologies, was planning to start hard disc drive production in Shenzhen since the early 2006, and requesting its suppliers to go over there. He replied that, to make a decision to expand into Shenzhen or not, he would consider expected market/production size in China, transport costs from Johor to Shenzhen, and the difference in costs between a new fixed investment in Shenzhen and an expansion of investment in Johor. His reply appears to support the Krugman's hypothesis.

[3] For instance, Hillberry and Hummels (2005) find that even within the United States, distance matters, resulting in industries that tend to be located close to each other.

export the goods. In Krugman's words, "countries will tend to export those kinds of products for which they have relatively large domestic demand" (Krugman, 1980, p. 955). The supposition is that when total transport costs become quite large, suppliers will shift their production facilities to a nearby market in order to reduce operating costs. Indeed, assemblers may wish to use neighboring suppliers in order to reduce transport. Therefore, it is possible that international trade can be partly substituted by "market-seeking" FDI.

Conversely, as Krugman and Venables (1995) argue, when transport costs fall enough so that the advantages of low wages in the "periphery" (the unindustrialized economy) offsets the disadvantages of being located remotely from markets and suppliers of the "core" (the industrialized economy), manufacturing in the core will move to the "periphery". Therefore, "efficiency-seeking" FDI can take place when transport costs fall such that lower wages offset the disadvantages of other conditions. While the core-periphery hypothesis assumes that production conditions are roughly the same everywhere and almost every resource can move across borders, in reality, production conditions are quite different by location. The core-periphery hypothesis that manufacturing moves from developed to developing countries, therefore, implies that reductions in trade costs and improvements in production conditions lead to increased OFDI from developed to developing countries.

2.3. *Driving Forces and Types of FDI*

Given the above discussions, what are the driving forces of OFDI? Roughly speaking, there are three primary drive forces of OFDI[4]:

(1) *Driving force 1*: better access to the markets of host countries and nearby countries (market-seeking FDI);

---

[4] "Efficiency-seeking" FDI can be regarded as one type of "resource-seeking" FDI since it seeks abundant labor resources. However, since "efficiency-seeking" FDI has special implications for the location of industry which differ from other "resource-seeking" FDI, we make a distinction between the two here.

(2) *Driving force 2*: the ability to take advantage of low wage rates in host countries (efficiency-seeking FDI); and

(3) *Driving force 3*: the ability to take advantage of resources in host country (resource-seeking FDI).

When developed country MNCs set up their overseas production plants in the large market, the "market seeking" forces come into effect. For instance, most of the OFDI from Japan to the United States and the European Union seek markets. On the contrary, when developed country MNCs set up their overseas production plants in developing countries, "efficiency-seeking" forces are mainly at work because there is a large difference in wage rates between developed and developing countries. Strategic functions such as headquarters (HQs), research & development (R&D), and highly capital intensive manufacturing processes often remain in the home country where high-skilled workers are available, while most of the manufacturing activities are located in host countries where wage rates are low. The last driving force of FDI is "resource-seeking" FDI. MNCs locate their R&D centers in the United States, and they seek natural resources in developing countries.

2.4. *Ricardian Model of Differences in Factor Prices*

The presence of MNCs in a foreign country has traditionally been explained in terms of differences in relative factor endowments among countries (Helpman, 1984; Helpman and Krugman, 1985). Given that transport costs are equal, the location of MNCs abroad is determined by the differences in endowments. Jones and Kierzkowski (1990) point out that different domestic locations are selected to take advantage of geographic difference in various factor costs such as land, labor, and technology. Besides factor prices, accessibility to suppliers or parts and components, determines location advantages. This approach can explain "vertical" FDI where firms locate different stages of production in different countries by taking advantage of differences in location advantages such as factor costs, accessibility to suppliers that determine production and trade costs.

2.5. *Production Fragmentation and Production Networks*

From the above arguments, that is, the core-periphery framework and the Ricardian model of difference in factor prices, what implications can be derived for Japan's OFDI in Asia? Japanese firms have extended their manufacturing enterprises across Asia. When wage rates and land prices increased, more capital intensive processes were implemented within Japan, and labor intensive processes were moved to labor-endowed countries. In the process of economic integration, then, production processes are becoming sequential stages of production, which locates across countries. Different stages of production are divided among different suppliers that are located in different countries. Products traded between firms in different countries are components instead of final products, and final products are sold outside the region. In this way the international division of labor in the production process happens both through intra-firm or inter-firm mechanisms. This phenomenon is known as many terms such as fragmentation (Jones and Kierzkowski, 1990), slicing up the value chain (Krugman, 1996), vertical specialization (Hummels *et al.*, 2001), production networks (Hanson *et al.*, 2003), or production sharing (Feenstra and Hanson, 2001).

Yi (2003) develops a theoretical model of vertical specialization and finds that a slight decline in trade costs induces large trade in intermediate goods, assuming close substitutes. This means that a decline in trade costs enable MNCs to increase FDI, and to expand the production networks. To simplify the discussion, Yi (2003) presents a model of two sequentially produced goods that are located in two countries.[5] After the processing, the good is imported back to country A again. In this case, the good crosses borders four times: at the export custom procedure when the good is exported from the country B; the import custom procedure when the good is imported into the country B; the export custom procedure when the good is exported from the country B; and the import custom procedure when the good is imported back to the country A. In the real world of

---

[5] That is, a good is produced in the country A and exported to the country B.

sequential production, one good can cross borders among several countries. Therefore, the reduction of trade costs, through not only trade liberalization, but also facilitation measures, could assist in the development of sequential production and expand intra-industry trade (IIT).

Production processes that are sliced into many stages and located in different countries have advanced in East Asia, in particular, in the electronics industry where trade costs are low due to light weight (Hiratsuka, 2006b). Two kinds of production fragmentation have advanced in East Asia (Hiratsuka and Kimura, 2007). The first is intra-firm production fragmentation in which MNCs split production processes at several stages, and locate them in different countries or cities according to location advantage. The other is inter-firm (arms length) production fragmentation in which MNCs outsource several parts production to different suppliers/countries.

3. New Asian Economic Landscape

3.1. *Changes of Trade Patterns Inside Asia*

In order to understand Japan's OFDI, this section reviews the trade patterns inside East Asia. Figure 1 depicts the trade share of East Asia (five ASEAN countries of Indonesia, Malaysia, the Philippines, Singapore, and Thailand, plus China, Japan, and Korea) between 1980 and 2003 by the Broad Economic Category (BEC) classification: primary (111, 21, and 31); processed goods (121, 22, and 32); parts and components (42 and 53); consumer goods (111, 122, 51, 522, 61, 62, 63) and capital goods (41 and 521).[6] Trade patterns have changed since the mid-1980s. In order to determine the transition of trade patterns inside East Asia, IDE-JETRO has converted the SITC Revised into BEC classification data. The distinction between processed goods, and parts and components is very important to understand the changes of trade patterns inside East Asia. Parts and components are just the intermediate goods in machinery industries.

---

[6] The Comtrade database, compiled by the United Nations has released the BEC classification trade series since 1991.

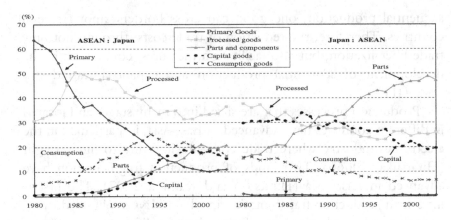

Figure 1:   Import share relation between Japan and ASEAN by commodity.

Note: ASEAN includes Indonesia, Malaysia, the Philippines, Singapore, and Thailand.

Source: IDE-JETRO/RIETI.

In the 1980s, primary commodity and processed goods occupied nearly 70 percent share of total trade within the East Asia. However, the trade share of primary commodity within the East Asia decreased from 29.3 percent in 1980 to 3.8 percent in 2003, and that of processed goods decreased from 37.3 percent in 1980 to 28.0 percent in 2003 also. In contrast, the trade share of parts and components within the East Asia increased throughout the period between 1980 and 2003, and the share in 2003 exceeded 30 percent.

Figure 1 depicts the import share of the five ASEAN countries with Japan and that of the latter with the former. It is apparent that Japan's trade patterns have changed. In the 1980s, Japan imported primary commodities from ASEAN, while ASEAN countries imported processed goods from Japan. The import share of parts and components of ASEAN from Japan increased rapidly, from 15.5 percent in 1980 to 47.3 percent in 2003. It exceeded the share of processed goods which decreased from 37.7 percent in 1980 to 26.1 percent in 2003. Japan's major imports to ASEAN have now become predominantly parts and components. On the other hand, exports of parts and components to Japan from ASEAN increased from 0.6 percent in 1980 to 20.8 percent in 2003. Trade patterns have changed not only in ASEAN-Japan relations, but also in the

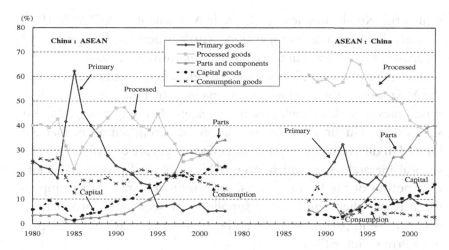

Figure 2: Import share relation between China and ASEAN by commodity.
Source: IDE-JETRO/RIETI.

case of ASEAN-China relations. Figure 2 summarizes the import share of ASEAN with China and that of China with ASEAN. The import share of parts and components of China from ASEAN increased from 5.7 percent in 1988 to 40.4 percent in 2003.[7] Similarly, the import share of parts and components to ASEAN from China increased from 3.5 percent in 1980 to 34.2 percent. The share of parts and components became the largest type of traded goods between China and ASEAN. Similarly, within ASEAN, the import share of parts and components increased from 7.2 percent in 1980 to 43.8 percent in 2003.

Overall, a review of the statistics reveals that trade patterns inside East Asia have been changing, from the traditional pattern that traded the primary commodity and the processed goods, to the pattern that has traded parts and components of machinery.

3.2. *Formation of Production and Distribution Networks*

Global competition has changed the traditional structure completely. The completion of the European Community integration in 1992 as

---

[7] The import share of China is available after 1988.

well as the North American Free Trade Agreement (NAFTA) in 1994 have accelerated global competition. North American, European, and Japanese firms have competed more intensively, resulting in the achievement of economies of scale. The global competition has forced the MNCs to divide production process into many stages, and achieve economies of scale at each production stage. Consequently, different stages of production are divided among different suppliers that are located in different countries. Production stages are organized around vertical hierarchies in which large MNCs sell final products, handle distribution of the final products, set production standards of inputs for part suppliers, and select suppliers. In sequenced production, products — in particular, parts and components — are traded, either intra-firm or inter-firm.

Figure 3 shows the parts procurement of a Japanese hard disc drive (HDD) assembler located in Thailand. The Japanese HDD

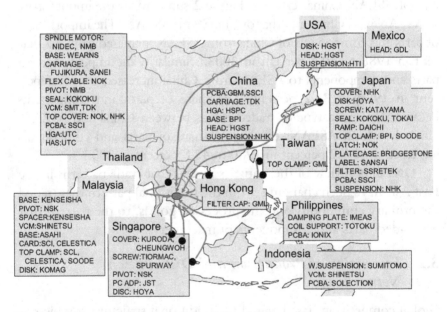

Figure 3:   Parts procurement of a hard disc drive assembler located in Thailand.

Source: Interviews by author with a Japanese HDD operated in Thailand.

assembler procures the same parts and component from multiple sources. For example, the assembler procures "carriage" from Fujikura and Sanei both in Thailand and TDK in China: They are Japanese suppliers. Most of HDD part and components suppliers are Japanese. There are a few American and Asian suppliers: "cover" from Cheungwoh (Singapore) and "base" from Wearns (Singapore firm operating in Thailand).[8] Japanese firms have extended their business activities overseas quite seamlessly as if they were operating in Japan. At present, Asian suppliers are increasing linkages with MNCs and have established overseas operations.

3.3. *Increasing Profits in Overseas Markets*

Due to the long historical production operations overseas, Japanese firms have traditionally relied on their profits from overseas economic activities. Table 1 summarizes the shares of operating profits of the Tokyo Stock Exchange listed manufacturing companies between the fiscal year of 1997 and 2005. The Table indicates two important factors. First, the shares of operating profits decreased from 76.6 percent in the fiscal year of 1997 to 70.8 percent in the fiscal year of 2005, respectively. The continuous declines in the domestic share and the corresponding increases in the overseas share result from the weak domestic sales and the expansion of overseas sales. Additionally, Japan's population is decreasing due to low fertility rates, and thus Japanese markets are matured in some sense. The importance of overseas markets is, therefore, increasing for Japanese firms. Second, the share in the Asia-Pacific region over total operating profits increased from 5.3 percent in the fiscal year of 1997 to 10.0 percent in 2005, respectively. The 2005 figures are almost the same as those in North America. It is therefore apparent that the Asian Pacific region will be the most significant region in sales and operating profits for Japanese manufactures in a few years.

---

[8] Cover and base are top and bottom cases to protect the inside.

Table 1: Share of operating profits for TSE-listed firms (by region) (%).

FY	No. of firms circulated	World market						
		Domestic	Overseas	The Americas	Europe	Asia Pacific	Other
1997	(582)	100.0	76.6	23.4	9.8	3.4	4.8	5.3
1998	(593)	100.0	73.4	26.6	13.8	4.8	4.4	3.6
1999	(643)	100.0	75.0	25.0	14.1	2.1	5.0	3.7
2000	(668)	100.0	79.9	20.1	10.4	0.7	6.0	3.0
2001	(715)	100.0	76.0	24.0	12.4	0.6	6.7	4.2
2002	(728)	100.0	72.9	27.1	13.0	2.8	7.2	4.1
2003	(738)	100.0	73.3	26.7	11.1	4.3	7.5	3.7
2004	(774)	100.0	71.8	28.2	10.9	4.7	8.6	4.0
2005	(804)	100.0	70.8	29.2	10.8	4.7	10.0	3.7

Notes:

1. The chart above shows results of firms listed on the Tokyo Stock Exchange (TSE), whose fiscal years ends between December and March, and who release sales and operating profits by region. (Firms in banking and insurance industries are excluded.)

2. Year-on-year growth rates for sales/operating profits are calculated to include the same group of firms (to allow for comparison).

3. "Europe" includes Africa and the Middle East. "Others" includes answers with multiple regions combined (e.g., "Europe and the United States").

Source: Prepared by JETRO based on Toyo Keizai Shimposha's "Kigyo Zaimu Karte 2007".

4. Distribution of Japan's OFDI

Two series are available for Japan's OFDI data: one is the balance of payment (BoP) series, and the other is on a report and notification basis (discussed below). Normally, the BoP series is used for analytical studies, since they reveal the accurate transaction of FDI by firms (for instance, see Chapter 3 by Hattari and Rajan). However, most of the studies on Japan's OFDI used the report and notification bases FDI data. Japan's BoP FDI series by region and country are available after 1995. In addition, only data on major FDI host countries are released, and data on relatively smaller countries such as Malaysia, Thailand, and the Philippines are not available. On the other hand, the report and notification-based FDI data are available by region and country between the fiscal years of 1965 and the fiscal year of 2004 which make it possible to analyze the long-term development of Japan's OFDI.[9] However, the report and notification base FDI series by country and region have some limitations since they only include data from firms whose registered capitals are more than 50 million yen. The report and notification FDI series is used in this study, and the BoP FDI series is used when necessary to complement the analysis.

Figure 4 depicted Japan's OFDI, based on reports and notification to the Ministry of Finance, Japan. The development of Japan's OFDI can be divided into two broad phases: the inactive phase before 1985; and the active FDI phase after the Plaza Accord in 1985.[10] Japan's OFDI has been active, meaning that Japanese firms became global. The globalization era of Japan's OFDI can be sub-divided into the three phases; the first boom-decline cycle between 1985 and 1992; the second boom-decline cycle between 1992 and 1998; and after the Asian currency crisis. Thus, in total, Japan's OFDI can be divided into four phases.

---

[9] The report and notification base data have not been released since 2005.
[10] The Plaza Accord was an agreement signed on 22 September 1985 by the then G5 nations (France, West Germany, Japan, the United States, and the United Kingdom). The G5 agreed to devalue the US dollar in relation to the Japanese yen and German Deutsche Mark by intervening in currency markets. The exchange rate of the US dollar against the yen declined over 50 percent in the two years after this agreement took place.

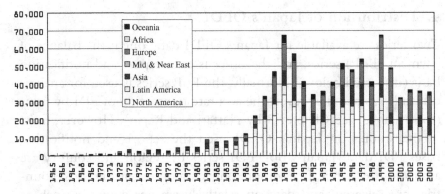

Figure 4: Japan's outward FDI (based on reports and notifications) by region (1965–2004, US$ million).

Note: Firms with capital of more than 100 million yen are to report to the Ministry of Finance, Japan.

Source: Original data from the Ministry of Finance of Japan, and converted from Japanese yen to the US dollar by JETRO.

4.1. *Inactive Japan's OFDI up to 1985*

Until 1985, Japan's OFDI was small — just US$4.9 billion even in 1979. The major host countries were spread around Asia, the Americas, and Europe. Between 1965 and 1979, Japan' OFDI to Asia reached at US$8.5 billion, followed by that to the North America (US$8.0 billion), Latin America (US$5.4 billions), and to the European Union (US$3.9 billion).

4.2. *First Boom-Decline FDI Cycle between 1986 and 1992*

Japan's OFDI increased from the mid-1980s. The 1985 Plaza Accord and subsequent revaluation of the Japanese yen was the turning point of Japan's OFDI. Since 1986, Japan's OFDI increased dramatically and amounted to US$67.5 billion in 1989. This was more than 10 times the figure in 1979, and about six times that in 1985. It has been usually understood that Japanese firms moved operations to Asia in response to the rise of yen against the US dollar resulting in Japan's FDI boom. However, there are other explanations.

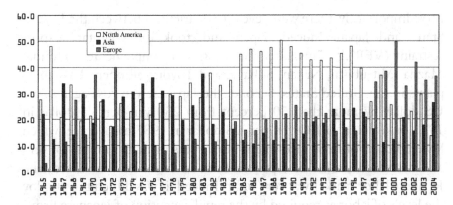

Figure 5: Distribution share of Japan's outward FDI (based on reports and notifications) by region (1965–2004, %).

Source: Original data from the Ministry of Finance of Japan, and converted from Japanese yen to the US dollar by JETRO.

During the 1980s, Japanese firms had targeted the large United States market. At that time, in fact, about a half of the OFDI was destined to the North American market, mainly to the United States. Japan's OFDI to the United States, on a report and notification basis, reached at US$33.9 billion, in 1989, which accounted for 50.2 percent of total Japan's OFDI, US$67.5 billion in the year (Figures 4 and 5). The European Union was the second largest host of the Japanese FDI, 14.8 billion US dollar in the year, 21.9 percent of total Japan's OFDI. The first boom of Japan's OFDI was led mainly by the United States and the European Union. The share of OFDI destined to the United States increased from 34.0 percent in 1980 to 50.2 percent in 1989. On the contrary, Asia's share of total Japan's OFDI decreased from 37.4 percent in 1981 to 10.4 percent in 1986, and 12.2 percent in 1989, although Japan's OFDI to Asia increased from about US$1 billion in 1986 to US$8.2 billion in 1980.

Since the 1985 Plaza Accord, Japanese firms have taken advantage of foreign resources. There were several reasons behind the aggressive advancement overseas markets, including the hike of yen, the severe trade frictions in the US market, and the tight labor market in Japan.

Most importantly, there were severe trade frictions between the United States and Japan. Indeed, Japan undertook the voluntary export restraint (VER).[11] Thus, after the VERs were implemented, Honda, Mazda, Mitsubishi, Nissan, Subaru, and Toyota, all opened assembly plants in the United States. Second, the Japanese yen rose against the US dollar by more than 50 percent from 250 yen per US dollar in 1985 on average to 130 yen per US dollar in 1987 on average, which lowered costs of fixed investment in overseas markets in terms of yen, and decreased profits of Japanese firms in terms of yen. Third, the Japanese labor market was very tight. Indeed, it was difficult to employ the levels of labor as required by the rapid expansion of Japanese firms' production in order to raise their market share in the world.

The first boom of Japan's OFDI ended in the early 1990s when the Japanese economy suffered from sluggish domestic demand arising from the bursting of the bubble and low population growth rates. Japan's OFDI decreased, in particular, those to the United States decreased to US$13.8 billion dollars in 1992, and its share declined at 42.3 percent. Similarly, Japan's OFDI to the European Union decreased to US$7.1 billion in the year but the share remained at 20.7 percent. Juxtaposed against the declining market-seeking FDI to the United States and Europe, Japan's OFDI to Asia, most of which was efficiency-seeking FDI, remained at US$6.4 billion, and the share increased at 18.8 percent.

4.3. *Second Boom-Decline Cycle between 1993 and 1997*

The second boom-decline FDI cycle was led by North America and Asia. In particular, FDI to Asia was noteworthy. In fact, Japan's OFDI to Asia increased remarkably from US$6.4 billion in 1992 to US$12.2 billion in 1997 (Figure 4). Asia's share of total

---

[11] The Japanese firms were faced with continuing calls by the United States automobile industry for legislated protection. Following discussions with the US trade representative's office, in 1981, eventually announced VERs on auto exports. The VERs were renewed regularly and lasted until the early 1990s.

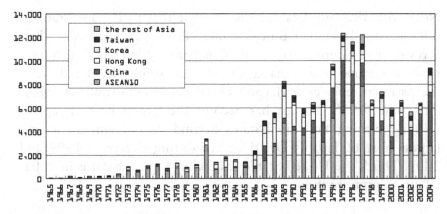

Figure 6: Japan's outward FDI (based on reports and notifications) inside Asia (1965–2004, US$ million).

Source: Original data from the Ministry of Finance of Japan, and converted from Japanese yen to the US dollar by JETRO.

Japan's OFDI jumped from 12.2 percent in 1989 to 24.2 percent in 1996 and 22.6 percent in 1997 (Figure 5). Asia became the second largest host area of Japan's OFDI, replacing Europe. (The reasons why Japanese firms increased their FDI to Asia will be discussed in the next section). FDI to the North America increased from US$14.6 billion in 1992 to US$23.0 billion in 1996, and the United States share increased 42.7 percent in 1992 to 47.9 percent in 1996. In contrast, the EU's share decreased from 20.7 percent in 1992 to 15.4 percent in 1996; although Japan's OFDI to the EU did not change at all — from US$7.1 billion in 1992 to US$7.4 billion in 1996.

4.4. *After the Asian Currency Crisis*

The second episode of Japan's OFDI boom came to an end when the Asian currency crisis erupted in 1997 in Thailand. The Asian currency crisis hit the Japanese economy through decreasing exports to Asia with the exception of China. Reflecting the sluggish economy, Japan's total OFDI decreased. In particular, FDI to

North America and Asia decreased, while that to Europe dramatically increased. At that time, Japanese firms were increasing their investments to Europe so as to establish production and distribution bases in Europe, where markets were increasingly integrated. After the Asian currency crisis, Japan's OFDI pattern drastically changed. First, since 1998, Europe has become the largest host of Japan's OFDI, replacing the United States. Second, Asia became the second largest host of Japan's OFDI except during the years 1999 and 2001. Third, the United States has lost its top host status in 2001, falling to number three.

5. Japan's OFDI Patterns Inside Asia

What are the main features of Japan's OFDI patterns inside Asia? Figures 7 and 8 present the development of Japan's OFDI patterns inside Asia, on a report and notification basis. As noted above, Japan's OFDI to Asia can be divided into four phases: (1) inactive Japan's OFDI up to 1985; (2) first boom-decline FDI cycle between 1986 and 1992; (3) second boom-decline cycle between 1993 and 1997;

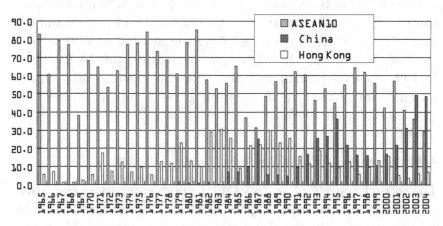

Figure 7:   Share of Japan's outward FDI (based on reports and notifications) inside Asia (1965–2004, %).

Source: Original data from the Ministry of Finance of Japan, and converted from Japanese yen to the US dollar by JETRO.

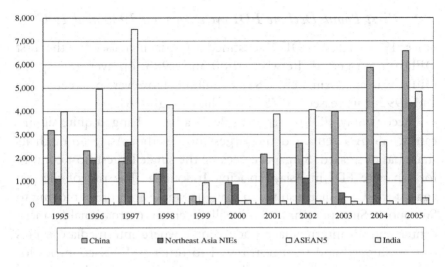

Figure 8: Japan's outward FDI inside Asia (based on balance of payments basis, net flow, US$ million).

Sources: Prepared by JETRO from Ministry of Finance Balance of Payments Statistics and Bank of Japan foreign exchange rates.

and (4) after the Asian currency crisis. The FDI patterns inside Asia have changed according to these phases.

5.1. *Inactive Japan's OFDI up to 1985*

Up to 1985, Japan's OFDI was inactive. About a half of Japan's OFDI was directed to Asia, and most of it destined to five ASEAN countries of Indonesia, Malaysia, the Philippines, Singapore, and Thailand. In this period, except for Singapore, Asian countries had adopted the so-called import substitution industrialization (ISI) policy in which high tariffs were imposed on the consumption goods meanwhile the tariff on intermediate goods were low. Because of the ISI policy, Japanese firms had been forced to produce goods in Asian countries in order to secure markets. However, the overseas production in Asia was operated at small volume for domestic markets, and therefore, Japan's FDI was very small. Indonesia, being the largest ASEAN member with the richest natural resources, was host to most of Japan's OFDI to the region.

5.2. *First Boom-Decline FDI cycle between 1986 and 1992*

Since 1986, Japan's OFDI destined to Asia increased in the first OFDI boom period. Between 1980 and 1985, on average, Japan's OFDI was approximately US$1.8 million. However, between 1986 and 1992 it increased to US$5.8 million (Figure 6).

Accordingly, FDI patterns inside Asia have changed quite significantly. ASEAN remained the largest host within Asia, although its share has decreased. Singapore became the single largest host country for Japanese FDI in Asia, replacing Indonesia. The rise of the yen against the US dollar resulted in many Japanese enterprises moving to Singapore. Singapore has traditionally been an international financial center and an intermediary trade center where intermediate goods can be shipped and then distributed to other ASEAN countries for manufacturing. Indeed, a number of electronics industries are concentrated in Singapore. The rise of yen empowered agglomeration forces of Singapore. However, the agglomeration forces did not last long. Because of the small population and labor force, wage rates rose in Singapore. Due to the congestion effect, Japanese firms had to find a new frontier. They chose Thailand where the regulations toward foreign capital participation were relaxed in 1985, substantially liberalizing foreign direct investment (FDI). At that time, in Thailand, supporting industries had developed to some extent, i.e., Minebea and Seagate operated metal engineering and HDD engineering parts, respectively there. In response to Thailand' pro-FDI policy, Japanese firms moved to the country for export production. Malaysia followed Thailand in relaxing the regulations of foreign capital participation. But, like Singapore, Thailand's and Malaysia's wage rates increased, which lowered profits of overseas affiliates, and weakened their agglomeration forces, resulting in the end of FDI boom.

5.3. *Second Boom-Decline Cycle between 1993 and 1997*

As discussed above, Japanese firms went to Asia where investment environments were relatively good: foreign capital was allowed to operate quite freely; generous tax incentives were provided; the industrial estates or parks were arranged; and to some extent supporting industries developed. But, due to a congestion effect in human resources and available land for industrial purpose, Japanese firms had to find new frontiers — moving investments from country to country. At that time, China made considerable efforts to improve its investment climate — in 1992, many Chinese cities were opened and provided incentives to foreign investors. Responding to the China's FDI liberalization policy, Japanese firms rushed to China. As mentioned, ASEAN and China have traded parts and components mutually, driven mainly by transactions by Japanese affiliates. However, Japan's OFDI wave to ASEAN and China ended when the Asian currency crisis erupted in 1997 in Thailand.

5.4. *After the Asian Currency Crisis: Rise of China and Resurgence of ASEAN*

The Asian currency crisis fundamentally altered the FDI patterns inside Asia. Due to the sharp drop of domestic demands in ASEAN, Japan's FDI destined to ASEAN decreased markedly. Instead, Japanese firms moved with even greater pace to China, responding also to China's entry into the World Trade Organization (WTO) at the end of 2001. By 2003 and 2004, China became the largest host of Japan's FDI among Asian countries (see Figures 6 and 7). Figure 8 depicted Japan's OFDI (on a BoP basis), which provides a more accurate picture than those of reports and notification bases. The same FDI patterns inside Asia can be observed, as seen in Figure 7 depicting the reports and notification basis. Since 2003, China has overtaken ASEAN in terms of Japan's OFDI host. Japan's FDI destined to China was US$4.0 billion in 2003, US$5.8 billion in 2004, and US$6.6 billion in 2005.

In contrast, Japan's FDI destined to ASEAN decreased drastically from US$4.1 billion in 2002 to US$ 0.3 billion in 2003. But, in 2005, ASEAN attracted a large amount of FDI, US$ 4.8 billion. Inside ASEAN, Thailand experienced a remarkable rise in FDI. The Thai government had imposed a 49 percent ceiling of foreign capital participation share in domestic sale business since the investment promotion act was enforced in 1983. However, a large number of domestic businesses suffered from the severe shrinkage of domestic sales. In order to rescue the troubled domestic sales business the government relaxed the regulations on foreign capital participation, and allowed foreign capital to hold more than a 50 percent in Thai firms. Responding to the FDI liberalization policy, Japanese firms allocated more FDI to Thailand than ever before.

There are two main factors which have resulted in the ASEAN resurgence: the rise of wages in China; and the rise of production risk. Rapid expansion of production activities in China, in particular, in coastal cities, raised wages in the cities. At the same time, concentration of manufacturing in China increased production risks in the country. Due to the congestion effect and the rise of production risks, Japanese firms tend to choose ASEAN in addition to China (i.e. the so-called "China plus one" strategy). In line with the "China plus one strategy," Thailand and Vietnam were selected. The "China plus one" strategy is in sharp contrast to the pattern of choosing China *instead of* ASEAN which emerged before the Asian currency crisis.

Looking back on the development of Japan's OFDI patterns in Asia we observe that when agglomeration forces work strongly, dispersion forces emerge in response to the congestion effects. The concentration of Japan's FDI in ASEAN induced Japan's FDI to China; and the concentration in China induced the FDI to ASEAN.

6. Evolution of Global Presence by Japanese Firms: Industrial Patterns and Motivations

6.1. *Industrial Patterns*

In order to facilitate trade, Japanese firms have employed a strategy of setting up trade offices prior to setting up of manufacturing sites. Finance, insurance, logistic, retail, hotel, restaurant, and so on have followed trade in merchandise. Consistent with this, in the first FDI boom after 1985, or the beginning of the globalization period, Japan's OFDI increased investment in the non-manufacturing rather than

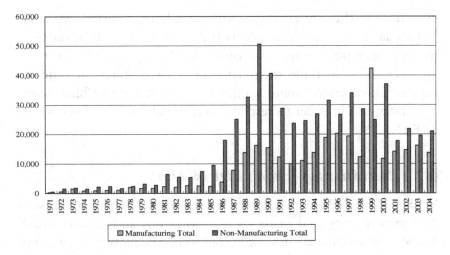

Figure 9: Japan's outward FDI (based on reports and notifications basis) by industry (US$ million).

Sources: Prepared by JETRO from Ministry of Finance (MOF) statistics for Japan's inward and
outward FDI, MOF Policy Research Institute Monthly Finance Review, and Bank of Japan foreign exchange rates.

manufacturing sectors. But, the manufacturing sector has gradually
increased its presence in FDI vis-à-vis non-manufacturing sector, since
Japanese firms are expanding FDI to produce goods overseas. Figure 9
indicates that share of FDI in manufacturing declined in the first
boom, i.e., 17.1 percent in 1985, but rose in the second FDI boom,
and after the Asian currency crisis. The manufacturing share
amounted to about 40 percent after 2001.

In the globalization era, Japan's OFDI was led by electrical industry. The electrical industry is a typical export industry where intermediate goods can be imported and special privileges given such as
exemption of tariff on intermediate goods and tax holiday of corporate tax. Thus, Japanese firms have explored location advantage of
countries/cities such as labor costs, pro-FDI policy, suppliers, and so
on; Singapore, Malaysia, Thailand, the Philippines, Indonesia, China,
and recently in Vietnam.

After 2000, the automobile industry became a major industry for
Japan's OFDI. Japanese automobile makers have expanded their

operations in the United States, Europe, China, Thailand, Malaysia, Indonesia, Korea, and recently in India. They have taken different overseas operation strategies according to the region and country — in order to avoid trade friction to the United States; in order to explore the expanded opportunities by liberalization to China, Korea and India; and in order to respond to regionalization to Europe and ASEAN.

6.2. *Motivations of Japan's FDI in Asia*

During the 1990s, investment and business environments in Asia greatly improved in terms of institutions and infrastructure. These improvements not only reduced production costs, but also, service link costs between manufacturing sites, and between manufacturing site and market. Improvements in investment and business environments have enabled Japanese firms to establish increasingly high level and complicated supply chain networks through optimum location of research and development (R&D), purchasing, manufacturing, and sales. Basic research activities remain in Japan, but some design aspects have been located in Asia and the United States. While capital intensive processes are located in Japan, other manufacturing processes (part and components) are located in various Asian countries according to location advantages.

Through a global wide strategy, resources in Japan have moved from inefficient industries that have lost the advantages to more efficient industries. Put differently, the inefficient industries were transferred to other countries through OFDI. These transfers have increased profits of Japanese firms through both channels of domestic and overseas operations, and eventually, have increased investments in R&D. As mentioned already, profits arising from overseas activities are increasing. On the other hand, in the host Asian countries, not only has income increased, but technology has also diffused to the local firms, which will require Japanese firms to innovate further to maintain their competitive advantage. This innovation cycle is realized through FDI.

6.3. *International Expansion by Japanese SMEs*

Since the 1990s, even average SMEs have resorted to overseas production. First, upon request from their MNC clients, many SMEs have moved to Asia, mostly to China (see Figure 10). In the 1990s, many large scale enterprises went to China for export purpose, but, at that time, they could not find enough credible suppliers. Eventually, large scale enterprises requested their smaller suppliers to shift to China. After strong urging from their clients, the SMEs had only two choices: to set up operations in China or to lose market. Since their customer base was not large enough to continue overseas operations, the SMEs had to find other customers other than their traditional clients. Since many SMEs have been moving operations to China, the pricing system and subcontratual relations collapsed in Japan. In addition, due to the slow population growth in Japan, domestic demand have decreased. Most of the SMEs have suffered from the decreasing demand. This in turn has pushed even more Japanese SMEs to operate in Asia — ASEAN and China in particular.

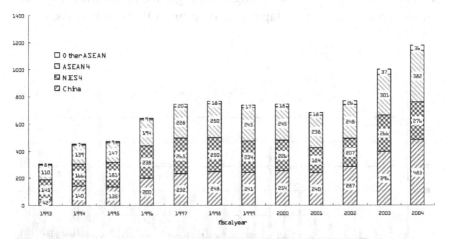

Figure 10: Number of firms operating in Asia by Japanese SMEs.

Notes: NIES4 (Hong Kong, the Republic of Korea, Singapore, and Taiwan), and ASEAN4 (Indonesia, Malaysia, the Philippines, and Thailand), and others are (India, Pakistan, Sri Lanka, Laos, Myanmar, Vietnam, and so on). SMEs are defined as less than 300 million yen of capita firms.

Source: Original source from METI.

7. Conclusion and Policy Implications

What perspectives can we draw on international operations by Japanese firms in Asia? Additionally, what role will they play in the future Asian economy?

Since the mid-1980s, for more than two decades, Japanese firms have operated in East Asia. Initially, they went to the five ASEAN countries (Indonesia, Malaysia, the Philippines, Singapore, and Thailand), extended to China, and in recent years to Vietnam. But, due to the long history, increasingly, Japan's new OFDI has been in the form of the expansion of the existing facilitates rather than new facilities. However, other Asian countries are investing aggressively in new facilities in these Asian countries. As a result, Japan's relative presence, in terms of amount of FDI has been declining against other Asian countries (Figure 11).

Nevertheless, Japan's OFDI remains at a high level in absolute terms. Japanese firms have established production and distribution networks in East Asia. The production and distribution networks have characteristics of self-organizing in the sense that they expand and enhance by themselves according to changes in the business environment. This suggests that Japan will continue OFDI in East Asia.

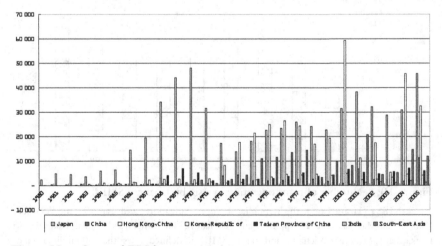

Figure 11:   Outward FDI by source region.

Source: UNCTAD, Key Data from UNCTAD, World Investment Report, Annex Tables.

In thinking about the regional perspective of Japan's OFDI, we have to consider at least three factors. First, there is the recent proliferation of FTAs in Asia. ASEAN Free Trade Area (AFTA) has proceeded and is scheduled to be fully established by 2015. The ASEAN-China FTA has also been implemented, and the ASEAN-Korea FTA has been concluded. The ASEAN-Japan FTA is expected to be concluded in 2007. The ASEAN-CER (Australia and New Zealand) and ASEAN-India FTA are under negotiation. Second, is the Chinese factor. China is geographically very close to Japan. Its large market is very attractive to Japanese investors. There are many industrializing cities. Considering market size, agglomeration of industry, and relative cheap labor, China will be the major host country of Japan's FDI. Third, is the Indian factor. Japan has not paid much attention to India so far. For Japanese investors, Asia was Korea, Hong Kong, and Taiwan in the 1960s. Singapore and the other middle income ASEAN economies (Indonesia, Malaysia, the Philippines, and Thailand) were included in the 1970s and China in the 1980s and 1990s. But, now, Japanese firms are looking to invest in new frontiers such as Vietnam and India. By how much Japanese firms undertake FDI in these new frontiers depends on the extent that these host locations improve their business and investment environments by implementing measures such as trade, service and investment liberalization and facilitation measures.

References

Anderson, JE and E van Winocoop (2004). Trade costs. *Journal of Economic Literature*, XLII, 691–751.

Ando, M and F Kimura (2004). The formation of international production and distribution networks in East Asia. NBER Working Paper No. 10167, December. Forthcoming in International Trade (NBER-East Asia Seminar on Economics, Vol. 14), T Ito and A Rose (eds.), Chicago: University of Chicago Press.

Feenstra, RC and G Hanson (2001). *Global Production Sharing and Rising Inequality: A Survey of Trade and Wages.* mimeo (June).

Fujita, M (2006). *Formation and Growth of Economic Agglomerations and Industrial Clusters: A Theoretical Framework From the Viewpoint of Spatial Economics* (forthcoming).

Hanson, GH, RJ Mataloni and MJ Slaughter (2003). Vertical production networks in multinational firms. NBER Working Paper 9723.

Helpman, E (1984). A simple theory of international trade with multinational corporations. *Journal of Political Economy*, 92, 31.

Helpman, E and P Krugman (1985). *Market Structure and Foreign Trade*, Cambridge Mass. MIT Press.

Hillberry, R and D Hummels (2005). *Trade Responses to Geographic Frictions: A Decomposition Using Micro-Data*.

Hiratsuka, D (2006a). Outward FDI from and intraregional FDI in ASEAN: Trends and drivers. Discussion Paper No. 77, Institute of Developing Economies.

Hiratsuka, D (2006b). Vertical intra-regional production networks in East Asia: A case study of the hard disc drive industry. In *East Asia's De Facto Economic Integration*, D. Hiratsuka (ed.), London: Palgrave Macmillan.

Hiratsuka, D and F Kimura (2007). *From De Facto to De Jure Economic Integration in East Asia: What has been Happening and will Happen in East Asia?* (Forthcoming).

Hummels, D, J Ishi, and K-M Yi (2001). The nature and growth of vertical specialization, *Journal of International Economics*, 54, 75–96.

Jones, RW and H Kierzkowski (1990). The role of services in production and international trade: A theoretical framework. In *The Political Economy of International Trade: Essays in Honor of Robert E. Baldwin*, Ronald W. Jones and Anne O. Krueger (eds.), pp. 31–48, Cambridge, MA: Blackwell.

Kimura, F (2006). The development of fragmentation in East Asia and its implications for FTAs. In *East Asia's De Facto Economic Integration*, D Hiratsuka (eds.), London: Palgrave Macmillan.

Krugman, P (1991). *Geography and Trade*. Cambridge: The MIT Press.

Krugman, P (1996). Does third world growth hurt first world prosperity? *Harvard Business Review* 72, 113–121.

Krugman, P and AJ Venables (1995). Globalization and the inequality of nations. *The Quarterly Journal of Economics*, 110, 857–880.

Yi, K-M (2003). Can vertical specialization explain the growth of world trade? *Journal of Political Economy*, 111(1), 52–102.

Chapter 5

The Pattern and Magnitude of China's Outward FDI in Asia*

Shaoming Cheng and Roger R. Stough

1. Introduction

Since 2002, China has surpassed the United States to become the world's top foreign direct investment (FDI) destination. Less well recognized is the fact that China is also an important source of FDI. By the end of 2004, China had established 8,299 overseas enterprises and had more than US$15 billion cumulative FDI in over 150 countries, based on statistics from China's Ministry of Commerce (MOFCOM). In 2005 itself, China recorded US$11 billion FDI outflows, accounting for one-tenth of all FDI outflow from developing countries (UNCTAD, 2006). The lack of research on China's OFDI hinders researchers and policymakers from understanding China's OFDI policy evolution, market development strategy, and Chinese firms' globalization strategies. The purpose of this chapter, therefore, is to document the pattern and magnitude of China's OFDI with a special emphasis on FDI destinations in Asia.

The chapter is organized as follows. Section 2 offers a brief overview of previous theories on OFDI from developing countries to provide an analytical and theoretical background for examining China's FDI outflows. Section 3 reviews China's political and ideological debates over FDI policy development and multinational operations to provide a historical and evolutionary policy and regulatory framework for examining the emergence and growth of China's OFDI. Section 4

* Comments by Rajat Khaturia at the ICRIER workshop are appreciated. The usual disclaimer applies.

discusses data sources and limitations of China's OFDI. Section 5 examines the characteristics, geographic distribution, and investment scale of Chinese FDI flows in Asia. Section 6 offers an assessment of past and present OFDI patterns as well as a discussion of both "push" and "pull" factors behind China's OFDI. Section 7 concludes with a discussion of future prospects for OFDI from China and some policy implications.

2. Theories on Outward FDI from Developing Countries

Research on developing countries' OFDI first emerged in the late 1970s in response to the rise of OFDI from developing countries. Lecraw (1977) was arguably the first study intended to examine the characteristics of developing countries' overseas firms. Lecraw surveyed over 20 firms from various Asian developing countries in Thailand and concluded that these firms tend to use labor-intensive technology and produce for both domestic and international markets. Taking advantage of Dunning's (1977, 1983) three dimensional paradigm of ownership, location, and internalization (OLI) advantages, other studies focused primarily on explaining what advantage(s) drive developing countries' multinational firms. Wells (1983) argued that multinational corporations (MNCs) from developing countries possess the same basic advantages as those from developed countries, but they are derived from different sources. For example, unlike the ownership advantage for FDI from developed countries which comes from sophisticated technology and management, the advantage for FDI from developing countries results from technology and management expertise which are suitable or adaptable to local conditions in other developing countries. Lall (1983) and Tolentino (1993) further added that such adapted advantages may help MNCs from developing countries overcome various disadvantages in host countries and predicted that OFDI from developing countries should choose countries with economic and cultural similarities and geographic proximity as destinations. Only after having gained international experience through overseas operations can firms invest on a relatively large scale in more developed and geographically distant countries (Dunning and Narula, 1996; Riemens, 1989). One of the strongest critiques of the mainstream OLI approach for explaining OFDI from developing countries is that this approach is erected on the observations of American and British experiences and thus may fail to capture the unique characteristics of MNCs from developing countries (Yeung, 1998).

In addition to the mainstream OLI framework, OFDI from developing countries have also been examined regarding their relation to both economic development, and knowledge and innovation transfer or spillover. Dunning (1981, 1986) proposed the investment development path (IDP) theory and argued that a country's outward and inward FDI position is related to its level of economic development. A country will initially experience increasing FDI inflows and then generate enlarged OFDI as its economy grows and its income increases (Dunning and Narula, 1996). Partly in response to the critique of the conventional OLI framework and partly in response to the critical role of technological innovation, OFDI from developing countries have been undertaken as effective vehicles for developing countries to access localized innovative assets and capabilities (Cantwell, 1989; Dunning, 1998; Porter, 1990, 1998; Wesson, 1993). Such asset-seeking FDI tries to enhance its dynamic competitive advantage by strategically locating itself around geographically dispersed local innovation centers in order to augment the competitive advantage of its parent company or parent country. This asset-seeking and innovation-enhancing interest in the FDI phenomenon may help explain the sharply increased amount of FDI inflows into the United States and other developed countries from many developing countries (Wesson, 1993).

3. History and Development of China's Outward FDI

This section discusses the evolution of the ideological and policy conditions that led to the dramatic growth of China's OFDI. Such evolution can be divided into four stages based on changes in attitudes toward China's MNCs and OFDI and, consequently, based on the growth in volume of China's OFDI. The first period from 1978 to 1986 witnessed strong ideological opposition toward MNCs and consequently any type of FDI activities. The second period from 1987 to 1991 involved heated debates on China's overall development strategy and China's overseas investment. The third period from 1992 to 2000 saw increasingly muted political opposition to developing China's transnational businesses and officially endorsed and encouraged overseas investment and operations. The most recent period since 2001 onward has involved the establishment of a consistent and coherent "going abroad" strategy that actively promotes China's OFDI as an integral part of China's economic development strategy and as a response to the growing competitive effects of globalization.

3.1. *Political Opposition Toward China's Outward FDI (1978–1986)*

Prior to 1978, China's ideological opposition and political denunciation were emphatic, primarily due to the fundamental viewpoint that MNCs were imperialist tools for economic exploitation and were an expression of neo-colonialism in the unjustifiable international economic order. Such ideological preconception was challenged after the publication of the Chinese version of Wells' (1983) *Third World Multinationals: The Rise of Foreign Direct Investment from Developing Countries* in 1986 (Zhang, 2003). Wells' pioneering work along with other studies by international organizations, especially UN subsidiaries, such as the United Nations Centre on Transnational Corporations (UNCTC) and the United Nations Industrial Development Organizations (UNIDO), elaborated possible economic and political benefits of third world MNCs to their home and/or host countries. Such discussions gradually eased the strong ideological antipathy toward MNCs and created support for China's own MNCs and OFDI.

3.2. *Political Debates and the Emergence of China's Outward FDI (1987–1991)*

The ideological prejudice and political bias against MNCs, however, lingered on in the late 1980s and together they resulted in an inconsistent and incoherent OFDI policy in China. China's OFDI's positive and legitimate role was strengthened by China's coastal-oriented export-led development strategy. Based on the results of debates on the adoption of import substitution or export promotion strategies, China adopted the latter and opened up 14 coastal cities in 1988 along with previous four special economic zones (SEZs) to participate in international competition. Internationalized operations (*guojihua jingying*) of Chinese firms, therefore, were necessary for taking advantage of international cooperation and international division of labor to promote economic growth in China's coastal regions. As a result, international operations of Chinese large state-owned enterprises were for the first time incorporated into China's economic reform agenda (Duan, 1995; Zhao and Li, 1991). However, in this period, only few state-owned foreign trade corporations were authorized to invest overseas (Tseng, 1996; Cai, 1999). In addition, their overseas investment activities were strongly linked with the government's political considerations of enhancing China's political and economic influence and expanding China's international trade relationships (Wu and Chen, 2001).

3.3. *Political Acceptance and the Early Boom of China's Outward FDI (1992–2000)*

The late *Deng Xiaoping*'s tour of the southern provinces and cities of China in 1992 ushered determined acceptance and encouragement of China's OFDI. The primary purpose of Deng's trip was to reaffirm the centrality of the export-oriented and FDI-led coastal development strategy in China's overall economic reform scheme. In September 1992, at the 14th National Congress of the Chinese Communist Party, Secretary Jiang Zemin formally stated and asserted that "we should encourage enterprises to expand their investment abroad and their transnational operations" (Beijing Review, 1992, p. 20). Since then, transnational operations of Chinese firms have been officially incorporated into China's national development strategy and explicitly regarded as one of the thrusts in China's economic integration into the global economy. In addition, as a prelude to joining the World Trade Organization (WTO), China further liberalized its trade, investment, and financial regimes and also accelerated the transnational operations of Chinese firms. National-level support for OFDI was mirrored at the provincial and municipal levels, that is, the support and encouragement of the Ministry of Foreign Trade and Economic Cooperation (MOFTEC) was paralleled by the support given by the provincial and municipal Foreign Economic Relations and Trade Commissions.

This period saw an enormous surge in local and provincial enterprises investing in overseas operations due to the relaxed requirements, particularly businesses in Hong Kong engaged in real estate and stock speculation. Among these overseas branches and businesses, corruption and nepotism were rampant and many of the businesses experienced heavy losses especially during the Asian financial crisis in 1997. Consequently, the Chinese government, specifically, MOFTEC, tightened approval requirements and procedures for OFDI projects. This tightening to a great extent resulted in a sharp decline in China's OFDI in the late 1990s.

3.4. *Political Enthusiasm and Rapid Expansion of China's OFDI (2001 onward)*

Despite the temporary adjustment and tightening of China's OFDI approval requirements, China's entry into the WTO in 2001 ignited both Chinese government's and its enterprises' enthusiasm to invest abroad. In 2001, Premier Zhu Rongji announced the "going abroad" (*zou chuqu*) strategy in China's 10th five-year plan (2001–2005), which pledged to establish favorable policies and coordinated schedules for Chinese enterprises to invest beyond Chinese borders. The "going abroad" strategy was envisioned in the late 1990s, formally adopted in 2001, and has been an integral part of China's overall strategy of economic development since then. This strategy is a deliberate one aimed at allowing and promoting capable Chinese enterprises to invest globally, be actively involved in international competition, and therefore enhance their international competitiveness. The Ministry of Commerce (MOFCOM) (the successor of the former MOFTEC) is responsible for the implementation and coordination of the strategy. As a focus of the strategy, FDI has been greatly encouraged by the gradual relaxation of foreign exchange controls and quotas, increasing investment incentives, and strengthened overseas FDI facilitation and protection mechanisms resulting from China's newly agreed bilateral, multilateral, and international investment and trade initiatives. The "going abroad" strategy was a necessary step to deepen China's opening to the outside world and economic reform. From political prejudice toward China's multinational firms in 1979, to political acceptance in 1992 and to political enthusiasm in 2001, China's OFDI has been fully embraced as an integral component of China's economic reform and as a powerful response to the increasing international competition and global integration.

4. Data Sources and Qualifications

China's outward investment activities can be categorized as either trading or non-trading. Non-trading investment activities refer to manufacturing (including processing and assembling), resource development (such as mining and forestry), and contracting works such as turnkey engineering/construction. Trading investment activities are generally service-oriented activities (such as financial intermediation, distribution, transport, and communications) which support international trade (Wong and Chan, 2003).

Typically, there are two types of data tracking of FDI. One is the financial data at the national level from a country's balance of payments (BoP) accounts, which records inward and OFDI flows. The other is business operation data at the individual firm level from FDI affiliates' and their parents' activities, including their sales, production, employment, assets, and expenditures on R&D. Both data sources are available in China, but each has its own limitations. The BoP financial data are provided by China's State Administration of Foreign Exchange (SAFE) (the successor of the former State Administration of Exchange Control) and are used by UNCTAD for

statistical purposes.[1] Though the SAFE data cover almost all the
countries in the world and document China's outward investment
flows from the late 1970s, they do not disaggregate the national-level
flow data based on different destination countries, i.e., this dataset
does not show the country-level distribution of China's OFDI. On
the other hand, firms' overseas operation and investment data are collected and provided by MOFCOM, the government agency responsible for the approval and administration of OFDI in China.
MOFCOM recodes every approved overseas investment project,
including its destination country, total amount, industrial sector etc.
(Wong and Chan, 2003). The MOFCOM data, however, only consists of approved overseas investment applications from enterprises
which need and actually pursue such permission. Consequently, the
MOFCOM data do not include overseas investment projects that do
not require MOFCOM approval or unauthorized outflows. Such
underestimation has been clearly shown by the significant and increasing discrepancy between the approved investment amount (MOF-
COM source) and actual monetary outflows (SAFE source).

Since one of the purposes of this chapter is to show the distribution of China's OFDI among Asian countries, the MOFCOM dataset
is the only official and country specific source and thus is used heavily for this paper. However, there are five qualifications in using this
dataset. First, OFDI may not take place in the same year of its
approval, if it takes place at all. Based on existing data sources, it is
impossible to track individual approved OFDI projects and clearly
understand when FDI is executed or whether the full authorized
investment amount is met. Second, the dataset does not include reinvested earnings from existing Chinese overseas affiliations since
MOFCOM (and previously MOFTEC) is responsible only for initial
screening and approval of OFDI projects (Zhan, 1995). Third, this
dataset includes only non-trade overseas investment activities. Fourth,
the pattern of China's OFDI derived from this dataset, particularly
the sectoral and country compositions, is heavily influenced by the

---

[1] Also see Chapter 3 by Hattari and Rajan for a more detailed discussion of BoP data on FDI
by UNCTAD.

state's overall, yet varying, objectives because the state may impose its own preferences and priorities in its overseas FDI project approval processes. Fifth and finally, the MOFCOM data do not include either unauthorized overseas investment or illegal and often personally motivated capital flight (Gunter, 1996; Wong and Chan, 2003). The size of such excluded capital outflows is very significant as indicated by the "Errors and Omissions" items in China's balance of payments statistics, for instance, the "Errors and Omissions" item was over US$27 billion in 2004 alone which is over eight-folds of the total recorded by MOFCOM that year. In sum, the MOFCOM data is likely a significant underestimate of the size of China's OFDI because it excludes reinvested earnings, trade-related FDI, unauthorized FDI, and illegal capital flight and may reflect the government's, rather than the enterprises' priorities and strategies through the stipulated OFDI approval criteria and procedures.

In addition to the above qualifications regarding the MOFCOM dataset, this data source also regards Hong Kong and Macau as "foreign" destinations, despite the fact that they are Chinese sovereign territories from 1997 and 1999, respectively. This is primarily because Hong Kong and Macau remain two independent economic entities under the "one country two systems" framework and are treated as two separate economies by international organizations. Explicitly stipulated in the "Basic Laws" of the Hong Kong and Macau Special Administrative Regions, both Hong Kong and Macau operate separate territory customs. Both capital and goods movements between Mainland China and Hong Kong and Macau, therefore, continue to be treated as foreign in the post-sovereignty period and recorded and compiled into official statistics (Cai, 1999). This approach is still accepted by major international organizations, such as the International Monetary Fund, United Nations, and World Trade Organization. Technically treating Hong Kong and Macau as foreign destinations in the MOFCOM data may distort the magnitude, distribution, and composition of China's OFDI in Asia and in the world, since Hong Kong and/or Macau may not be the ultimate destinations of China's FDI outflows, for example, the phenomenon of "round-tripping" FDI, which takes place when mainland China's capital lands in Hong Kong and then returns to the mainland to take advantage of the favorable FDI policies. This is particularly true in light of Hong Kong's traditional role as a springboard for Mainland China's inbound and outbound FDI flows (Cai, 1999; Chan, 1995; UNCTAD, 2006) and in light of the ease of transferring capital, both legally and illegally, to Hong Kong from the rest of China (Wall, 1997).[2]

5. Characteristics and Geographic Distribution of China's Outward FDI in Asia

China has become one of the largest FDI exporting countries in the world. China's OFDI has grown tremendously — from merely US$0.53 million in 1979 to over US$3.7 billion in 2004 based on MOFCOM statistics; and from US$0.5 million in 1979 to over US$6.8 billion in 2001 and US$1.8 billion in 2004 based on "balance of payments" statistics. China's FDI outflows have accelerated since 2001. This spike in OFDI cannot necessarily be attributed to China's rapid GDP growth which started in the early 1990s, a time when China's OFDI was quite steady (Figure 1). Indeed, while China's rapid growth corresponded with a sharp increase of China's FDI inflows, over the entire 1990s, China's FDI outflows remained quite stable (Figure 2). A partial reason for the spurt in China's OFDI may be rooted in FDI home countries' policy regime changes (UNCTAD, 2006). Specifically, China has actively encouraged its firms to go abroad since 2001, the reason for which will be discussed in Section 6.

Geographically, China's OFDI spreads over 150 countries, but the majority of such FDI outflows are concentrated in its neighboring economies. Over the period of 1979–2004, about 70 percent of cumulative China's OFDI was clustered in 11 economies, including Hong Kong, Korea, ASEAN-5 (Indonesia, Malaysia, Philippines, Singapore, and Thailand), Russia, United States, Canada, and Australia (see Table 1). Also from 1979 to 2004, over half of China's

---

[2] See Chapter 7 by Aminian, Fung, Lin for a discussion of OFDI from Hong Kong and Taiwan.

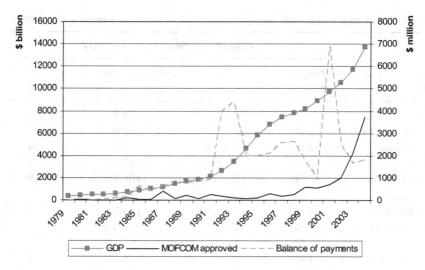

Figure 1:   Relation between China's FDI outflows and GDP, 1979–2004.

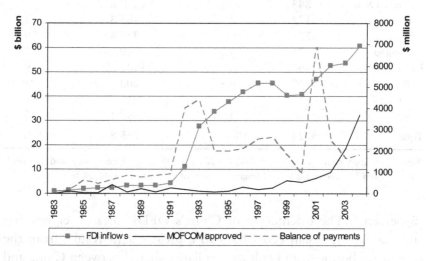

Figure 2:   Relation between China's FDI outflows and inflows, 1983–2004.

OFDI, both in terms of total number of projects and accumulated investment amounts, was destined to Asia. Europe (12 percent) was the second most popular destination, followed by North America (10 percent), Africa (9 percent), Latin America (9 percent), and Oceania

Table 1:   China's cumulative approved outward FDI (by continent, 1979–2004).

Region	No. of Projects	Share (%)	Investment Amount (US$ million)	Share (%)
		Cumulative from 1979 to 2004		
Asia	4237	51	8224.7	54
Hong Kong	2258	27	5298.0	35
Macau	248	3	217.6	1
Japan	276	3	117.4	1
Korea	91	1	1408.5	9
India	17	0.2	22.8	0.1
Middle East	169	2	194.2	1
ASEAN-5*	599	7	900.3	6
Europe	1473	18	1765.1	12
Germany	186	2	110.7	1
Russia	575	7	657.0	4
North America	1077	13	1556.5	10
United States	883	11	1089.3	7
Canada	173	2	467.3	3
Africa	717	9	1357.5	9
Zambia	21	0.3	149.7	1
Latin America	465	6	1422.3	9
Peru	23	0.3	202.1	1
Oceania	353	4	819.7	5
Australia	256	3	695.4	5
Total	8322	100	15145.8	100

Note: *ASEAN-5 countries include Indonesia, Malaysia, Philippines, Singapore, and Thailand.
Source: *China Commerce Yearbook*, China's Ministry of Commerce, 2004, 2005.

(5 percent). The orientation of China's OFDI toward neighboring and developing Asian economies to a great extent results from the economic, business, and cultural similarity shared between China and the Asian economies (UNCTAD, 2003; Wall, 1997; Wu and Chen, 2001).[3] The lion's share, over a quarter, of Chinese FDI outflows went to Hong Kong, the top destination of China's OFDI in the

---

[3] The determinants of Asian FDI flows are explored more formally in Chapter 3 by Hattari and Rajan.

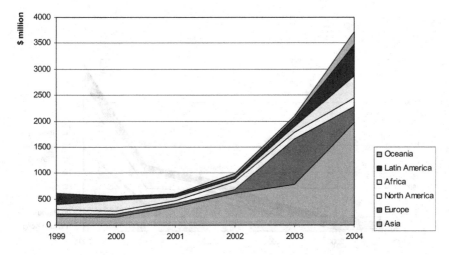

Figure 3: Geographical distribution of China outward FDI, 1999–2004.

world. The United States (7 percent) was the second most popular host country for China's OFDI, followed by Australia (5 percent) and Russia (4 percent). These four economies accounted for more than half of the cumulative approved FDI outflows during 1979–2004. Despite this concentration, China's OFDI flows reach a growing number of countries and regions.

Most recently, from 1999 to 2004, the geographic concentration of China's OFDI in Asia has become deeper. As shown in Figure 3, all major continents have experienced growing Chinese FDI inflows since 2001, but the majority has gone to Asia, thus strengthening Asia's position as the primary location for China's OFDI in the world. In addition, Europe witnessed significant growth in hosting China's FDI in 2002–2003, but lost most of its share to Asia the following year and became the fourth largest destination continent for China's OFDI in 2004, following Asia, Latin America, and Africa.

As the global distribution of China's OFDI is highly skewed toward Asia, its geographic distribution in Asia is highly skewed toward Hong Kong. As shown in Figure 4, Hong Kong is the single economy hosting the largest amount of China's OFDI in Asia, followed by Korea and the ASEAN-5 countries. Hong Kong is also the

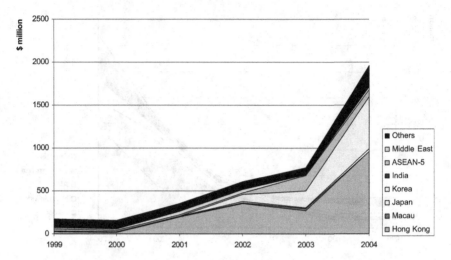

Figure 4:   Geographic distribution of China's outward FDI in Asia (in total investment amounts, 1999–2004).

single economy that attracts the largest number of China's OFDI projects in Asia, followed by the ASEAN-5 countries, Japan, and Korea. In addition to Hong Kong, Korea has experienced rapidly growing Chinese FDI inflows since 2001 and has outperformed other Asian countries becoming the second most favorable destination for China's OFDI. On the contrary, limited amounts of China's OFDI goes to the Middle East, India, and Japan.

In 2004 alone, specifically, over one quarter of China's OFDI went to Hong Kong and 16 percent to Korea, compared to only 4 percent to the United States and 6 percent to Australia (see Figure 5). Figure 5 also shows that China's OFDI is concentrated in a very small number of countries, particularly Asian economies.

In addition to the continued rise of China's OFDI, both in terms of its total volume and number of FDI projects, the average investment scale of China's overseas FDI projects has also increased. As shown in Figure 6, the average FDI project scales in the first two of the three Chinese OFDI policy development stages are almost the same with a slight decrease occurring in the second stage. The average scale in the third stage, however, increases considerably from less

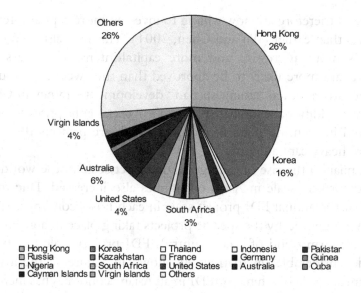

Figure 5:   China's approved outward FDI among countries, 2004.

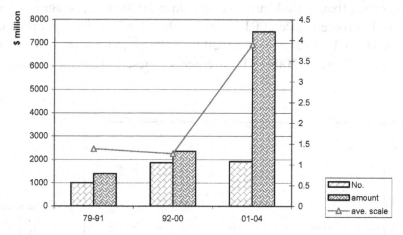

Figure 6:   Average project scale of China's outward FDI.

than US$1.5 million per project in 1979–1991 and 1992–2000 to over US$4 million per project in 2001–2004. This may imply that through learning and trial experiences over two decades, China's enterprises have gained adequate management skills to operate multinational firms and therefore are now willing to invest in more capital-intensive projects than earlier (Wu and Chen, 2001). This may also imply that China's more aggressive and more capital-intensive overseas FDI projects are more likely to be approved than they were as a result of the recently adopted "going abroad" development strategy in China. This may additionally imply that China's overseas enterprises are more involved in securing natural resources which are projects that often require heavy capital inputs.

Similar to the rise of average FDI project scale in the world, the average project scale in Asian economies also increased. Due to the fact that the annual FDI project scale in each host economy is significantly influenced by the specific projects taking place in a given year, the long-term trend of each country's FDI project scale has experienced considerable fluctuation. As shown in Figure 7, the average investment scale of China's OFDI in all Asian economies has increased slightly from 1999 to 2004 except for a slight dip in 2003. Hong Kong is the only economy whose average Chinese OFDI project scale is larger than that of all Asian countries since 2000. The average scale in Korea has soared since 2001, from less than US$1 million per project in 2001 to US$12 million in 2002, US$19 million in 2003, and US$32 million in 2004. The average Chinese FDI project scale in

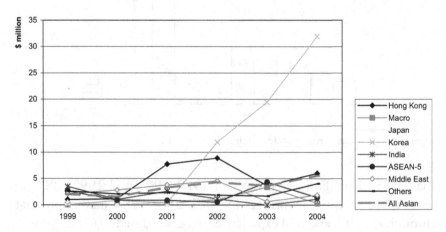

Figure 7:   Average project scale of China's outward FDI in Asia, 1999–2004.

India, on the contrary, is much less than that of all Asian countries except for a temporary increase in 2003. The average project scale in the ASEAN-5 countries remains quite stable despite a brief rise in 2003 contradicting previous observations and arguments that China's OFDI was primarily resource-seeking in the ASEAN countries (Frost, 2004; Zhang and Hock, 1996). The average project scale in the Middle East decreased from 2002 onward in contrast to a steady increase from 1999 to 2002.

In sum, China's OFDI has grown rapidly particularly since 2001 when China's "going abroad" strategy was adopted. China's FDI flows are highly concentrated in a handful of national economies, though they reach almost every country in the world. Among various continents, Asia is the top destination for China's OFDI with Hong Kong alone accounting for 35 percent of the entire accumulative Chinese OFDI from 1979 to 2004. Parallel to the significant rise of China's FDI outflows, the average FDI project scale has increased over time but continues to be variable across Asian countries.

6. Determinants of China's Outward FDI: Push and Pull Factors

The literature on FDI has identified four types of OFDI: (1) resource-acquisition FDI that aims at acquiring and securing resources, mainly natural resources, in FDI host countries; (2) market-expanding FDI that expands domestic production and sales in host and other overseas markets; (3) efficiency-improving FDI that improves productivity by avoiding trading barriers and taking advantage of inexpensive production inputs abroad; and (4) asset-seeking FDI that accesses localized knowledge and technology base (Dunning, 1998; UNCTAD, 2006). Despite Wang's (2002) emphasis on political motivations behind

---

[4] The first survey is titled: "Chinese Enterprises' Expansion into European and North American Market" and was conducted by Chinese Academy of International Trade and Economic Cooperation and Welsh Development Agency in 2005. The other one is titled: "From Middle Kingdom to Global Market: Expansion strategies and success Factors for China's Emerging Multinationals" and was carried out by the Shanghai office of Germany-based Roland Berger strategy Consultants.

China's OFDI practices, two recent surveys[4] of leading Chinese corporations on their OFDI motivations and factors clearly indicate that China's OFDI is not oriented by political or governmental agendas, at least to a much less degree, but by a combination of resource-, market-, efficiency-, and knowledge-seeking objectives, in consistent with prevailing theories (Hong and Sun, 2004; Wu, 2005; Wu and Chen, 2001).

Resource acquisition has been one of the key strategic considerations for China's OFDI. This consideration has been highlighted by a number of "blockbuster" acquisitions in the world. For example, Capital Iron and Steel's acquisition of Hierro Peru Mining Ltd. in 1992 helped Peru become the largest Chinese FDI host country in the period of 1992–1996 (Wu and Chen, 2001). Similar acquisitions also include China Metallurgical Industrial Corporation's (CMIC) investment (US$180 million) in Channar Mine in Australia, China International Trust and Investment Corporation (CITIC) and China National Non-ferrous Metal Industrial Corporation's investment (US$120 million) in the Portland Aluminum Smelter in Australia, and China National Chemical Import and Export Corporation's investment (US$105 million) in Atlantis subsidiary in Norway. Due to increasing domestic and international demand on energy and natural resources, it is foreseeable that China's resource-securing FDI will not end with China national Offshore Oil Corporation's (CNOOC) unsuccessful bid for Unocal in 2005, which ignited a prolonged congressional debate on the specter of the "China threat" and national/ economic security in the United States. Resource acquisition is also a leading motivation for China's OFDI in Asia, particularly in Southern Asia, and Asia may play a significant role in China's efforts in accessing and securing foreign resources. In 2002 alone, major resource-driven acquisitions in ASEAN countries included CNOOC's US$585 million purchase of nine oil and gas subsidiaries of Repsol-YPF SA in Indonesia, CNOOC's US$275 million equity of the Tangguh Gas Fields in Indonesia, and Petro China Co. Ltd.'s 100 percent stake (US$262 million) of Devon Energy-Indonesian Oil in Indonesia.

Efficiency-improving and market-expanding OFDI are often intertwined and complementary to each other. Efficiency-improving

FDI is characterized by an intent to avoid trade barriers and quotas in FDI host countries and third-country markets. Avoiding trade quotas for exports to developed countries has prompted some Chinese firms to invest in South–East Asian countries (UNCTAD, 2003). For instance, some Chinese textile companies invested in Cambodia and Thailand to take advantage of quota-free access for exporting to the United States and the European Union. By investing in ASEAN countries, Chinese enterprises can transfer their mature low-tech and labor-intensive production manner into these countries and take advantage of these countries' abundant labor in response to escalating wages at home (Wu and Sia, 2002). As a result, Chinese firms can lower their production costs, achieve economic efficiency, circumvent trade barriers, and expand international markets at the same time. Such efficiency-enhancing and market-expanding OFDI could grow significantly in ASEAN countries.

Asset-seeking FDI is driven by desire to access technology and other strategic assets such as brand names and distribution networks in foreign countries and is typically seen in developed countries. Such motivation has been well demonstrated by recent widely publicized Chinese acquisitions and bids for recognizable major corporations in the United States and countries in the European Union, such as Lenovo's takeover of IBM, China Electronic Corporation's acquisition of Netherlands-based Philips Electronics' mobile handset division, Huali Group's acquisition of US-based Philips' CDMA R&D department, and TCL's merger with French-based Thomson. In addition to the United States and Europe Union, Korea is a leading destination country in Asia for asset-seeking OFDI. Major acquisitions include Shanghai Automotive Industry Corporation's purchase of 51 percent stake of Korea's Ssangyong Motor for US$419 million and BOE Technology's acquisition of Hynix Semiconductor's flat panel display unit (Republic of Korea) for US$380 million. These massive buyouts may explain why Korea's rapidly growing share of China's OFDI and its soaring average FDI project scale, as shown in Figures 6 and 7.

All of these motivations discussed above can be summarized as "pull" factors for China's rapidly growing OFDI, that is, favorable natural and economic endowments abroad lure Chinese corporations invest and expand their businesses overseas. Complementing the pull factors, there are also "push" factors inside China that facilitate, if not force, Chinese firms to actively participate in international and global investment and production. These push factors mainly come from increasing domestic competition, excess production capacity and sliding profit margins, from abundant foreign exchange reserves, from huge and still rising demands for natural resources, and from Chinese governments' determination and associated policy and financial support to help Chinese firms go abroad.

Increasingly severe competition and overcapacity are among the most important factors pushing out FDI from China, particularly in China's home appliance sector. Woetzel (2003) estimated that there was 30 percent excess production capacity in washing machines, 40 percent in refrigerators, 45 percent in microwave ovens, and 87 percent in televisions. Such production surplus in turn reduces prices and encourages Chinese firms to seek sales abroad in response to diminishing profits at home. It is natural for Chinese manufacturers to tap into existing overseas distribution networks and seek out new international markets through cross-border mergers and acquisitions (M&As), such as TCL's merger with Thomson (France), TCL's acquisition of Schneider (Germany), and Haier's bid for Maytag (United States). Such M&As can provide Chinese manufacturers, almost instantly, brand name reorganization and existing distribution channels in North American and European markets.

China's foreign exchange reserves have ballooned from foreign trade surplus and inward investment and exceeded a record of US$1 trillion in November 2006, accounting for more than one-tenth of global reserves (*The Economist*, 2006). On one hand, such massive reserves can financially back up China's increasing foreign acquisitions. On the other hand, China's burgeoning foreign exchange reserves will intensify demands and pressures, both economically and politically, that China appreciates the value of its currency, which to many appears to be undervalued. Though China is generally unwilling to appreciate the renminbi yuan enough to hinder exports and dampen growth, the renminbi yuan has appreciated modestly against the US dollar. A stronger currency will greatly enhance Chinese firms' purchasing strengths in international M&As and therefore lead to rising Chinese FDI outflows. If the Chinese currency appreciates against other major currencies, more Chinese corporations will be potentially pushed to invest abroad because of relatively lower investment cost and less competitive export prices at home.

With China's economy growing at more than 10 percent for over a decade and China's recent efforts to develop its vast western region, China has developed a huge demand for natural resources and energy. China, the world's sixth largest economy, accounted for between a fifth and a third of the world's consumption of alumina, iron ore, zinc, copper, and stainless steel (*Financial Times*, 15 November 2003). China was also the second largest oil importer in the world in 2005 (*BBC News*, 16 February 2006). In light of China's surging global needs for natural resources, securing overseas resource reserves to fuel China's economic growth is essential, despite China's strong interests and financial commitments in finding alternative and renewable energy. Consequently, at least in the near future, Chinese firms will continue to pour money into expanding production and capacity in resource-rich countries.

7. Conclusion and Policy Implications

China's OFDI has grown tremendously, from initial political opposition, to selective approval, and to enthusiastic encouragement. Guided by a recently adopted strategy of "going abroad", OFDI has been fully embraced as an integral component of China's economic reform and as a response to the increasing international competition and global integration. Although China's OFDI reaches almost every country in the world, the majority of China's FDI is concentrated in Asia — in terms of both total FDI amounts and in terms of the number of FDI projects. Despite Hong Kong's role of being China's primary OFDI destination, South–East Asia and Korea have also become more important destinations, serving, respectively, as China's overseas production base and as a provider of important technology and know-how. In terms of strategic orientation of China's OFDI, while the natural resource-seeking type of FDI has continued its expansion since the 1970s, Chinese policymakers and firms have placed an increasing emphasis on access to advanced foreign technologies, managerial know-how, R&D establishments, distributional networks, and even brand names in developed economies. In addition to the pull factors overseas, China's OFDI is also pushed out by the country's increasing needs to secure overseas energy and raw material resources, intensified domestic competition and because of overcapacity in a number of key sectors, as well as continuously rising foreign exchange reserves and associated pressures on currency appreciation.

The Chinese government is determined to stand behind its recently adopted "going abroad" strategy with newly enacted policies that can further enable Chinese corporations to act on OFDI opportunities. For example, Chinese Premier Wen Jiabao declared in a speech in 2003 that "The Chinese Government will encourage more of its companies to make investment and establish their businesses in Asian countries".[5] This stance has also been articulated by Chinese Vice-Premier Wu Yi when she noted that the Chinese government would "actively foster our own multinational companies...(by creating)...all kinds of [favorable] conditions to help our multinational companies further explore overseas markets and engag(ing) more strongly in global economic competition and cooperation"(*China Daily*, 7 November 2003). Guided by such determination, MOFCOM has relaxed its OFDI approval system, the Export–Import Bank of China has provided easier access to loans and foreign exchanges, and China has signed bilateral investment treaties with 103 countries and double taxation treaties with 68 countries to support Chinese enterprises' transnational expansion and operations. All of these favorable policy measures will greatly facilitate Chinese firms to internationalize their operations. As such, recent high-profile international acquisitions and takeover bids by Chinese companies should only be

---

[5] Speech of Mr. Wen Jiabao, Premier of the State Council of the People's Republic of China, titled "China's Development and Asia's Rejuvenation", presented at the ASEAN Business and Investment Summit on 7 October 2003, in Bali, Indonesia.

seen as the tip of the iceberg that is set to usher in the globalization of Chinese corporations. China is clearly set to emerge as a major source of FDI in the near future.

References

Cai, KG (1999). Outward foreign direct investment: A novel dimension of China's integration into the regional and global economy. *China Quarterly,* 160, 856–880.

Cantwell, J (1989). *Technological Innovation and Multinational Corporations.* Oxford, UK: Basil Blackwell.

Chan, H (1995). Chinese investment in Hong Kong: Issues and problems. *Asian Survey,* 35(10), 941–954.

Duan, Y (1995). *Zhongguo Qiye Kuaguo Jingying yu Zhanlue* [Chinese enterprises' transnational operations and strategies]. Beijing: China Development Press. [In Chinese].

Dunning, JH (1977). Trade, location of economic activities and the MNE: A search for an eclectic approach. In *Proceedings of a Nobel Symposium Held at Stockholm,* B Ohlin, PO Hesselborn and PM Wijkman (eds.), pp. 395–431, London: Macmillan.

Dunning, JH (1981). Explaining the international direct investment position of countries: Toward a dynamic or developmental approach. *Weltwirtschaftliches Archiv,* 117(1), 30–64.

Dunning, JH (1983). Market power of the firm and international transfer of technology: A historical excursion. *International Journal of Industrial Organization,* 1(4), 333–351.

Dunning, JH (1986). The investment development cycle revisited. *Weltwirtschaftliches Archiv,* 122(4), 667–677.

Dunning, JH (1988). The eclectic paradigm of international production: A restatement and some possible extensions. *Journal of International Business Studies,* 19(1), 1–31.

Dunning, JH (1998). Location and the multinational enterprises: A neglected factor? *Journal of International Business Studies,* 29, 45–67.

Dunning, JH and R Narula (1996). The investment development path revisited: Some emerging issues. In *Foreign Direct Investment and governments: Catalysts for Economic Restructuring,* JH Dunning and R Narula (eds.), pp. 1–41. London: Routledge.

Frost, S (2004). Chinese outward direct investment in Southern Asia: How big are the flows and what does it mean for the region? *Pacific Review,* 17(3), 323–340.

Gunter, FR (1996). Capital flight from the People's Republic of China: 1984–1994. *China Economic Review,* 7, pp. 77–96.

Hong, E and L Sun (2004). Go overseas via direct investment: Internationalization strategy of Chinese corporations in a comparative prism. Discussion Paper No. DP40. Centre for Financial and Management Studies, University of London.

Lall, S (ed). (1983). *The New Multinationals: The Spread of Third World Enterprises.* New York: John Wiley & Sons.

Lecraw, D (1977). Direct investment by firms from less developed countries. *Oxford Economic Papers*, 29(3), 442–457.

Porter, M (1990). *The Competitive Advantage of Nations.* New York: Free Press.

Porter, M (1998). *On Competition.* Cambridge, MA: Harvard Business School Press.

Riemens, P (1989). *On the Foreign Operations of Third World Firms.* Amsterdam: Koninklijk Nederlands Aardrijkskundig Genootschap, Insituut voor Sociale Geografie, Faculteit Ruimtelijke Wetenschappen, Universiteit van Amsterdam.

Tolentino, PE (1993). *Technological Innovation and Third World Multinationals.* London: Routledge.

Tseng, C (1996). Foreign direct investment from the People's Republic of China. In *Business Transformation in China*, H de Bettignies (ed.), pp. 121–128. London: International Thomson Business Press.

UNCTAD (2003). *China: An Emerging FDI Outward Investor.* New York: United Nations.

UNCTAD (2006). *World Investment Report 2006: FDI From Developing and Transition Economies: Implication for Development.* New York: United Nations.

Wall, D (1997). *Outflows of capital from China.* OECD Working Paper No. 123. Paris: OECD.

Wang, M (2002). The motivations behind China's government-initiated industrial investments overseas. *Pacific Affairs*, 75(2), 187–206.

Wells, LT (1983). *Third World Multinationals: The Rise of Foreign Direct Investment from Developing Countries.* Cambridge, MA: MIT Press.

Wesson, TJ (1993). An alternative motivation for foreign direct investment. Unpublished Doctoral Dissertation, Harvard University.

Woetzel, J (2003). *Capitalist China: Strategies for a Revolutionized Economy.* Singapore: John Wiley & Sons.

Wong, J and S Chan (2003). China's outward direct investment: Expanding worldwide. *China: An International Journal*, 1–2, 273–301.

Wu, F (2005). The globalization of corporate China. *NBR Analysis*, National Bureau of Asian Research. 16(3).

Wu, H and C Chen (2001). An assessment of outward foreign direct investment from China's transnational economy. *Europe-Asia Studies*, 53(8), 1235–1254.

Wu, F and Y Sia (2002). China's rising investment in Southeast Asia: Trends and outlook. *Journal of Asian Business*, 18(2), 1–19.

Yeung, H (1998). *Transnational Corporations and Business Networks: Hong Kong Firms in the ASEAN Region.* London: Routledege.

Zhan, JX (1995). Transnationalization and outward investment: The case of Chinese firms. *Transnational Corporations*, 4(3), 67–100.

Zhang, Y (2003). *China's Emerging Global Businesses.* Hampshire: Palgrave Macmillan

Zhang, Z and O Hock (1996). Trade interdependence and direct foreign investment between ASEAN and China. *World Development*, 24(1), 155–170.

Zhao, K and Z Li (eds.), (1991). Kuaguo Jingying Zhilu [The path to transnational operations]. Beijing: China Social Sciences Press. [In Chinese].

Chapter 6

Emerging MNCs: Trends, Patterns, and Determinants of Outward FDI by Indian Enterprises*

Nagesh Kumar

1. Introduction

Growing outward foreign direct investment (OFDI) from some developing countries, especially in Asia, over the past decade is an important aspect of their growing economic integration with the world economy. UNCTAD's *World Investment Report 2004* noted that India stood out among Asian developing countries, not only because of the recent significant increase in the OFDI flows, but also because of "its potential to be a large outward investor" with annual outflows averaging US$1 billion during the period 2001–2003 (UNCTAD, 2004, p. 27). A growing number of Indian enterprises are beginning to see OFDI as an important aspect of their corporate strategies and are emerging as multinational corporations (MNCs) in their own right.

Although a few Indian enterprises were investing abroad in the mid-1960s (Lall, 1983, 1986), OFDI activity became significant only since the onset of economic reforms in 1991. OFDI underwent a considerable change in the 1990s in terms not only of magnitude, but also the geographical focus and sectoral composition of the flows

* This chapter draws upon an earlier paper (co-authored with Jaya Prakash Pradhan) prepared as part of a larger study on the competitiveness of Indian enterprises at Research and Information System (RIS), supported by the Department of Scientific and Industrial Research (DSIR), Government of India. An earlier version appeared in a special issue of *Transnational Corporations* and has benefited from comments of anonymous reviewers. Comments by Andrea Goldstein at the ICRIER workshop are appreciated. The usual disclaimer applies.

(Kumar, 2004). Kumar (1996, 1998) has argued that this change in the geographical and sectoral composition of OFDI has in line with the change in their motives from essentially market-seeking to more asset-seeking ones to support exporting with a local presence.

The theory of international operation of the firm — which evolved over the years with the contributions from Hymer (1976), Caves (1971), and Dunning (1979) among many others — posits that some unique advantages such as having a revenue generating potential abroad combined with the presence of internalization and locational advantages leads to OFDI. Enterprises based in the industrialized countries have emerged as MNCs on the strength of ownership advantages derived from innovative activity that is largely concentrated in these countries. Very little is known about the sources of the strength of enterprises based in developing countries, such as India, that enables overseas investment. It is of potential analytical and policy interest to examine the determinants of the OFDI activity of Indian enterprises. However, the lack of corporate statistics giving information on OFDI from India has prevented such analysis.

This chapter quantitatively analyzes the patterns and determinants of OFDI activity of Indian enterprises using an exclusive panel dataset covering 4271 Indian enterprises in manufacturing for the period from 1989/1990 to 2000/2001. The rest of the chapter is organized as follows. Section 2 briefly discusses government policy toward OFDI and broad trends and patterns of Indian OFDI. Section 3 develops a framework for analyzing the determinants of Indian OFDI. Section 4 presents the results of the quantitative analysis and draws some inferences. Section 5 concludes with a few remarks on policy implications.

2. Liberalization and Patterns of OFDI by Indian Enterprises

Alongside the liberalization of policies dealing with inward FDI, the policy governing OFDI from India has also been liberalized since 1991. The Guidelines for Indian Joint Ventures and Wholly Owned Subsidiaries Abroad, as amended in October 1992, May 1999, and

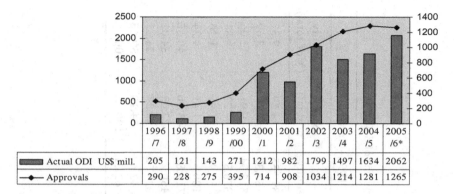

	1996 /7	1997 /8	1998 /9	1999 /00	2000 /1	2001 /2	2002 /3	2003 /4	2004 /5	2005 /6*
▬ Actual ODI US$ mill.	205	121	143	271	1212	982	1799	1497	1634	2062
—◆— Approvals	290	228	275	395	714	908	1034	1214	1281	1265

Figure 1: Indian outward investments, 1996–1997 to 2005–2006.

Source: India, Ministry of Finance
* Up to February 2006.

July 2002, provided for automatic approval of OFDI proposals up to a certain limit. This limit was expanded progressively from US$2 million in 1992 to US$100 million in July 2002. In January 2004, the limit was removed altogether and Indian enterprises are now permitted to invest abroad up to 100 percent of their net worth on an automatic basis.

The magnitudes of OFDI flows as well as their numbers have risen considerably over the past few years as shown in Figure 1. In 2005/2006, the latest fiscal year for which the data are available, India's OFDI flows crossed the US$2 billion mark. A more detailed examination of the patterns of OFDI has been carried out with the help of the RIS database compiled from published and unpublished sources.[1] As is apparent from Table 1, the pattern of OFDI activity has also undergone a considerable change in the post-liberalization period in terms of the geographical focus as well as the sectoral composition. In the pre-1991 period, as much as 86 percent of Indian OFDI was concentrated in other developing countries. However, in the 1990s, an overwhelming (nearly 60 percent) proportion of these investments was directed to developed countries.

---

[1] See Annex for details.

Table 1: Geographical distribution of approvals of outward FDI from India, 1975–2001 (millions of dollars)

Region	1975–1990				1991–March 2001			
	No	Equity	No (% of total)	Equity (% of total)	No	Equity	No (% of total)	Equity (% of total)
South–East and East Asia	67	80.79	29.26	36.32	379	399.35	14.79	9.37
South Asia	30	20.91	13.10	9.40	197	157.39	7.69	3.69
Africa	29	37.83	12.66	17.01	254	513.94	9.91	12.06
West Asia	19	21.54	8.30	9.68	185	376.5	7.22	8.83
Central Asia	4	23.2	1.75	10.43	49	50.99	1.91	1.20
Latin America & the Caribbean	2	0.58	0.87	0.26	36	180.6	1.41	4.24
Developing Countries	165	191.52	72.05	86.09	1176	1719.82	45.90	40.35
Western Europe	40	17.29	17.47	7.77	565	1450.2	22.05	34.02
North America	23	13.51	10.04	6.07	749	1029.52	29.23	24.15
Developed Countries	64	30.89	27.95	13.89	1386	2542.6	54.10	59.65
Total	229	222.46	100	100	2562	4262.52	100	100

Source: RIS database.

Similarly, Table 2 shows that Indian OFDI before 1990 was largely concentrated in manufacturing, which accounted for over 65 percent of the flows. Since 1991, however, nearly 60 percent of these flows have gone to services. Within these broad groups, OFDI is concentrated in industries like drugs and pharmaceuticals in the manufacturing sector, and IT, communication and software and media, broadcasting and publishing services in the services sector, viz. areas where Indian enterprises have a competitive advantage.

Many have argued that the OFDI activity in the pre-1991 period was of the market-seeking type where Indian enterprises established a presence in developing countries on the basis of their intermediate technologies in relatively low technology industries such as light engineering (Lall, 1983, 1986; Kumar, 1996). Since the 1990s, however, OFDI has been undertaken by Indian enterprises to improve their global competitiveness with a local presence in major markets, acquiring strategic assets and access to markets in emerging trading blocs in the context of the increased emphasis on outward orientation as part of the reforms (Kumar, 1996, 1998). Therefore, it is concentrated in countries that are key destinations for Indian exports (viz. European Union and North America) and in the sectors of their strength.

A number of Indian enterprises are establishing growing webs of overseas operations. They include pharmaceutical companies such as Ajanta Pharma (with 18 overseas investment approvals by 2001), Ranbaxy Laboratories (14 approvals), and Dr Reddy's Laboratories (9 approvals); IT software development enterprises such as NIIT Ltd. (15 approvals), Aptech (12 approvals), Infosys Technologies (10 approvals), Mastek (9 approvals); engineering companies like L&T, Voltas, and Usha Beltron (11 approvals each); Asian Paints (13 approvals); Essel Packaging (12 approvals), among others. Of late, Indian enterprises have also started using overseas acquisitions as a mode of establishing a foreign presence. The motives of the acquisitions are often similar to those of greenfield entries (viz. building marketing networks in foreign markets), but they are sometimes strategic with a view to filling gaps in their capabilities or, obtaining access to technologies, brands, natural resources or other assets. Hence, these

Table 2: Sectoral composition of outward FDI flows from India, 1975–2001 (millions of dollars).

Sector	1975–1990				1991–March2001			
	No	Equity	No (% of total)	Equity (% of total)	No	Equity	No (% of total)	Equity (% of total)
Exploration & refining of oil	1	0.02	0.43	0.01	5	61.10	0.20	1.43
Exploration of minerals & precious stones	2	4.02	0.87	1.81	2	0.04	0.08	0.00
Extractive	3	4.04	1.30	1.82	7	61.14	0.27	1.43
Oilseeds, food products & processing	10	9.06	4.35	4.07	91	69.34	3.55	1.63
Textiles and garments	12	9	5.22	4.05	158	112.56	6.17	2.64
Wood, pulp and paper	3	11.51	1.30	5.17	11	17.72	0.43	0.42
Leather, shoes & carpets	4	20.55	1.74	9.24	63	28.41	2.46	0.67
Chemicals, petro-chemicals & paints	18	7.82	7.83	3.52	94	92.13	3.67	2.16
Drugs & pharmaceuticals	8	4.72	3.48	2.12	163	270.24	6.36	6.34
Rubber, plastic & tyres	6	2.32	2.61	1.04	45	85.80	1.76	2.01
Cement, glass & building material	2	4.19	0.87	1.88	58	79.78	2.26	1.87
Iron and steel	10	16.17	4.35	7.27	47	50.65	1.84	1.19
Electrical & electronic equipment	6	2.11	2.61	0.95	63	90.86	2.46	2.13
Automobiles and parts thereof	6	3.21	2.61	1.44	26	24.00	1.02	0.56
Gems & jewellery	1	0	0.43	0.00	56	17.85	2.19	0.42
Electronic goods & consumer durables	2	0.27	0.87	0.12	29	20.75	1.13	0.49
Beverages & tobacco	7	3.24	3.04	1.46	37	142.05	1.44	3.33

(*Continued*)

Table 2: (*Continued*)

Sector	1975–1990				1991–March2001			
	No	Equity	No (% of total)	Equity (% of total)	No	Equity	No (% of total)	Equity (% of total)
Engineering goods & metallurgical items	18	8.53	7.83	3.83	84	66.24	3.28	1.55
Fertilizers, pesticides & seeds	5	39.93	2.17	17.95	27	326.96	1.05	7.67
Miscellaneous	10	2.59	4.35	1.16	184	183.58	7.18	4.31
Manufacturing	**128**	**145.22**	**55.65**	**65.28**	**1236**	**1678.92**	**48.26**	**39.39**
IT, communication & software	6	5.64	2.61	2.54	761	1354.49	29.71	31.78
Hotels, restaurants, tourism	24	24.96	10.43	11.22	53	112.45	2.07	2.64
Civil Contracting & engineering services	6	1.8	2.61	0.81	44	16.57	1.72	0.39
Consultancy	7	0.43	3.04	0.19	31	8.07	1.21	0.19
Trading & marketing	27	12.47	11.74	5.61	146	96.45	5.70	2.26
Media broadcasting & publishing	2	0.01	0.87	0.00	61	739.64	2.38	17.35
Financial services & leasing	17	26.32	7.39	11.83	96	95.49	3.75	2.24
Transport services	3	0.55	1.30	0.25	44	48.33	1.72	1.13
Other professional services	7	1.05	3.04	0.47	82	50.69	3.20	1.19
Services	**99**	**73.2**	**43.04**	**32.91**	**1318**	**2522.17**	**51.46**	**59.17**
Total	**230**	**222.45**	**100.00**	**100.00**	**2561**	**4262.23**	**100**	**100**

Source: RIS database.

are also generally concentrated in the areas of the competitive advantages of Indian companies.

For instance, Ranbaxy acquired RPG Aventis in France, Dr Reddy's Labs acquired Beetapharm in Germany; Cadila acquired the generics business of Alpharma in France; Asian Paints acquired Berger International, thus obtaining a foothold in 22 countries across the world; Tata Steel set up an affiliate in South Africa and acquired NatSteel in Singapore; Tata Tea acquired Tetley of the United Kingdom (UK), one of the world's biggest tea companies for US$430 million, thus gaining the control of a full value chain in tea processing; Titan Industries has set up a network of foreign affiliates in Europe and Asia to conduct its overseas business and emerged as a watch maker trying to build its brand in this highly skill-intensive and competitive industry. Indian companies are also acquiring stakes abroad to strengthen their access to resources. These include ONGC Videsh Ltd.'s investments/acquisitions of oil-related equity abroad, the Aditya Birla Group's acquisition of two copper mines in Australia and, Reliance Group's acquisition of Flag International.

3. Determinants of OFDI: Analytical Framework and Hypotheses

According to the ownership, location, and internalization theory, a prerequisite for a firm to become international is the ownership of unique advantages that outweigh the disadvantages of being "foreign" in overseas markets. Therefore, a key question in identifying the determinants of overseas investment is the nature of the ownership advantages or unique assets of Indian enterprises that allow their outward expansion. It has been argued that the main source of the advantage enjoyed by Indian enterprises was their ability to absorb, adapt, and build upon the technologies imported from abroad rather than produce completely novel technologies. Indian enterprises had accumulated considerable learning and technological capabilities as well as managerial and technical expertise during the first four decades of independence when the Government pursued a strategy of import substitution industrialization (Lall, 1986; Kumar, 1996). Sometimes, these included adaptation of imported designs to make them appropriate for local climatic conditions and more cost-effective, given their experience of dealing with highly price conscious and demanding customers in India. A number of Indian pharmaceutical and chemical enterprises developed cost-effective processes of known chemical entities, helped by the absence of product patents in India. With this capability, they began to enter the generics market in the United States and other developed countries after the expiry of product patents. Therefore, the strengths of Indian enterprises are likely to be concentrated in relatively standardized and mature technologies in industries characterized by competition based on price. They are not likely to move abroad primarily on the strength of their novel innovative proprietary technologies or globally recognized brand names like established developed country MNCs.

We develop a model for explaining the probability of an Indian enterprise investing abroad in the light of these observations. To explain the OFDI decision of Indian manufacturing firms, we have formulated a simple qualitative response model where the dependent variable takes the value one if the enterprise has invested abroad and zero if otherwise. Denoting X_{it} as a vector of k ($k = 1 \ldots k$) elements capturing ownership advantages and other factors explaining the ith firm's overseas investment decision in the tth time period. These factors are expected to provide the outward investing Indian enterprise some edge over local rivals in order to overcome the cost of "foreignness" in the host location. Thus, our empirical model is as follows:

$$L_{i_t} = X_{it}\beta + u_{it}, \qquad (1)$$

where β is the vector of logit coefficients and u_{it} is a normally distributed error term. L_i is the log of odds ratio, viz. the probability of an Indian enterprise undertaking OFDI. L_i viz., logit is linear in X and in the parameters.

We now identify different factors in X_{it} that are the sources of the ownership advantages for Indian enterprises investing abroad. We have specified X_{it} to include three sets of factors: firm-specific intangibles, industry-specific characteristics, and policies. The firm-specific intangibles, in turn, are assumed to be dependent upon a host of firm-specific characteristics such as age, technology, product differentiation, managerial skill, firm size, export orientation, and ownership. The theoretical basis for including these variables in the model is provided in the following discussion.

3.1. *Ownership Advantages of Enterprises*

Here, we identify certain variables that can be measured objectively to capture the possible sources of the ownership advantages of Indian enterprises.

(a) *Accumulated learning and managerial skills*: Accumulated production experience is a source of considerable learning and absorption of know-how. This learning is a source of incremental innovations on the shop floor that are not captured by indicators of more formal innovatory activity. Accumulated experience also helps an enterprise acquire managerial skills, knowledge of the market and reputation, among other advantages. These advantages can be valuable for overseas investments especially in relatively mature and standardized industries, if not in more skill- or knowledge-intensive ones. Hence, other things being equal, we expect accumulated learning (*LEARNING*) measured in terms of the years the enterprise has been in production to affect favorably its probability of undertaking OFDI.

(b) *Technological effort*: Further technological effort at the enterprise level is often required for absorption and adaptation of knowledge imported from abroad before it can lend an advantage to the firm, except possibly in very mature and low technology industries. Technological effort is also likely to capture the ability of the enterprises to replicate processes and methods at a foreign location. It is also a source of the cost effective process development in which Indian firms have been engaged, in the chemicals and pharmaceuticals industries. Hence, technological effort (*TECHEFFORT*) of the enterprises, measured in terms of research and development (R&D) intensity is posited to increase their probability of being outward investors.

(c) *Product differentiation*: Developing country firms are not likely to be strong in terms of the ability to differentiate their products with brand/trade names having good reputations worldwide. However, enterprises that are able to differentiate their product and build their brand names in domestic markets would be better placed to tap the opportunities abroad than others. This ability of branding (*BRANDS*) or differentiating the product, measured in terms of advertising intensity, may be valuable, at least in certain knowledge-intensive industries where quality enjoys a relatively high premium. Hence, it may favorably affect the probability of OFDI being undertaken by the enterprises.

(d) *Cost effectiveness of processes*: As argued earlier, one of the unique advantages enjoyed by Indian enterprises could be their ability to bring about adaptations and incremental changes to production processes to make them more cost effective, in view of their experience of operating in a highly price competitive environment. Hence, we expect the ownership of cost effective processes or methods of production (*COSTEFFECT*) measured in terms of profitability to be positively associated with the probability of investing abroad.

(e) *Firm size*: Larger firms are more likely to venture abroad than smaller firms, because they often have better access to market information and possess financial strength, allowing them to bear greater risks. A number of studies have found that firm size is an important determinant of overseas operations for developed as well as developing country enterprises (Caves, 1996). Hence, firm size (*SIZE*) is posited to have a favorable effect on the probability of the enterprise crossing the border. The effect of size, however, is generally observed to be nonlinear in many firm level studies of research and development activity and export performance. To check the possible nonlinearity of the effect, a quadratic term of SIZE will be used in the estimation.

(f) *Export-orientation*: In the product cycle theory of Vernon (1966), overseas investment is postulated to follow the initial exploration of overseas markets through exporting. It has been argued that the recent boom of overseas investment by developing country enterprises has been motivated by the need to support exporting with a local presence (i.e., developing marketing networks, providing after-sales services etc.) (Kumar, 1998). Exporting activity enhances the international competitiveness of the enterprise and may also provide valuable information on emerging opportunities in other countries. Hence, the export-intensity ($EXPORT$) of Indian enterprises is posited to be positively linked to the probability of establishing overseas operations. One may argue that there could be a simultaneity bias in the export intensity and overseas operations as the network of overseas operations may also generate exports for the firm. Studies for developed countries find exports and OFDI to be related.[2] Indian enterprises, however, appear to be at a rather early stage of evolution on the international scene with overseas operations following exports. In any case, a verification of simultaneity bias in the present context is constrained by the limited availability of methodological tools.

(g) *Technological dependence*: OFDI activity is posited to be based on firms' own "created" assets, which may be adapted from knowledge imported in the past. They are unlikely to have an edge over other enterprises in foreign markets on the basis of imported know-how and imported equipment. Therefore, the dependence of enterprises on imported technology ($TECHIM$) and capital goods ($MACHIM$) is likely to be negatively related to the probability of being outward investors.

(h) *Local ownership*: The overseas expansion of operations from India is likely to be limited to domestic enterprises, as foreign owned enterprises in India come to India primarily to explore the Indian market. Any overseas expansion of foreign affiliates in India would be subject to corporate decisions at headquarters. Hence,

---

[2] For instance, see Lipsey and Weiss (1984) and Liu and Graham (1998).

a dummy identifying foreign owned firms (*FOREIGN*) is likely to be negatively related to overseas expansion.

3.2. *Liberalization of Outward Investment Policy*

In the pre-1991 phase, government policy toward OFDI was rather restrictive and required overseas investments to be only through the capitalization of exported machinery and know-how fees. Outflows of liquid investment were generally restricted. However, as noted above, the policy has been progressively liberalized since 1991 along with the policy governing inward investment. Hence, a dummy identifying the 1991 liberalization (*LIBERAL*) is expected to have a positive effect on the probability of undertaking OFDI.

3.3. *Industry Effects*

The incidence of overseas activity is expected to vary across industries because of industry-specific comparative advantages and the specialization of the country. In particular, Indian enterprises are likely to be active abroad in industries that require adaptations, large inputs of skilled manpower or managerial resources. The inter-industry differences in the intensity of outward orientation are controlled in the estimation with the help of a set of industry dummies (*INDDUM$_n$*).

Having identified various components of vector X_i, we may now expand Equation (1) as follows:

$$
\begin{aligned}
Li = {} & \beta + \beta_1 LEARNING + \beta_2 SIZE + \beta_3 SIZE^2 \\
& + \beta_4 TECHEFFORT + \beta_5 TECHIM + \beta_6 MACHIM \\
& + \beta_7 BRANDS + \beta_8 COSTEFFECT + \beta_9 EXPORT \\
& + \beta_{10} FOREIGN + \beta_{11} LIBERAL + \sum_n \delta_n INDDUM_n + u_{it}. \quad (2)
\end{aligned}
$$

4. Empirical Estimations

The model as expressed in Equation (2) is estimated using an exclusive RIS dataset described earlier, compiled by pooling company annual report statistics for 4271 Indian manufacturing firms listed on stock exchanges from the Centre for Monitoring Indian Economy (CMIE)'s Prowess database and linking it with the OFDI information gathered from various published and unpublished sources from 1988/1989 to 2000/2001. (See Annex for more details and measurements of variables.)

The logit model has been estimated using the maximum likelihood method with robust standard errors. The statistical package STATA provides the robust standard errors using the Huber–White sandwich estimators that can effectively deal with the violations of some assumptions like normality, homoscedasticity, or some observations that exhibit large residuals, leverage or influence. Standardized logit coefficients, which are free of scale and hence are useful in assessing the relative strength of the independent variables in addition to marginal effects, are estimated.

4.1. *Full-sample Estimations*

Table 3 presents estimation results for model (2) for the full sample. The overall fitted model in terms of Wald Chi-squares is statistically highly significant. The explanatory power in the case of total manufacturing is about 16 percent. The performance of individual variables is discussed below.

The variable, *LEARNING*, capturing accumulated learning by the firm comes up with a strong positive effect on the probability of Indian enterprises undertaking OFDI. Therefore, accumulated learning from production experience is an important source of ownership advantage for Indian enterprises. It is likely to give them an edge, especially in other developing countries and in relatively low technology and mature industries.

The variable capturing the technological effort of enterprises, *TECHEFFORT*, turns out to have a significant positive effect on the probability of OFDI by Indian enterprises as expected. Enterprise-level technological effort, as represented by in-house R&D activity, leads to adaptations and innovations in the products and processes that could often lend Indian enterprises an advantage abroad.

Table 3: Determinants of probability of outward investments of Indian enterprises.

Independent Variables	Coefficients	Robust Z-Statistics
LEARNING	0.01404869***	14.87
TECHEFFORT	0.04872711***	2.74
BRANDS	0.02689367*	1.66
COSTEFFECT	0.00017099	1.51
SIZE	0.00287626***	22.74
SIZE²	−0.00000034***	10.6
EXPORTS	0.01977054***	25.28
FOREIGN	−1.35730201***	9.29
TECHIM	−0.00010668	0.39
MACHIM	−0.00161704***	3
LIBERAL	0.46447587***	6.77
DTEXTIL&LEATHER	0.41846904***	4.73
DWOOD&PAPER	0.15081544	0.96
DRUBBER&PLASTICS	0.59830256***	5.27
DNONMETALICMINERAL	−1.49406861***	3.19
DCEMENT&GLASS	0.56007601***	4.22
DBASICMETAL	0.35157936***	3.28
DCHEMICALS	0.29241594***	2.73
DELECTRICALS	0.51836462***	4.24
DMACHINERY	0.28631712**	2.08
DAUTOMOTIVE	−0.09043282	0.57
DPHARMACEUTICALS	0.97833303***	9.34
DELECTRONICS	0.40439671***	2.9
Constant	−4.28644974***	39.96
Pseudo R-square	0.1564	
Wald chi²	1723.8	
Log likelihood	−6688.3925	
Number of obs.	29051	

Note: * Significant at 10%; ** Significant at 5%; *** Significant at 1%. Food & beverages products has been treated as the base industry.
Source: Estimations as explained in the text.

Similarly, *BRANDS*, capturing the ability of Indian enterprises to differentiate their products, certainly increases the likelihood of undertaking OFDI.

As expected, *SIZE* and *SIZE²* have statistically significant positive and negative impacts, respectively, suggesting a favorable but a nonlinear effect of firm size on the probability of undertaking OFDI. Size increases the probability of undertaking OFDI up to a limit beyond which it turns negative.

As expected, *EXPORTS*, a variable capturing the export intensity of enterprise, has a positive effect on the probability of OFDI being undertaken. It appears that a part of Indian OFDI is undertaken by exporters to support their exporting activity with a local presence.

The two variables capturing technological dependence, viz. *TECHIM* and *MACHIM*, have expected negative signs and the latter also reaches statistical significance.

Obviously, OFDI activity is not possible on the basis of borrowed knowledge and capital goods alone. An enterprise needs to develop a base of created assets to be able to move abroad. Similarly, *FOREIGN*, a variable capturing the foreign ownership of Indian enterprises, also comes up with a statistically significant negative effect indicating that foreign MNCs come to India for exploring the Indian market and not to go abroad from India. Outward investment activity is undertaken by Indian enterprises on the strength of their own created assets.

LIBERAL, the variable capturing the effect of the 1991 liberalization of the Government's policy toward investment — inward as well as outward — is robustly positive. Liberalization has removed the policy constraints on OFDI in addition to promoting the external orientation of enterprises.

The sectoral dummy variables are generally significant with a positive sign but, being intercept coefficients, they only indicate that compared to the food and beverages industries, these industries have a better probability of OFDI. A more direct analysis of inter-industry patterns of OFDI is carried out with sectoral estimations, which are reported later.

4.2. Technology Intensity and Determinants of OFDI: Sub-sample Estimations

The full sample estimations were followed up with separate estimations for four sub-samples of Indian manufacturing, grouped by the technology-intensity of the industry following the revised OECD technological classification (see Annex 1), viz. high technology, medium-high technology, medium-low technology, and low technology. We also estimate the determinants of the probability of OFDI being undertaken for each of the 13 broad industry groups that are summarized in Table A.1. These sub-sample estimations may provide additional insights into the relative importance of the ownership advantages across industries. The estimations summarized in Tables 4 and A.1 are broadly similar to the full sample estimation except for some variations across technology classes and industries in terms of the relative importance of individual variables. Hence, we confine ourselves to a discussion of the major differences from the general pattern.

LEARNING continues to have a positive and statistically significant effect on the probability of OFDI in all technology classes except for high technology industries where it actually has a significant negative effect. Apparently, because of rapidly changing technology, accumulated experience is not an advantage in high technology industries. Younger firms are perhaps more dynamic and flexible in responding to the challenges of fast changing technologies in these industries. At the industry level, 8 out of the 13 industries (viz. textiles and leather, rubber and plastics, cement and glass, metals, chemicals, electrical machinery, non-electrical machinery, and transport equipment) follow the general pattern of having a significant positive effect on OFDI. In the rest of the industries (food and beverages, pharmaceuticals, electronics, wood and paper, and non-metallic mineral products), it has a negative effect.

Enterprise level technological effort (*TECHEFFORT*) has a statistically significant positive effect in the case of the medium-high technology and medium-low technology groups. However, it has a coefficient that is not significantly different from zero in statistical terms in the case of the low technology group. Apparently, in these industries, because of mature and standardized technology, the ownership advantage based on accumulated production experience is generally adequate. In the high technology group, *TECHEFFORT*

Table 4:   Determinants of probability of outward investments of Indian enterprises: Sub-samples by technology-intensity.

Independent variables	High technology	Medium-high technology	Medium-low technology	Low technology
LEARNING	-0.01225145**	0.01983054***	0.02839336***	0.0060186 8***
	(2.55)	(9.35)	(12.94)	(4.28)
TECHEFFORT	0.03825016	0.0373665*	0.14036360**	-0.04089900
	(1.60)	(1.92)	(2.51)	(0.34)
BRANDS	0.00070178	0.17323670***	0.01918220	0.01431513
	(0.09)	(9.81)	(0.67)	(1.32)
COSTEFFECT	0.00035855	0.00002231	0.00004253	0.00031543**
	(1.07)	(0.34)	(0.38)	(2.48)
SIZE	0.00721355***	0.00220079***	0.00218862***	0.00524463***
	(9.05)	(11.30)	(13.66)	(16.23)
SIZE²	-0.00000220***	-0.00000025***	-0.00000026***	-0.00000054***
	(3.78)	(5.41)	(9.81)	(13.60)
EXPORT	0.01846809***	0.02167980***	0.02491160***	0.01883140***
	(8.23)	(12.08)	(13.09)	(16.37)

(Continued)

Table 4: (*Continued*)

Independent variables	High technology	Medium-high technology	Medium-low technology	Low technology
FOREIGN	-1.79946462***	-1.79051006***	-3.31540517***	-1.25973224***
	(4.61)	(7.54)	(3.38)	(3.11)
TECHIM	0.00089860	-0.01566338	-0.00502218	-0.07882066
	(1.30)	(1.33)	(1.11)	(0.49)
MACHIM	-0.00169882**	-0.00110926	-0.00028239	-0.00134145
	(2.12)	(1.51)	(0.95)	(1.14)
LIBERAL	0.75100189***	0.32023588***	0.49989376***	0.32389356***
	(3.27)	(2.59)	(3.71)	(2.75)
Constant	-4.16541252***	-4.01165425***	-4.02677182***	-4.21724622***
	(15.93)	(26.94)	(25.40)	(29.53)
Pseudo R-square	0.2318	0.1608	0.1832	0.1747
Wald chi²	345.29	526.93	628.55	567.08
Log likelihood	-812.36787	-1776.4646	-1649.1752	-2243.1509
Number of obs	3198	8282	7227	10344

Note: Robust z-statistics in parentheses; * Significant at 10%; ** Significant at 5%; *** Significant at 1%. Relevant industry dummies have been included in the estimations but suppressed here.

Source: Estimations as explained in the text.

just misses the statistical significance, suggesting that in these industries, local technological effort alone may not be adequate and firms would need other advantages to be able to operate abroad. In the estimations at the level of individual industries, *TECHEFFORT* has a significant positive effect in the case of food and beverages, non-metallic metal products, chemicals, non-electrical machinery and pharmaceuticals; and a positive and nearly significant effect in rubber and plastics, cement and glass, automotive, electrical machinery and electronics. Its effect is not significantly different from zero only in those industries that are highly mature like textiles, leather, and metals. It is, therefore, clear that the enterprise level technological effort of the firms is an important source of their unique ownership advantages.

BRANDS also has a positive impact on OFDI in a significant positive manner only in the case of the medium-high technology group. In other groups, its coefficient is not significantly different from zero. Evidently, the ability of Indian enterprises to differentiate their products as a source of the advantage has been effective only in selected industries that are characterized by moderate technology intensity. Industry level estimations suggest that product differentiation or branding is a source of the advantages for Indian enterprises in food and beverages, textiles and clothing (nearly significant), cement and glass, chemicals, electrical machinery, non-electrical machinery, and pharmaceuticals. It is clear that enterprises that develop their brand identities and pay attention to their quality do better in international markets.

Finally, *COSTEFFECT* is relevant only in the case of the low technology group. At the industry level, the cost advantage has a strong positive effect in the case of textiles and leather, cement and glass, chemicals and electronics. Therefore, the experience of Indian enterprises in developing cost effective processes and products could be a source of the advantages in their overseas forays, at least in certain industries.

The technology dependence variables follow the general pattern of having either a negative or not significantly different from zero effect except in the pharmaceuticals industry, for which *TECHIM* has a significant positive effect. The Indian pharmaceuticals industry has a long tradition of building on knowledge imported from abroad and absorbing other spillovers with its own technological effort. Hence, it could be interpreted as indicating that a source of the unique owner-ship advantages of Indian enterprises in this industry is in the adapta-tion of imported know-how as reflected by the significant positive effect of both their own technological efforts as well as imported knowledge variables.

A striking finding is the consistent performance of *SIZE, FOREIGN, EXPORT* and *LIBERAL* across different technology classes and across most of the industries. Apparently, economic reforms and policy liberalization have had an important effect on the outward orienta-tion of Indian enterprises. Export-orientation exposes Indian enter-prises to the opportunities available in foreign markets and hence facilitates OFDI.

5. Conclusion and Policy Implications

This chapter has analyzed the trends, patterns, and determinants of OFDI by Indian enterprises. OFDI from India has increased notably over the past decade following the reforms and liberaliza-tion of policies undertaken by the Government since 1991. OFDI has emerged as an important mechanism through which the Indian economy is integrated with the global economy, along with grow-ing trade and inward FDI. The sharp rise in OFDI since 1991 has been accompanied by a shift in the geographical and sectoral focus. Indian OFDI is now more evenly distributed across the world com-pared to the pre-1990 period when it was heavily concentrated in poorer developing countries. They have also diversified sectorally to focus on the areas of India's emerging comparative advantages such as in pharmaceuticals and IT software. Indian enterprises have also started to acquire companies abroad to obtain access to mar-keting networks, brands, natural resources, technology, and other strategic assets.

This chapter has developed a framework for explaining the probability of an Indian enterprise investing abroad. This analytical framework was applied to assess the probability of OFDI being undertaken by Indian enterprises with an exclusive panel dataset covering over 4270 manufacturing companies for the 1989–2001 period. The empirical estimations suggest that, in line with hypotheses, Indian enterprises draw their ownership advantages from their accumulated production experience, the cost effectiveness of their production processes and other adaptations to imported technologies made with their technological effort, and sometimes with their ability to differentiate the product. Firm size exerts a positive effect but in a nonlinear manner. Enterprises that are already engaged in exporting are more likely to be outward investors. Outward orientation however, is unlikely to arise if the enterprise is heavily dependent on foreign technology, machinery or under foreign ownership. Finally, the policy liberalization of the 1990s is shown to have pushed Indian enterprises abroad.

The sub-sample estimations highlighted some variations across industries in terms of the relative importance of explanatory variables. In the low technology industries, accumulated production experience and cost effectiveness are sufficient, and enterprise level technological effort does not appear to be crucial for OFDI. In the high-technology industries, younger enterprises rather than those with longer production experience appear more dynamic, given their technological dynamism and flexibility in responding to the rapidly changing technological frontier in these industries.

The key lesson emerging from the above analysis is the importance of enterprises' own technological efforts and the focus on absorption and adaptation of knowledge that gives them the confidence to move beyond the confines of the domestic markets. Enterprises also need to pay attention to building brand identities and position them as a provider of qualitatively superior products or services. Firm size is certainly an advantage in international markets at least up to a level. Hence, some consolidation of the fragmented capacity in some industries may be useful. Finally, an enabling policy framework and macroeconomic environment, such as those that are developing with the progressive liberalization of policy, appear to foster the external orientation of Indian enterprises.

Annex: Dataset and Measurements of Variables

This chapter uses the exclusive RIS database on Outward Investments of Indian Enterprises. The RIS database has been compiled mainly from the published data of the India Investment Centre (IIC), supplemented by unpublished data from the Ministry of Commerce and the Ministry of Finance, Government of India. The dataset contains information on Indian enterprises investing abroad, the sectors of investment, the amount and share of Indian ownership, year of approval of projects, and the status of implementation of the projects. The constructed database on Indian investment abroad over the period 1975–March 2001 was then merged with the firm-level financial data obtained from the Prowess Data Base (2002) of the Centre for Monitoring Indian Economy (CMIE). The outcome is a panel dataset covering 4271 Indian enterprises in manufacturing for the period 1989/1990–2000/2001.

Variable Measurements

OFDI:	A dummy variable for Indian firms taking value 1 for firms undertaking outward FDI and 0 otherwise.
LEARNING$_{it}$:	The age of ith firm in number of years.
SIZE$_{it}$:	Total sales of ith firm in tth year.
SIZE$^2_{it}$:	The squared term of the sales of ith firm in tth year.
TECHEFFORT$_{it}$:	Total R&D expenditure as a percentage of total sales of ith firm in tth year.
TECHIM$_{it}$:	Royalties, technical and other professional fees remitted abroad by ith firm as a percentage of sales in the year t.

MACHIM$_{it}$:   Imports of capital goods by ith firm as a percentage of sales in tth year.

BRANDS$_{it}$:   Advertising expenditure of the ith firm as a percentage of sales in the year t.

COSTEFFECT$_{it}$:   The ratio of profit before tax (PBT) of the ith firm to net worth (%) in tth year.

EXPORT$_{it}$:   Exports of ith firm as a percentage of sales in the year t.

FOREIGN: Dummy variable for majority foreign owned firm taking value 1 for firms with 25% or more foreign equity participation and 0 otherwise.

LIBERAL: Liberalization dummy taking 1 for post-reform period 1993–1994 to 2000–2001 and 0 for the pre-reform period 1989–1990 to 1992–1993.

INDDUM$_j$:   denotes sectoral dummies included in the estimation.

Technological Classification of Indian Manufacturing Industries

Technology category	Industry
Low technology	1. Food, beverages & tobacco products 2. Textile, leather & footwear 3. Wood, paper & paper products
Medium-low technology	4. Rubber & plastic products 5. Other non-metallic mineral products 6. Cement & glass 7. Basic metal & metal products
Medium-high technology	8. Chemicals excluding pharmaceuticals 9. Electrical machinery 10. Non-electrical machinery 11. Automotives
High technology	12. Pharmaceuticals 13. Electronics

Source: The above technological classification is based on OECD (2001) 'OECD Science, Technology and Industry Scoreboard, 2001'

Table A.1: Determinants of probability of outward investments of Indian enterprises: Industry-wise estimations.

Industry Independent Variables	Food, bev, & tobacco	Textiles & leather	Wood & paper	Rubber & plastics	Other non-metallic mineral products	Cement & glass	Metals
LEARNING	-0.00747009**	0.01005395***	-0.00623802	0.02406590***	-0.90597974***	0.03698831***	0.02823189***
	(2.39)	(5.98)	(0.93)	(6.65)	(3.07)	(6.28)	(9.39)
TECHEFFORT	0.10175822**	-0.07647313	-7.35617829**	0.07046386	6.66783085***	0.44935156	-0.00368027
	(2.13)	(1.04)	(2.32)	(1.55)	(2.91)	(1.38)	(0.02)
BRANDS	0.02134473	0.01685106	-0.07653573	-0.02291589	-5.25637265**	0.26485907***	-1.91587103***
	(1.61)	(1.48)	(0.78)	(0.44)	(2.04)	(2.74)	(2.77)
COSTEFFECT	0.00012532	0.00126456**	0.00194693	-0.00052320**	-0.00687360*	0.00066816*	0.00016222
	(1.39)	(2.25)	(1.44)	(2.03)	(1.82)	(1.74)	(0.30)
SIZE	0.00555460***	0.00892902***	0.00430171***	0.00249933***	0.68481605	0.00409309***	0.00180214***
	(10.37)	(12.18)	(2.64)	(7.69)	(1.29)	(6.82)	(9.05)
SIZE^2	-0.0000054***	-0.00000474***	0.00000165	-0.00000033***	-0.02590137	-0.00000104***	-0.00000021***
	(8.95)	(5.42)	(1.12)	(4.65)	(0.99)	(4.42)	(7.08)
EXPORTS	0.01029237***	0.02310179***	0.03808611***	0.02187285***	0.05081438*	0.02795647***	0.02733743***
	(4.52)	(15.00)	(4.42)	(7.84)	(1.87)	(4.07)	(9.11)
FOREIGN	-2.02568237**	-0.50660449		-2.76729307***			
	(2.33)	(1.16)		(2.82)			
TECHIM	-0.71152894	-0.01886787	-0.02065755	-0.04656017		-0.00376338*	0.01053096
	(1.42)	(0.17)	(0.39)	(0.80)		(1.69)	(0.60)
MACHIM	-0.00298487	-0.00115727	-0.01403288	-0.00024432	0.00011892	-0.00008515	-0.00100808
	(1.52)	(0.97)	(0.69)	(0.28)	(0.06)	(1.15)	(0.67)
LIBERAL	0.11459941	0.41448666***	0.28905317	0.38381885		0.76956380*	0.45745358**
	(0.53)	(2.65)	(0.76)	(1.64)		(1.93)	(2.42)
Constant	-3.48877965***	-4.38465087***	-3.63931168***	-3.78051629***	-5.24456562**	-5.20789075***	-4.10096000***
	(16.02)	(26.53)	(9.47)	(15.20)	(2.31)	(11.93)	(20.10)
Pseudo R-square	0.1892	0.1911	0.2124	0.1521	0.5842	0.2698	0.1879
Wald chi2	162.21	561.10	87.99	199.84	26.96	161.60	331.72
Log likelihood	-690.15802	-1302.3585	-178.96438	-573.36415	-9.475484	-261.4862	-764.05338
Number of obs	3890	5249	1158	2343	178	1197	3317

(*Continued*)

Table A.1: (*Continued*)

	Chemicals	Electrical machinery	Non-electrical machinery	Transport equipment	Pharmaceuticals	Electronics
LEARNING	0.01855550***	0.02306959***	0.01981240***	0.01061348***	-0.02737287***	-0.04630854***
	(4.85)	(4.79)	(4.32)	(2.64)	(3.15)	(4.52)
TECHEFFORT	0.09014240**	0.15454497	0.02738876*	0.11454221	0.03469031*	0.04933230
	(2.07)	(1.57)	(1.75)	(1.36)	(1.80)	(1.56)
BRANDS	0.18287934***	0.17951839***	0.21412778***	0.01923598	0.10029626***	-0.16750628*
	(7.91)	(2.75)	(3.51)	(0.12)	(3.02)	(1.96)
COSTEFFECT	0.00075075**	-0.00041418	0.00003403	-0.00002435	0.00008224	0.00159732*
	(2.55)	(0.89)	(0.37)	(0.34)	(0.11)	(1.65)
SIZE	0.00336443***	0.00467657***	0.00793652***	0.00149688***	0.01719057***	0.00423678***
	(12.08)	(5.77)	(7.47)	(7.74)	(11.37)	(6.07)
SIZE²	-0.00000054***	-0.00000187***	-0.00000436***	-0.00000012***	-0.00000828***	-0.00000060*
	(5.50)	(3.00)	(4.00)	(5.06)	(7.29)	(1.68)
EXPORTS	0.01934662***	0.02309955***	0.01840023***	0.03972878***	0.01749393***	0.01486872***
	(7.79)	(5.43)	(2.99)	(6.22)	(5.05)	(4.07)
FOREIGN	-2.42700671***		-1.48559935***	-0.90903682	-3.31551633***	-1.57986211***
	(5.62)		(3.66)	(1.30)	(5.30)	(2.63)
TECHIM	0.01093690	-0.02124700	-0.01617508*	-0.89579637**	0.18339891*	-0.04626719
	(0.49)	(0.43)	(1.85)	(2.56)	(1.87)	(0.59)
MACHIM	-0.00018232	-0.00210436	-0.00036276	-0.00624566	-0.01022129*	-0.00088192
	(0.72)	(0.65)	(0.08)	(0.67)	(1.92)	(0.55)
LIBERAL	0.20719872	0.74848122**	0.62088083***	-0.49205187**	0.09137886	1.45054567***
	(1.04)	(2.41)	(1.97)	(2.11)	(0.36)	(3.41)
Constant	-4.11667846***	-4.60694798***	-4.69081972***	-3.14900133***	-3.34818376***	-3.67815205***
	(18.90)	(12.69)	(13.81)	(11.98)	(11.72)	(8.32)
Pseudo R-square	0.2334	0.1764	0.1799	0.1838	0.3583	0.2093
Wald chi²	319.84	163.96	153.34	140.54	219.81	150.15
Log likelihood	-646.543	-357.47414	-332.59283	-338.31366	-433.84898	-294.91317
Number of obs	3148	1489	1842	1613	1829	1369

Note: Robust z-statistics in parentheses; * Significant at 10%; ** Significant at 5%, *** Significant at 1%. In many industries, *FOREIGN* is found to predict failure perfectly and hence has been dropped from the estimation. In the case of other non-metallic mineral products *TECHIM* and *LIBERAL* have been dropped for the same reason.

Source: Estimations as explained in the text.

References

Caves, RE (1971). International comparisons: The industrial economics of foreign investment. *Economica*, 38, 1–27.

Dunning, JH (1979). Explaining changing patterns of international production: In defence of the electric theory. *Oxford Bulletin of Economics and Statistics*, 41, 269–296.

Hymer, SH (1976). *The International Operations of National Firms: A Study of Direct Foreign Investment*. Cambridge, MA: MIT Press.

Kumar, N (1996). India: Industrialization, liberalization and inward and outward foreign direct investment, In *Foreign Direct Investment and Governments*, JH Dunning and R Narula, (eds.), pp. 348–379. London: Routledge.

Kumar, N (1998). Emerging outward foreign direct investment from Asian developing countries: Prospects and implications, In *Globalization, Foreign Direct Investment and Technology Transfers*, N Kumar (ed.), pp. 177–194. London and New York: Routledge.

Kumar, N (2004). India. In *Managing FDI in a Globalizing Economy: Asian Experiences*, DH Brooks and H Hill (eds.), pp. 119–152. New York: Palgrave Macmillan for ADB.

Lall, S (1983). Multinationals from India. In *The New Multinationals: The Spread of Third World Enterprises*, S Lall (ed.), New York: John Wiley & Sons.

Lall, RB (1986). *Multinationals from the Third World: Indian Firms Investing Abroad*. Delhi: Oxford University Press.

Lipsey, RE and MY Weiss (1984). Foreign production and exports of individual firms. *The Review of Economics and Statistics*, 66(2), 304–308.

Liu, L and EM Graham (1998). The relationship between trade and foreign direct investment: Empirical results for Taiwan and South Korea. IIE Working Paper 98–7, Washington, D.C.: Peterson Institute for International Economics.

Vernon, R (1966). International investment and international trade in the product life cycle. *Quarterly Journal of Economics*, 80, 190–207.

Wells, Jr LT, (1983). *Third World Multinationals: The Rise of Foreign Investment from Developing Countries*. Cambridge, MA: MIT Press.

Section III

FDI from East and South–East Asia

Chapter 7

Outward FDI from East Asia: The Experiences of Hong Kong and Taiwan*

Nathalie Aminian, K. C. Fung and Chelsea C. Lin

1. Introduction

Foreign direct investment (FDI) flows into and out of East Asia has been quite active since 1990. Apart from Japan, Taiwan, Hong Kong, Korea and Singapore were the main sources of FDI flows to the region as well as outside the region.[1] During the 1990s and the early 2000s, the geographic composition of FDI from developing economies has changed, mainly reflecting the growing importance of East Asia as a source of FDI. By 1990, Taiwan was second after Brazil in the list of top FDI sources. Since 2000, Hong Kong has been the main outward investor among developing countries. The Asian financial crisis has caused the direction of the FDI flows to change. This is particularly evident in the allocation of FDI flows between crisis countries in East Asia and China. For example, FDI flows from Taiwan and Hong Kong to China increased for the period 1999–2005. The proportion of FDI going to China compared with those to the countries affected by the Asian financial crisis increased steadily after 1997. Moreover, the outward-looking pattern initiated by China and trade liberalization measures institutionalized in the process of China's accession to World Trade Organization (WTO) have undoubtedly helped to accelerate this trend and to promote tighter intra-regional trade relations.

---

* Comments by Abhijit Sen Gupta at the ICRIER workshop are appreciated. The usual disclaimer applies.
[1] See Chapter 3 by Hattari and Rajan for more details.

This reallocation of OFDI from Hong Kong and Taiwan and the growing importance of China as a recipient country show an increased dependency on intra-regional investment, which has emerged out of a non-institutional (i.e, informal) economic integration among the three economies. The purpose of this chapter is to investigate the magnitude and the allocation of OFDI from Hong Kong and Taiwan for the period 1999–2005, and to analyze the determinants of such FDI outflows from both the home and host countries' viewpoints.

The chapter is organized as follows. Section 2 describes the position of Hong Kong and Taiwan in the regional and international contexts as sources of FDI. Section 3 outlines the main characteristics of outward direct investment from Hong Kong and Taiwan, detailing the major recipient countries and the sectors benefiting from this investment. As will be apparent, the direct investment outflows from Hong Kong and Taiwan are largely dominated by China as a key destination. Section 4 analyzes the determinants of these outflows of direct investment (including both push and pull factors), with a particular emphasis on the relationship between OFDI and trade patterns, in the context of regional integration. Section 5 concludes with a summary and some policy implications.

2. General Trend in Outward FDI Flows from East Asia

In the regional context, as Figure 1 indicates, outward stock of direct investment for most Asian countries in the 2000s increased and reached a relatively high level. Hong Kong, Taiwan, Singapore, and South Korea were leading investors. It is noteworthy that Hong Kong is the major outward investor, leaving other Asian investors far behind. However, the FDI outflows from East Asian economies fell in 2001, 2003, and 2005, as can be seen in Figure 2. Asian NIEs, namely Hong Kong, Taiwan, Singapore, and South Korea exhibited a significant decline in their total outflows, while outflows from China also surged in 2005, reaching US$11 billion.

The pattern of OFDI in terms of absolute values does not, however, provide a full picture of the significance of OFDI for different

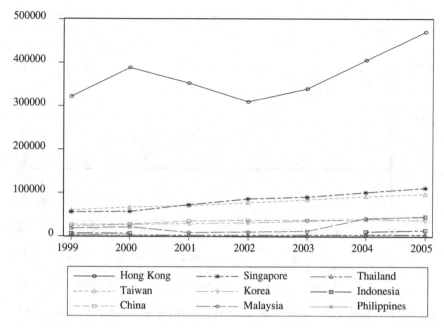

Figure 1: Total outward FDI stock for selected East Asian economies (Millions of US dollars).

Source: UNCTAD, FDI/TNC database.

countries. The sizes of source economies have to be taken into account. Table 1 presents the evolution of the FDI outflow as a percentage of gross fixed capital formation (GCFC) and the FDI outward stock as a percentage of GDP for selected Asian countries. Outflows as a percentage of GCFC and FDI outward stock as a percentage of GDP are significantly higher for both Hong Kong and Singapore compared to other East Asian countries. Hong Kong shows a sharp increase in both of these ratios in recent years. The share of OFDI to GDP for Hong Kong increased from 15.7 percent in 1999 to 264.7 percent in 2005. Its share of OFDI to GFCF rose from 16.4 percent in 1990 to 129.5 percent in 2000, before falling to 88 percent in 2005. The same trend is noticeable for Singapore to a lesser extent. The high shares of OFDI to GCFC ratios underline Hong Kong's status as a hub for regional headquarters and businesses, as well as being an international financial center.

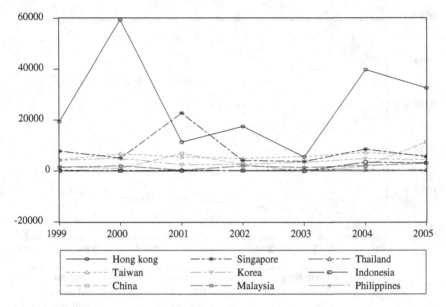

Figure 2:   Total FDI outflows of selected East Asian economies (Millions of US dollars).

Source: UNCTAD, FDI/TNC database.

Table 1:   FDI outflows as a percentage of gross fixed capital formation (GFCF) and FDI stocks as a percentage of Gross Domestic Product (GDP).

	FDI/GFCF (%)			FDI/GDP (%)		
Economy	2003	2004	2005	1990	2000	2005
China		0.2	1.4	1.2	2.6	2.1
Hong Kong	16.4	129.5	88.0	15.7	234.9	264.7
Taiwan	10.4	10.5	8.5	18.9	21.7	28.1
Korea, Rep. of	1.9	2.3	1.9	0.9	5.2	4.6
Indonesia		6.2	5.0	0.1	4.6	5.0
Malaysia	6.0	8.5	11.4	6.1	25.3	34.0
Philippines	2.3	4.1	1.1	0.3	2.1	2.1
Singapore	14.1	33.3	21.7	21.2	61.3	94.1
Thailand	1.4	0.3	0.5	0.5	1.8	2.3

Source: UNCTAD, World Investment Report (2006).

Table 2: Top 12 developing countries in terms of stocks of outward FDI (*Millions of US dollars*).

Rank	Economy	1990	Economy	2000	Economy	2005
1	Brazil	41 044	Hong Kong	388 380	Hong Kong	470 458
2	Taiwan	30 356	Taiwan	66 655	British Virgin Islands	123 167
3	South Africa	15 004	British Virgin Islands	64 483	Russian federation	120 417
4	Hong Kong	11 920	Singapore	56 766	Singapore	110 932
5	Singapore	7808	Brazil	51 946	Taiwan	97 293
6	Argentina	6057	South Africa	32 319	Brazil	71 556
7	China	4455	China	27 768	China	46 311
8	Panama	4188	South Korea	26 833	Malaysia	44 480
9	Kuwait	3662	Malaysia	22 874	South Africa	38 503
10	Mexico	2672	Argentina	21 141	South Korea	36 478
11	Malaysia	2971	Cayman Islands	20 553	Cayman Islands	33 747
12	Korea	2301	Russian federation	20 141	Mexico	28 040

Source: UNCTAD, World Investment Report (2006).

An international comparison can broaden our perspective on OFDI from Asian countries. This gives us a few interesting observations. Table 2 indicates the top 12 developing economies in terms of stocks of OFDI in the 1990s and the early 2000s. It is noteworthy that the geographical composition of FDI from developing economies has changed significantly in the 1990s, mainly reflecting the growing importance of Asian countries as outward investors. By 1990, Taiwan was ranked second after Brazil. The Asian NIEs, Hong Kong, South Korea, Singapore, and Taiwan as well as China and Malaysia were among the top 12 outward investors. Ten years later, Hong Kong led the list of top FDI sources, followed by Taiwan. As a whole, the Asian NIEs, China and Malaysia improved their position, being among the top nine sources. In 2005, Hong Kong was the largest source of FDI from developing countries and the sixth largest in the world in terms or FDI outward stock.

In addition to comparing countries in terms of FDI in absolute values, it is also useful to consider OFDI patterns in relative terms and from the perspective of the source country. The OFDI performance index determined by UNCTAD can be an indicator comparing OFDI from different economies in relative terms. It compares a country's share of world OFDI against its share of world GDP.[2] Table 3 presents the OFDI performance index for selected economies. Hong Kong, Malaysia, and Singapore have seen increases in their index values over the past 10 years. The index value for Hong Kong has risen at a very fast pace to reach 9.97 for the period 2003–2005. According to this

Table 3:   Outward FDI Performance Index,[a] average (Ranked by 2003–2005)

Rank	Economy	2003–2005	1993–1995
1	Hong Kong	9.97	4.63
2	Norway	5.80	1.40
3	Luxembourg	4.99	
4	Switzerland	4.42	4.32
5	Netherlands	4.22	4.13
6	Belgium	4.00	
7	Singapore	3.97	3.61
8	Panama	3.36	5.45
9	United Kingdom	2.47	2.72
10	Sweden	2.46	2.80
20	Malaysia	1.39	1.07
21	Taiwan	1.19	1.68
59	Republic of Korea	0.18	0.18
71	China	0.09	0.26

Source: UNCTAD, World Investment Report (2006).

[a] The outward FDI performance index measures the world share of an economy's OFDI as a ratio of its share in world GDP. The index in Table 3 has been calculated on the basis of OFDI stocks.

---

[2] The UNCTAD Outward FDI Performance index is a measure of the extent to which a source country has OFDI relative to its economic size. It is calculated as the ratio of a country's share in global FDI outflows to its share in global GDP, World Investment Report, UNCTAD (2006).

index, FDI from Hong Kong was about 10 times larger than would have been expected given its share of world GDP. On the other hand, the value for Taiwan fell significantly and the value for Korea remained unchanged.

3. Characteristics of Outward Direct Investment of Hong Kong and Taiwan

The previous section highlighted the leading role of Hong Kong, in particular, as an outward investor both in the regional or in the international context, as well as Taiwan. We now turn to the main characteristics of these two countries as outward investors. We examine the major recipient countries and the sectors benefiting from such investment.

3.1. *Hong Kong*

Given that Hong Kong is a leading FDI source, it is useful to provide a better idea of its FDI patterns, taking into account both inward and OFDI. Figures 3 and 4 present the outward and inward FDI in terms of flows (Figure 3) and stocks (Figure 4), and FDI net balance. It is noteworthy that, in terms of stocks, Hong Kong has recorded a steady positive position, as inward FDI has surpassed OFDI every year from 1999 to 2005, with a sharp decline in 2002. However, in terms of flows, FDI patterns are quite different. Hong Kong experienced an unprecedented FDI boom in 1999 and 2000 after it recovered from the economic turmoil of the Asian financial crisis. The surge reflects Hong Kong's role as a financial hub for businesses in the region, particularly in China. At the same time, investments from Hong Kong to China have increased. This is why the net FDI position of Hong Kong is only slightly positive in 2000. From 2000 to 2002, Hong Kong experienced an abrupt decline in its FDI inflows, resulting in the net position becoming negative.

Hong Kong has been experiencing another surge in FDI inflows during recent years. This partly reflects the Closer Economic Partnership Arrangement (CEPA) signed between Hong Kong and China which

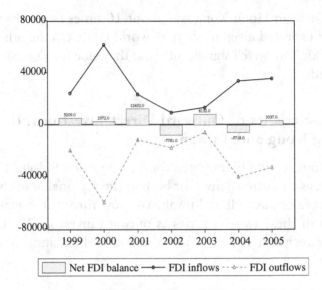

Figure 3:   Hong Kong Net FDI flows balance (Millions of US dollars).
Source: UNCTAD, FDI/TNC database.

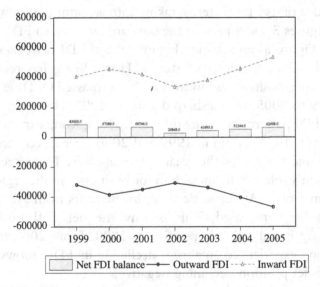

Figure 4:   Hong Kong Net FDI balance in terms of FDI stocks (Millions of US dollars).
Source: UNCTAD, FDI/TNC database.

opened up new opportunities not only for firms in Hong Kong, but also for foreign investors that operate in Hong Kong. The CEPA came into force in the beginning of 2004 with two main measures, being the first formalized institution of economic integration within Greater China. One measure is aimed at promoting exports from Hong Kong into China by granting preferential treatment of zero tariffs. The other is to provide lower thresholds and easier entry permits for FDI of the service industries from Hong Kong to China. At the same time, outflows from Hong Kong to China increased as Hong Kong played an important role for investment into and out of China. Most of the FDI outflows from Hong Kong are by affiliates of multinational corporations (MNCs) from developed countries and from China. This is why the net position became negative again in 2004. FDI inflow to Hong Kong decreased slightly in 2005 and, FDI outflow from Hong Kong decreased significantly because of the negative outflows in inter-company debt transactions arising from repayment of debts by non-resident affiliates of some Hong Kong firms. Taking inflow and outflow together, there was a net inflow in 2005.

It is noteworthy that official data on outward direct investment from Hong Kong are available only since 1998. The statistics are compiled on the basis of data obtained from the "Survey of External Claims, Liabilities and Income" conducted by Census and Statistics Department of the government. Hong Kong government does not publish detailed distributions of OFDI at individual industry levels and regional level for any country. The recently released statistics (2005) on Hong Kong's OFDI indicated the major recipients of OFDI from Hong Kong, as can be seen in Table 4. The bulk of its OFDI is related to investment in offshore financial centers in the Caribbean. The immediate destination is by far the British Virgin Islands (BVI), followed by the Cayman Islands and Bermuda. The BVI remained the most popular tax haven economy for indirect channeling of FDI funds, accounting for 44 percent of the total of Hong Kong's outward direct investment in 2005. However, the actual destination of these funds is elsewhere. Some of these funds are channeled to China; others to other parts of the world; and an important portion went back to Hong Kong. Statistics show these "tax haven" economies

Table 4: Stock of outward direct investment of Hong Kong at market value by major recipient countries (*HK$ billion*).

Destination	1999	Destination	2000	Destination	2001	Destination	2002
BVI	1395.6	BVI	1569.4	BVI	1437	BVI	1437.0
China	620.6	China	1011.6	China	844.0	China	843.0
Bermuda	93.2	Bermuda	88.9	Bermuda	91.9	Bermuda	76.8
Cayman Is.	86.1	Cayman Is.	71.1	Panama	32.4	Panama	39.0
New Zealand	31.5	New Zealand	27.1	USA	28.7	USA	32.2
Panama	30.9	Singapore	25.9	Malaysia	24.8	Malaysia	27.9
UK	26.0	USA	24.3	Singapore	24.5	Singapore	26.0
USA	22.5	Panama	23.5	Thailand	20.6	Thailand	20.8
Singapore	18.9	UK	23.5	UK	20.6	UK	20.5
Japan	17.4	Japan	18.3	Japan	11.5	Japan	11.9
Others	157.2	Others	144.4	Others	213.2	Others	166.6
Total	2499.9	Total	3027.9	Total	2749.2	Total	2412.9

(*Continued*)

Table 4: (*Continued*)

Destination	2003	Destination	2004	Destination	2005
BVI	1270.3	BVI	1402.1	BVI	1609.3
China	931.2	China	1211.6	China	1477.4
Bermuda	88.4	Bermuda	129.7	Bermuda	126.1
UK	47.3	UK	55.3	UK	59.6
Singapore	30.0	Japan	42.1	Singapore	40.0
Malaysia	24.2	Singapore	34.2	Japan	29.7
Panama	24.2	Panama	28.6	Panama	29.7
Thailand	21.6	Thailand	24.8	USA	26.3
USA	20.4	USA	22.6	Cayman Is.	25.1
Japan	15.2	Malaysia	22.2	Thailand	23.0
Others	163.8	Others	160.4	Others	207.7
Total	2636.7	Total	3133.6	Total	3653.9

Source: Census & Statistics Department Hong Kong External Direct Investment of Hong Kong (various issues).

are also the largest source of FDI into Hong Kong. Indeed, the BVI became the fourth largest source of FDI in China during 1999–2000 (UNCTAD, 2001).

Apart from offshore financial centers, China is the most important destination for Hong Kong's OFDI. The investment from Hong Kong to China increased steadily from 1999 to 2005, with a share of 40.4 percent of the total stock at end-2005. Guangdong Province is the favorite location for Hong Kong's investment in Mainland China, accounting for 37.1 percent of the total stock of OFDI to the Mainland. Hong Kong is by far the largest foreign investor in China. A significant portion of Hong Kong investment to China originates from China itself. Most of China's capital outflow that takes place either through legal or illegal channels to Chinese firms located in Hong Kong finds its way back to China as FDI. This type of "round tripping" of funds is mostly used to escape regulations such as barriers to trade or to gain eligibility to incentives available to only foreign investors (e.g, tax concessions). It is estimated that around one-third of Hong Kong's FDI outflows were "round tripping" from China, and another one-third were from other countries (Petri, 1995, Fung, 1997). Hong Kong is also used as a stepping stone for investment to China.

A large number of foreign firms use affiliates in Hong Kong to invest in China on their behalf. Many overseas companies have regional offices as well as regional headquarters in Hong Kong. Apart from China, the other Asian destinations of Hong Kong's FDI are Singapore and Japan and from 2001 onwards, Malaysia and Thailand.

Table 5 indicates the economic activities that benefited from such investment in 2004 and 2005. The bulk of Hong Kong's overseas FDI has been in services. Outward FDI engaged in investment holding, real estate and various business services took up the largest share at 69 percent of the total stock in 2005. This was followed by wholesale, retail and import/export trades (with a share of 10.9 percent), and manufacturing (4.5 percent).[3]

---

[3] See Chapter 2 of this volume by Aykut on the importance of FDI to the services sector in Hong Kong and other developing economies.

Table 5: Stock of outward direct investment of Hong Kong at market value by economic activity (Ranked by 2005).

Economic Activity	Stock of outward DI at the end of year	
	2004	2005
Investment holding, real estate and various business services	1925.6	2520.1
Wholesale, retail and import/ export trades	380.6	398
Manufacturing	158.5	165.6
Banks and deposit-taking companies	58.9	96.5
Transport and related services	84	89.3
Communications	145.6	84.1
Financial institutions other than banks and deposit-taking companies	72.3	83.2
Restaurants and hotels	52.6	53.2
Insurance	29.4	30
Construction	21.6	25.9
Other activities	204.6	107
Total	3133.6	3653.9

Source: Census & Statistics Department Hong Kong External Direct Investment of Hong Kong (2005).

3.2. *Taiwan*

Figures 5 and 6 show the outward and inward FDI to and from Taiwan in terms of flows and stocks, and well as its FDI net balance. It is noteworthy that in terms of both stocks or flows, from 1999 to 2005 (and even before, since the late 1980s) Taiwan has recorded a steady, consistent negative position, as OFDI has always exceeded inward FDI. In the mid-1980s, FDI outflows from Taiwan started to grow significantly to South–East Asia and to China. This trend has been driven by two main factors, viz. difficult conditions in the domestic investment environment (land prices increased sharply and the wage rate rose), and rapid appreciation of the Taiwan dollar (40 percent in nominal terms) during 1986–1988. Taiwanese firms attempted to escape from the worsening domestic environment and turned to foreign

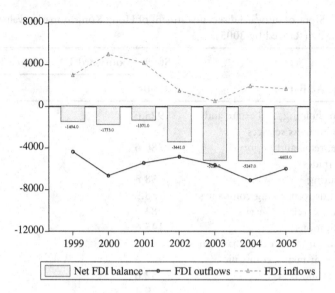

Figure 5:   Taiwan net FDI balance (Millions of US dollars).
Source: UNCTAD, FDI/TNC database.

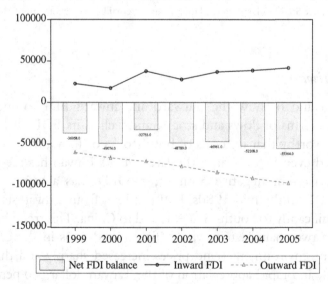

Figure 6:   Taiwan FDI balance in terms of stocks (Millions of US dollars).
Source: UNCTAD, FDI/TNC database.

investment to maintain their export market shares and competitiveness. Outward FDI appears to play a defensive role in retaining export markets and to be a substitute for domestic production. However, from the mid-1990s, Taiwanese firms increased OFDI to exploit their assets, such as patents, other technological assets, reputation, skills in production, marketing and advertising. FDI outflows therefore appear to play an expansive role in the international market, and it is quite complementary to domestic production in Taiwan.

In terms of FDI flows (Figure 5), Taiwan's FDI inflows grew rapidly in 2000 due to a large-scale reform of various laws and regulations on FDI inflows as well as further opening of the financial sector.[4] However, FDI inflows plunged by nearly 40 percent in 2001 and dropped still further in the next two years. The year 2004 marked the start of a recovery; since then, FDI inflows have grown by over 20 percent annually. The FDI outflows were significant with a downturn during 2001–2002.

Table 6 indicates the major recipient countries of OFDI from Taiwan. It is important to note that in most empirical studies on Taiwanese inward and outward FDI, these flows are under-estimated as far as direct investment to China is excluded because the statistics for China are not systematically compiled. However, we fill this gap here, using data including OFDI to China (see Table 9 for details).

As Table 6 indicates, the number one destination for Taiwanese outward direct investment is China for the whole period of our study. Apart from China, the favorite destination for OFDI from Taiwan is other East Asian economies (Hong Kong, Japan, Singapore, Malaysia, Thailand, Vietnam, and the Philippines). In the 1990s, Taiwanese FDI was concentrated in less-developed areas, such as China and South–East Asia. The pattern shifted toward the United States and Europe after 1996 under the "go slow, be patient" policy. However, since 2000, FDI outflows from Taiwan toward China surged due to high economic growth in China and perceived political instability in

---

[4] In 1995 a plan to make Taiwan an Asia-Pacific regional operation center was approved. The purpose was to promote Taiwan to become a regional financial hub for business, following Hong Kong and Singapore.

Table 6: Stock of approved direct investment of Taiwan by major recipient countries[a] (*Millions of US dollars*).

Destination	1999	Destination	2000	Destination	2001	Destination	2002
Caribbean Sea	1 359 373	China	2 607 142	China	2 784 147	China	3 858 757
China	1 252 780	Caribbean Sea	2 248 064	Caribbean Sea	1 693 367	Caribbean Sea	1 575 077
USA	445 081	USA	881 638	USA	1 092 748	USA	577 781
Singapore	324 524	Bermuda	571 076	Bermuda	383 632	Bermuda	170 336
Panama	222 664	Japan	312 222	Singapore	378 300	Hong Kong	167 063
Bermuda	141 381	Singapore	219 531	Japan	169 033	Samoa	139 616
Japan	121 867	Panama	212 103	Hong Kong	94 901	Philippines	82 833
Thailand	112 665	Korea	93 053	Philippines	46 200	Netherlands	56 421
Hong Kong	100 318	Thailand	49 781	Malaysia	45 515	Vietnam	55 192
Korea	80 906	Hong Kong	47 512	Canada	248 983	Malaysia	31 956
Others	360 234	Others	442 082	Others	238 975	others	513 771
Total	4 521 793	Total	7 684 204	Total	7 175 801	Total	7 228 803

(Continued)

Table 6: (*Continued*)

Destination	2003	Destination	2004	Destination	2005
China	4 594 935	China	6 940 663	China	6 006 953
Caribbean Sea	1 997 245	Caribbean Sea	1 155 198	Caribbean Sea	1 261 566
Hong Kong	641 287	Singapore	822 229	USA	314 635
USA	466 641	USA	557 036	Netherlands	256 750
Panama	169 091	Japan	149 330	Hong Kong	107 559
Vietnam	157 369	Hong Kong	139 702	Singapore	97 701
Japan	100 370	Vietnam	95 128	Vietnam	93 932
Malaysia	50 215	Bermuda	86 706	Samoa	71 420
Samoa	52 810	Samoa	67 633	Japan	42 552
Thailand	48 989	Panama	55 566	Malaysia	28 195
Others	284 571	Others	253 494	Others	173 139
Total	8 563 573	Total	10 322 685	Total	8 454 402

Source: Investment Commission of the Ministry of Economic Affairs.
[a] Total amount of OFDI includes OFDI to China.

Taiwan. It is expected that Taiwanese FDI to China will continue to increase in the future, since the "go-slow" policy has been abandoned and replaced with the new "active openness and effective management" policy. In addition, both Taiwan and China have become members of the WTO since December 2001. Trade-related investment is already large and will be further enhanced. In 2005, Taiwanese firms have invested some US$8.45 billions in Asia alone (79.6 percent), of which some US$6 billion of OFDI was to China (67.2 percent). By way of comparison, Table 7 shows the total OFDI from Taiwan to Asian recipient countries. FDI to the Americas and Europe was US$1.6 billions and US$0.3 billion, respectively (Table 8). This indicates that there is a clear geographical preference in favor of East Asia.

Table 9 describes the outward direct investment from Taiwan by economic activity. Major items for outward investment in 2004 and 2005 include electronics and electric product manufacturing, finance and insurance, services industry, chemical production as well as wholesale and retails. In 2005, some 57.1 percent of Taiwanese investment abroad was in financial industry, followed by electronics and electric product manufacturing (15.5 percent), services, wholesales and retail and chemical production, making up 5.9 percent, 3.6 percent, and 1.5 percent, respectively. FDI to China has been concentrated in the manufacturing sector, whereas investments made outside of China has been concentrated in the services sector.

4. Drivers of Outward Direct Investment

After taking a close look at the FDI in Hong Kong and Taiwan, we next consider the factors that determine outward direct investment from these two economies. Before doing so, however, we outline some theoretical development on the topic that can give us some guidance for our analysis.

4.1. *Theoretical Framework*

Theories of FDI attempted largely to shed light on the drivers of inward or outward FDI. The crucial issue in this area is either the

Table 7: Approved outward direct investment from Taiwan to Asian Countries (Unit: US$ 1000).

| Area | | | No China | Asia (Amount) | | | | | | | | | | |
Year	Total	China	Total	Sub-total	Japan	South Korea	Hong Kong	Singapore	Indonesia	Malaysia	Philippines	Thailand	Vietnam	Others
1952~1996			12419781	4729658	119041	12692	763949	458460	453662	1283612	367601	692371	514142	64128
1997	4508368	1614542	2893826	818743	32342	345	141593	230310	55861	85088	127022	57546	85414	3222
1998	4815511	1519209	3296302	580819	29596	1831	68643	158176	19541	19736	38777	131186	110078	3255
1999	4521793	1252780	3269013	836378	121867	80906	100318	324524	7321	13700	29403	112665	34567	11107
2000	7684204	2607142	5077062	851065	312222	93053	47512	219531	33711	19406	12971	49781	54046	8832
2001	7175801	2784147	4391654	814981	169033	12103	94901	378300	6124	45515	46200	16287	30911	15607
2002	7228803	3858757	3370046	530055	23554	5186	167063	25760	9163	31956	82833	5960	55192	123388
2003	8563573	4594985	3968588	1063915	100370	10666	641287	26403	12751	50215	2374	48989	157369	13491
2004	10322685	6940663	3382022	1275089	149330	6369	139702	822229	2445	35475	2393	8663	95128	13355
2005	8454402	6006953	2447449	430673	42552	3613	107559	97701	9115	28195	14937	20265	93932	12804
2006	11957761	7642335	4315426	1390621	10926	15910	272021	806303	8798	31236	13483	81672	123736	26536

Source: Investment Commission of the Ministry of Economic Affairs.

Table 8: Approved outward direct investment from Taiwan to North America and Europe (Unit: US$ 1000).

Area	North America			Amount	Europe				
Year	Sub-total	Canada	United States of America	Sub-total	United Kingdom	France	Germany	Netherlands	Others
1952~1996	3 038 395	61 114	2 977 281	581 003	303 640	12 963	48 609	55 202	160 589
1997	563 285	15 869	547 416	131 235	13 412	127	3821	11 113	102 762
1998	601 862	3271	598 591	33 903	9724	6488	6394	8574	2723
1999	454 222	9141	445 081	82 382	10 263	1790	21 549	17 800	30 980
2000	866 559	4921	861 638	125 432	31 250	1669	8878	3245	80 390
2001	1 341 731	248 983	1 092 748	46 870	29 218	47	5297	5797	6511
2002	582 008	4227	577 781	154 416	43 028	614	17 066	56 421	37 287
2003	467 402	761	466 641	76 724	25 257	2008	10 860	15 137	23 462
2004	559 853	2817	557 036	61 913	17 931	567	7822	22 781	12 812
2005	317 969	3334	314 635	299 314	10 789	465	6262	256 750	25 048

Source: Investment Commission of the Ministry of Economic Affairs.

Table 9: Stock of outward direct investment of Taiwan by economic activity (Millions of US dollars)

Economic activity	2004	Economic activity	2005
Manufacturing	152 922	Finance & insurance	143 121
Finance & insurance	135 760	Manufacturing	662 472
Electronic Parts & Components	101 584	Electronic Parts & Components	208 343
Wholesale & retail trade	250 853	Wholesale & retail trade	178 801
Computers, electronic & optical	153 134	Electrical equipment	71 588
Information & communication	109 676	Fabricated metal products	58 086
Transportation & Storage	87 752	Information & communication	55 409
Medical goods	54 338	Support services	30 133
Textile mills	42 697	Machinery & equipment	2873
Chemical material	396	Textiles Mills	23 259

Source: Investment Commission of the Ministry of Economic Affairs.

question of why a firm is involved in FDI, i.e., why FDI outflows take place, or the question of what factors make an attractive FDI location, i.e., why FDI inflows come about in a specific country. The first question is addressed in a microeconomic perspective, mainly taking into account firm-specific assets in the context of FDI decisions. The second question, related to the location determinants of FDI and characteristics of the host country, is discussed in a macroeconomic perspective.

A large number of variables have been considered in the literature as possible drivers of FDI flows (Lipsey, 2000). There are a number of ways to classify them, one of which is in terms of home country drivers ("push factors") and host country drivers ("pull factors"). Home country drivers, which refer to conditions that influence firms to move abroad, consist of four main types: market and trade conditions, costs of production, domestic business conditions, and home government policies. Host country drivers, encouraging foreign firms to invest in particular countries, are exactly symmetrical to the previous ones. In fact, however, few are considered to be significant across the empirical studies that have been carried out.

As far as East Asia is concerned, industrial restructuring, cost of production, and domestic business conditions have been shown as main drivers, in terms of home country drivers. The outflows of direct investment from investors have been viewed as the continuation and extension of the "flying geese" phenomenon. This phenomenon started in the 1960s when OFDI from Japanese labor-intensive industries contributed to the industrial upgrading of the first-tier NIEs, (Hong Kong, South Korea, Singapore, and Taiwan) and their emergence as outward investors. Their successful restructuring helped create new home countries, and, with the liberalization of inward FDI policies in the region, their investment in turn helped in the restructuring of a second-tier of NIEs (Malaysia, the Philippines, and Thailand). This second group has since then also become a source of outward investment targeting lower income countries such as China and Vietnam.

Kojima (1973) argued that Japanese firms started to invest abroad because of changes in macroeconomic conditions in Japan, which made it impossible for firms to continue producing at home. Home country drivers ("push factors") were stressed as the key determinants of FDI outflows from Japan. Moreover, OFDI that originated from Japan has been specified by Kojima and distinguished from OFDI originated from the United States. Kojima (1975) claimed that FDI originating in Japan was in line with the host country's comparative advantages ("pull factors") and resulted in a trade promotion effect. In contrast, FDI that originated in the United States did not conform to the host country's comparative advantages and resulted in a trade reduction effect. This is because most US FDI was concentrated in capital-intensive and high technology industries in which the United States of America has comparative advantages.

On the contrary, Japanese firms invested in the sectors in which the host country had a comparative advantage to employ low cost production factors. Since this leads to part of the production process being relocated to the host country, the semi-finished goods would have been re-exported from the host country to the home country or other regions for the final stage of production process. This inevitably increases trade between the host and the source country. The difference between

Japanese and US OFDI flows was that Japanese FDI emanated from competitive industries while the US FDI came from an oligopolistic industry. This is why Japanese FDI outflows were efficiency-seeking and "trade-oriented" while US FDI outflows were market-seeking and "anti-trade-oriented." The differences in domestic market structures and FDI strategies led to the differences in the overseas operations, which in turn accounted for the various effects of FDI.

The flying geese phenomenon highlighted the pattern of division of labor through outward and inward FDI and trade. A similar pattern has emerged with respect to FDI from newer outward-investor economies from East Asia, such as Hong Kong and Taiwan that are investing within and beyond the region. Hong Kong and Taiwanese firms are similar to Kojima's Japanese firms as far as they are highly competitive, involved in labor-intensive industries, and realizing efficiency-seeking FDI. In addition, like Japanese firms, they faced adverse conditions in the domestic economic investment environment. The expansion of labor-intensive manufacturing industries in the 1980s drew up the wage level, as well as the land prices, compelling domestic firms to move into lower costs countries. Taking advantage of the open-door policy of China in the early 1980s, firms from Hong Kong and — in a lesser extent and only after 1987[5] — Taiwanese firms were attracted by the abundant supply of cheap labor and available land and, invested a large amount of capital into China. Although Hong Kong and Taiwan faced quite similar push factors to invest abroad, it appears that they evolved along two different industrial restructuring paths: while Taiwan was trying to keep its lead in high-technology industries, Hong Kong has transformed itself into a financial and service-based economy.

More recently, Antras (2005) argued that the sequence of events that happen over time in terms of trade and outward investment from the source country is as follows: First, the richer economies will only export finished products to the less-developed economies; Second, the source economies will invest in the less-developed country to take

---

[5] The year when foreign exchange control was liberalized and Taiwanese dollar largely appreciated.

advantage of lower labor costs; and finally, the source economies will outsource their production to the local firms in the poorer countries. In the Hong Kong and Taiwanese cases, some products like electronics may follow a pattern similar to this trade- and FDI-related product cycle. Furthermore, Helpman, *et al.* (2004) provided a model of heterogeneous firms that show that firms that invest abroad as well as do exporting have a higher productivity than firms that only export, which in turn are more productive than firms that only serve the domestic markets. If this model is applicable to the case of Hong Kong and Taiwanese firms, then it seems that these firms are increasingly productive, since more and more of firms from Hong Kong and Taiwan are not only exporting, but they are also investing.

As far as Hong Kong is concerned, Qiu and Wu (2001) explained the development of OFDI by the evolution of industrial restructuring in Hong Kong. They showed that the first wave of outflows to China led Hong Kong industrial firms to establish the labor intensive production process into China, in particular in the Southern China (in Guandong Province, in particular), while they kept and expanded the high value added economic activities in Hong Kong. At the same time, Chinese firms were also attracted into Hong Kong to set up "window" companies to take advantage of better infrastructure and faster access to the world market. Hong Kong became then the center of corporate operations that could provide business services such as marketing, finance, and transportation. The growing demand, from not only regional but also international firms, for those services led the evolution of industrial restructuring in Hong Kong during the 1980s and 1990s, and drove Hong Kong toward specialization of services.

As for Taiwan, the industrial restructuring offered a different path. According to Hsu and Liu (2004), in the 1980s Taiwan started to make substantial FDI in South–East Asia, and its most important export markets were the United States and Japan. In the 1990s, Taiwan invested massively in China, to the detriment of ASEAN countries. Taiwanese firms that relocated to China produced intermediate goods for Taiwan-based firms in order to produce labor-intensive manufactured goods for the United States and Japanese markets. Since 2000, China gradually became an important export market for

Taiwan, and by 2002, China was the largest market for Taiwanese products. This growing trade relationship points to the dependency of Taiwanese economy on China. According to the "2005 survey of the manufacturing sector investments abroad" conducted by the Ministry of Economic Affairs, Taiwanese choice of investments has seen a decline from the five ASEAN countries (Singapore, Malaysia, Thailand, Indonesia, and the Philippines) to other countries, mainly to China. In terms of the industry choice, electric and electronics made up 41 percent and 8.5 percent, respectively. Sixty three percent of the investors took the decision to invest abroad mainly due to the local market potential; 55 percent were taking the advantage of cheaper local labor cost and 28.6 percent of the investments were following their Taiwanese clients. Another key reason for investing abroad was the deteriorating Taiwanese business environment.

4.2. *Trade Intensity Indices*

To evaluate the trade and FDI links for these countries we propose to determine the absolute and relative importance of trade and FDI flows between each of these two countries and their main partners.[6] As for trade, we investigate the extent and intensity of bilateral East Asian trade for all goods and to other countries such as North America and the European Union for the year 2005. We have illustrated our results in Table 10.

In absolute value, it can be seen that the main trade partners for Hong Kong in terms or its export value are China, Japan, and Korea. In terms of the share of imports, Hong Kong's share in Chinese import is 36 percent and Hong Kong represents the main importing source for China. Its share in Japanese imports is 7.5 percent, representing the third importing source for Japan. The major trade partners for Taiwan in terms or its export values are China, Hong Kong, Japan, and Singapore. In terms of the share of imports,

---

[6] The comparison of countries in terms of trade or FDI in absolute values tends to overestimate the role of large countries; this is why it is interesting to consider also relative values taking into account the importance of individual countries in world's total direct investment outflow.

Table 10: Matrix of intra-regional trade in East Asia, 2005.

Partner (Importer)	Exporting country										
	China	Hong Kong	Indonesia	Japan	Korea, Rep.	Malaysia	Philippines	Singapore	Taiwan	Thailand	E Asia (10)
Export Value of Total Trade in All Goods ($ million)											
China	0	130426	6662	80074	61915	9302	4077	19757	40879	9134	362227
Hong Kong	124473	0	1492	35960	15531	8242	3339	21522	30721	6128	247408
Indonesia	8350	1265	0	9214	5046	3322	476	22103	2336	3960	56073
Japan	83986	15304	18049	0	24027	13184	7203	12532	14481	15029	203796
Korea, Rep.	35108	6540	7086	46630	0	4739	1391	8052	5575	2250	117371
Malaysia	10606	2419	3431	12531	4608	0	2457	30385	4154	5685	76277
Philippines	4688	2635	1419	9057	3220	1974	0	4184	4220	2050	33448
Singapore	16632	6046	7837	18436	7407	22009	2706	0	7656	7459	96187
Taiwan	16550	6769	2475	43578	10863	3912	1887	8976	0	2694	97704
Thailand	7819	3001	2246	22451	3381	7586	1169	9402	3718	0	60773
East Asia (10)	308213	174405	50698	277932	135997	74272	24704	136913	113739	54390	1351264
EU (27)	145613	42942	10347	87819	44354	16614	7008	27907	22124	15019	419745
Nam (13)	192173	53088	11478	158201	54543	29879	7945	26411	33272	19702	586691
World	761953	292119	85660	594941	284418	140963	41221	229652	189393	110110	2730431

(*Continued*)

Table 10: (Continued)

Partner (Importer)	Exporting country										
	China	Hong Kong	Indonesia	Japan	Korea, Rep.	Malaysia	Philippines	Singapore	Taiwan	Thailand	E Asia (10)
Share of Intra-Regional Trade in All Goods from Importer (%)											
China	0	36.0	1.8	22.1	17.1	2.6	1.1	5.5	11.3	2.5	100.0
Hong Kong	50.3	0	0.6	14.5	6.3	3.3	1.3	8.7	12.4	2.5	100.0
Indonesia	14.9	2.3	0	16.4	9.0	5.9	0.8	39.4	4.2	7.1	100.0
Japan	41.2	7.5	8.9	0	11.8	6.5	3.5	6.1	7.1	7.4	100.0
Korea, Rep.	29.9	5.6	6.0	39.7	0	4.0	1.2	6.9	4.7	1.9	100.0
Malaysia	13.9	3.2	4.5	16.4	6.0	0	3.2	39.8	5.4	7.5	100.0
Philippines	14.0	7.9	4.2	27.1	9.6	5.9	0	12.5	12.6	6.1	100.0
Singapore	17.3	6.3	8.1	19.2	7.7	22.9	2.8	0	8.0	7.8	100.0
Taiwan	16.9	6.9	2.5	44.6	11.1	4.0	1.9	9.2	0	2.8	100.0
Thailand	12.9	4.9	3.7	36.9	5.6	12.5	1.9	15.5	6.1	0	100.0
East Asia (10)	22.8	12.9	3.8	20.6	10.1	5.5	1.8	10.1	8.4	4.0	100.0
EU (27)	34.7	10.2	2.5	20.9	10.6	4.0	1.7	6.6	5.3	3.6	100.0
Nam (13)	32.8	9.0	2.0	27.0	9.3	5.1	1.4	4.5	5.7	3.4	100.0
World	27.9	10.7	3.1	21.8	10.4	5.2	1.5	8.4	6.9	4.0	100.0

(Continued)

Table 10:   (*Continued*)

Trade Balance of Total Trade in All Goods ($ million)

Partner (Importer)	Exporting country										
	China	Hong Kong	Indonesia	Japan	Korea, Rep.	Malaysia	Philippines	Singapore	Taiwan	Thailand	E Asia (10)
China	0	-4540	819	-28403	23267	-3871	1026	-759	20951	-2024	6466
Hong Kong	112248	0	1201	34389	13488	5390	1344	17314	28834	4626	218835
Indonesia	-87	-659	0	-11603	-3139	-1052	-610	11656	-2202	832	-6865
Japan	-16421	-17732	11143	0	-24376	-3450	-827	-6702	-31460	-11020	-100845
Korea, Rep.	-41713	-6723	4217	22215	0	-946	-887	-548	-7629	-1622	-33635
Malaysia	-9487	-4935	1283	-2138	-1403	0	685	3050	-1039	-2404	-16388
Philippines	-8182	-2506	1097	1357	904	-1246	0	-464	1435	168	-7437
Singapore	118	-11374	-1634	11741	2089	8594	-1024	0	2716	2078	13304
Taiwan	-58131	-14874	1134	25514	2813	-2419	-1561	-4347	0	-1808	-53679
Thailand	-6173	-3049	-1201	6893	692	1544	-489	1888	851	0	956
East Asia (10)	-27827	-66393	18059	59966	14335	2544	-2345	21089	12457	-11173	20712
EU (27)	71641	20169	4488	28976	16940	3260	3328	4612	4599	4211	162224
Nam (13)	110889	34689	5809	69776	14849	13045	-1154	552	7622	8528	264606
World	102001	-8042	27959	79074	23183	26379	-5732	29602	7801	-8054	274171

(*Continued*)

Table 10: (Continued)

Trade Intensity Index of Total Trade in All Goods

Partner (Importer)	Exporting country										
	China	Hong Kong	Indonesia	Japan	Korea, Rep.	Malaysia	Philippines	Singapore	Taiwan	Thailand	E Asia (10)
China	–	8.0	1.4	2.4	3.9	1.2	1.8	1.5	3.9	1.5	2.4
Hong Kong	5.1	–	0.5	1.9	1.7	1.8	2.5	2.9	5.0	1.7	2.8
Indonesia	1.5	0.6	–	2.1	2.4	3.1	1.5	12.8	1.6	4.8	2.7
Japan	2.7	1.3	5.2	–	2.1	2.3	4.3	1.4	1.9	3.4	1.9
Korea, Rep.	2.2	1.1	4.0	3.8	–	1.6	1.6	1.7	1.4	1.0	2.1
Malaysia	1.3	0.8	3.6	1.9	1.5	–	5.4	12.1	2.0	4.7	2.5
Philippines	1.2	1.8	3.3	3.0	2.2	2.8	–	3.6	4.4	3.7	2.4
Singapore	1.4	1.3	5.8	2.0	1.6	9.9	4.1	–	2.6	4.3	2.2
Taiwan	0.8	0.8	1.0	2.6	1.3	1.0	1.6	1.4	–	0.9	1.3
Thailand	1.1	1.1	2.8	4.1	1.3	5.8	3.1	4.4	2.1	–	2.4
East Asia (10)	49	7.3	7.2	5.7	5.8	6.4	7.3	7.3	7.3	6.0	6.1
EU (27)	1.7	1.3	1.0	1.3	1.4	1.0	1.5	1.1	1.0	1.2	1.3
Nam (13)	2.2	1.6	1.2	2.3	1.7	1.8	1.7	1.0	1.5	1.5	1.9

Source: Computations based on UN COMTRADE statistics.

East Asia (10) = China, Hong Kong, Indonesia, Japan, Korea Rep., Malaysia, Philippines, Singapore, Taiwan, and Thailand.

EU (27) = European Union 25 members plus Bulgaria and Romania.

Nam (13) = Canada, United States, Argentina, Bolivia, Brazil, Chile, Colombia, Ecuador, Mexico, Paraguay, Peru, Uruguay, and Venezuela.

Taiwan's share in Chinese imports is 11.3 percent and Taiwan represents the fourth importing source for China. Its shares in Japanese, Singaporean, and Hong Kong's imports are, respectively, 7.4 percent, 7.8 percent, and 2.5 percent. It can easily be seen that China appears as the single most important trading partner for Hong Kong and Taiwan; this underlines the dependence of these countries on the Chinese economy.

We also examined the relative importance of bilateral trade using the trade intensity index. The trade intensity index is defined as

$$\frac{X_{ij}/X_i}{X_{wj}/X_w},$$

where, X_{ij} and X_{wj} are country i and world exports to country j; X_i and X_w are country i and world total exports. The numerator indicates that the share of country i's export to country j in total export of the country i, and the denominator indicates the share of world's export to country j in its total export. If the bilateral trade intensity index has a value greater than one, the export of country i outperforms in country j. It implies that country j is relatively important to country i's export.

Results show that for Hong Kong, the most prominent trade partners are, respectively, China (8), the Philippines (1.8), and Japan (1.3). The main trade partners for Taiwan are, respectively, China (3.9), Hong Kong (5), the Philippines (4.4), and Singapore (2.6). These results show that the trade intensity with China is higher for Hong Kong than for Taiwan.

After taking a look at trade between Hong Kong, Taiwan and their principal partners, we now turn to examine the absolute and relative importance of bilateral direct investment for Hong Kong and Taiwan with their major partners. In absolute values, the main recipient countries for each country under study are examined previously. Apart from offshore financial centers, we found the same Asian partners for trade as for outward investment. We focus on several important investment recipients. For Hong Kong, we have selected: China, Japan, Singapore, and as an outside region's destination,

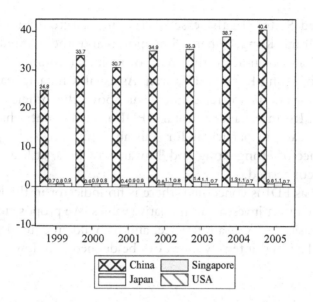

Figure 7: Share of selected recipients of outward FDI from Hong Kong (%).
Source: Authors' own calculations based on data from Tables 4 and 6.

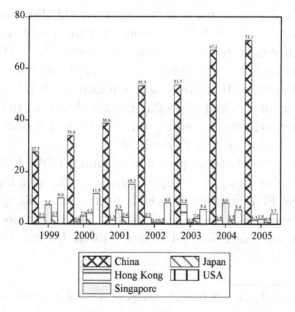

Figure 8: Share of selected recipients of outward FDI from Taiwan (%).
Source: Authors' own calculations based on data from Tables 4 and 6.

the United States. In the case of Taiwan, selected countries are: China, Hong Kong, Japan, Singapore, and the United States. Figures 7 and 8 indicate the share of recipient countries' in total outward of Hong Kong and Taiwan. As usual, China appears as the most important recipient country far above the others for both countries. Its importance in total OFDI of each country has grown over the years, in particular for Taiwan. This shows the growing dependence of Hong Kong and Taiwan on China, at least as far as OFDI is concerned.

As far as FDI is concerned, there is no indicator in the literature to evaluate direct investment in relative values. We propose to use the trade intensity index as a reference, and to build an equivalent index for FDI. The FDI intensity index can be defined as follows:

$$\frac{\Upsilon_{ij}/\Upsilon_i}{\Upsilon_{wj}/\Upsilon_w},$$

where, Υ_{ij} and Υ_{wj} are the country i and world direct investment toward country j; Υ_{ii} and Υ_w, are country i and world total OFDI. The numerator indicates that the share of country i's OFDI to country j in total OFDI of the country i, and the denominator indicates the share of world's OFDI to country j in its total OFDI. If the bilateral FDI intensity index has a value greater than one, the OFDI of country i outperforms in country j. It implies that country j is relatively important to country i's total OFDI.

In Figures 9 and 10, we present calculations of the FDI intensity indices for Hong Kong, Taiwan and partners.[7] We have found many cases of low FDI intensity indices between Hong Kong, Taiwan, and their respective partners (see Tables 11 and 12 for more details). The indices for Hong Kong–US, and Taiwan–US are, respectively,

---

[7] Our calculations are based on OFDI stocks. In the case of Taiwan, total OFDI includes OFDI to China.

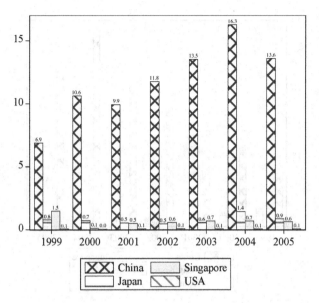

Figure 9:   FDI Intensity Index for Hong Kong.

Source: Authors' own calculations based on Census & Statistics Department, External Direct Investment of Hong Kong, various issues, and Investment Commission of the Ministry of Economic Affairs of Taiwan for bilateral FDI; UNCTAD, FDI/TNC database for global FDI. For more details, see Tables 10 and 11.

0.04 and 0.24 only in 2005. This supports the idea that the United States is obviously important but not over-represented as a FDI destination for Hong Kong and Taiwan.

The favorable ranking of the United States as recipient country can partly be explained by large FDI in the form of mergers and acquisitions (M&As) in recent years. In fact, an increasing number of mega deals have been realized in the United States. For example, in 2005 a group of Hong Kong investors acquired Bank of America Center in San Francisco for US$1 billion. The index for Hong Kong–Japan in 2004 is 1.43, which implies that Japan is not a very important FDI recipient for Hong Kong, although it is not unimportant. In the case of Taiwan, it is noteworthy that indices for Taiwan–Japan and Taiwan–Singapore were relatively high from 1999 to 2001. Since 2000, these indices fell to 0.53 and 0.65, respectively, in 2005. The

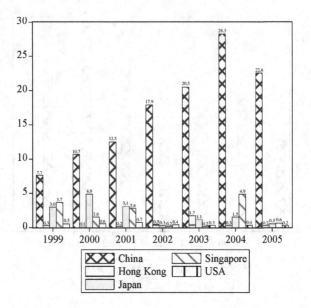

Figure 10:   FDI Intensity Index for Taiwan.

Source: Authors' own calculations based on Census & Statistics Department, External Direct Investment of Hong Kong, various issues, and Investment Commission of the Ministry of Economic Affairs of Taiwan for bilateral FDI; UNCTAD, FDI/TNC database for global FDI. For more details, see Tables 10 and 11.

Table 11:   FDI intensity index for Hong Kong.

	1999	2000	2001	2002	2003	2004	2005
HK-China	6.87	10.62	9.92	11.76	13.50	16.26	13.57
HK-Singapore	1.46	0.11	0.48	0.57	0.68	0.67	0.62
HK-Japan	0.77	0.73	0.54	0.46	0.56	1.43	0.85
Hong Kong-USA	0.04	0.03	0.04	0.07	0.04	0.05	0.04

Source: Authors' own calculations based on Census & Statistics Department, Hong Kong, External Direct Investment of Hong Kong, various issues for bilateral FDI and UNCTAD, FDI/TNC database for global FDI.

highest indices are those related to the FDI outward to China and are comparable to those on OFDI in absolute terms.

It can be easily observed that the high indices for China exhibited a sharp upward trend since 2002 for both Hong Kong and Taiwan,

Table 12: FDI intensity index for Taiwan

	1999	2000	2001	2002	2003	2004	2005
TW-China	7.67	10.78	12.53	17.97	20.51	28.28	22.57
TW-Hong Kong	0.28	0.08	0.20	0.50	1.71	0.30	0.25
TW-Singapore	3.65	1.56	2.84	0.18	0.18	4.92	0.65
TW-Japan	3.01	4.96	3.07	0.30	1.14	1.54	0.53
TW-USA	0.53	0.56	0.74	0.43	0.34	0.37	0.24

Source: Authors' own calculations based on Investment Commission of the Ministry of Economic Affairs for bilateral FDI and UNCTAD, FDI/TNC database for global FDI.

with a peak in 2004. The Hong Kong–China index was 6.87 in 1999, reaching 11.76 in 2002 and 16.26 in 2004, before falling at 13.57 in 2005. The Taiwan–China index was 7.67 in 1999, reaching 17.97 in 2002 and 28.28 in 2004, before falling to 22.57 in 2005. It is worth mentioning that, for the period of our study, there is a general trend showing the decreasing importance of most major recipient countries, and a rising importance of China for outward direct investment from Hong Kong and Taiwan, since 2002. One can easily conclude that China is a substitute for other destinations for FDI outflows. According to "2002 survey of the manufacturing sector investments abroad," conducted by Taiwanese Ministry of Economics Affairs, early Taiwanese investments to China have reaped the benefits of China's labor cost advantage. This led to increased productivity and an enlarged base of manufacturing. The early investors were mostly small and medium-sized enterprises (SMEs) investing in labor-intensive industries. Input components were exports from Taiwan. However, the survey conducted in 2005, showed that this model has changed. 40 percent of the orders in Taiwan were filled in China.

5. Conclusion and Policy Implications

This chapter has investigated the trends, magnitude and rationale of outward direct investment from Hong Kong and Taiwan for the period 1999–2005. We have shown that the geographical composition of FDI from developing economies has changed significantly since 1990, reflecting the growing importance of Asian countries as outward investors.

In the 2000s, Hong Kong led the list of top FDI sources, and as a whole the Asian NIEs, China and Malaysia improved their position, being among the top nine sources. Apart from offshore financial centers, China is the most important destination for Hong Kong's OFDI. In terms of economic activity, OFDI from Hong Kong engaged in investment holdings, real estate and various business services were the most prominent.

Taiwan's OFDI has outpaced its inward FDI during the whole period under study, showing that it is a capital-exporting country. The immediate destination for Taiwan's OFDI over the whole period under study has been China. Apart from China, the favorite destination of OFDI from Taiwan is East Asia. The drivers of these OFDI can be viewed as the continuation and extension of the "flying geese" phenomenon. The newer outward-investor economies from East Asia, such as Hong Kong and Taiwan, are investing within and beyond the region. In these countries, labor costs and land prices have become relatively high, compelling domestic firms to move into lower costs countries, in a context of regional integrated production systems. FDI outflows and trade are thus positively linked. In this context, we have used the same kind of indicators to evaluate the expansion and the intensity of trade and OFDI, namely trade and FDI intensity indices; we have shown that China is the largest partner for trade and direct investment for both Hong Kong and Taiwan. Its importance increased since 2002, mainly as a favorite destination for direct investment flows, to the detriment of other East Asian recipient countries.

China's importance as a source of FDI can be explained by the emergence of Greater China as a *de facto* economic integration among the three economies. The dynamics of East Asia have shifted drastically since China initiated the "open-door" policy in the late 1970s. The economic reform and opening up policy has made China a center for both FDI and trade. This integration has resulted in a mass departure of the manufacturing sector from Hong Kong and Taiwan to China. In addition, it has driven Hong Kong toward specialization of the services and Taiwan to the high-technology industry, with a relocation of labor-intensive production into China.

The emergence of China poses an economic threat as well as an economic opportunity for Hong Kong, Taiwan as well as for other Asian economies. Both Hong Kong and Taiwan have gone through painful adjustments. Hong Kong is now completely "hollowed out," while Taiwan has also lost a significant segment of its high technology sector to China. At the same time, both economies have grown richer by taking advantage of the growing Chinese market. Hong Kong has further specialized to become the trading and financial hub of the region, while Taiwan has some successes in fostering innovations and designs. In the face of a growing China, other economies in Asia have little choice but to adjust. Some of the complementary policies include paying more attention to education, spending more on research and development, adopting a more business-friendly environment, shoring up the domestic infrastructure and promoting more domestic and foreign competition. One policy that we think other Asian economies should not adopt is protectionism. Protectionist policies that shut out imports or inward direct investment may provide some breathing room for the domestic industries in the short run, but in the long run, they reduce competition, stifle innovation and ultimately will be self-defeating.

References

Antras, P (2005). Incomplete contracts and the product cycle. *American Economic Review*, 95(4), 1054–1073.

Census and Statistics Department (2002). External Direct Investment of Hong Kong in 2002, available on: www.info.gov.hk

Census and Statistics Department (2005). External Direct Investment of Hong Kong in 2005, available on: www.info.gov.hk

Fung, KC (1997). *Trade and Investment: Mainland China, Hong Kong and Taiwan*, City University of Hong Kong Press.

Helpman, E, MJ Melitz and SR Yeaple (2004). Export versus FDI with heterogenous firms. *American Economic Review*, 94(1), 300–316.

Hsu, CM and WC Liu (2004). The role of Taiwanese foreign direct investment in China: Economic integration or hollowing out? In *Economic Integration and Multinational Investment Behaviour, European and East Asian Experiences*, P-B Ruffini (ed.), pp 403–421, UK: Edward Elgar.

Kojima, K (1973). A macroeconomic approach to foreign direct investment. *Hitotsubashi Journal of Economics*, 14(1), 1–21.

Kojima, K (1975). International trade and foreign investment: Substitutes or complements? *Hitotsubashi Journal of Economics*, 16(1), 1–12.

Lipsey, RE (2000). Interpreting developed countries' foreign direct investment. NBER Working Paper 7810.

Petri, PA (1995). The interdependence of trade and investment in the Pacific, In *Corporate Links and Foreign Direct Investment in Asia and the Pacific*, Edward KY Chen and Peter Drysdale (eds.), Pymble: Harper Educational Publishers.

Petri, PA (2006). Is East Asia becoming more interdependent? *Journal of Asian Economics*, 17(3), 381–394.

Petri, PA and MG Plummer (1998). The determinants of foreign direct investment: A survey with applications to the Unites-States. In *Economic Development and Cooperation in the Pacific Basin: Trade, Investment, and Environment Issues.* H Lee and DW Roland-Holst (eds.), New York: Cambridge University Press.

Qiu, LD and C Wu (2001). Development of foreign direct investment and evolution of industrial Structure: Case of Hong Kong. *Report written for the Institute of Developing Economies, Japan External Trade Organization.*

UNCTAD (2006). *World Investment Report*. New York: United-Nations.

UNCTAD, FDI/TNC database, available on www.unctad.org/fdistatistic

Chapter 8

New Multinationals from Singapore and Thailand: The Political Economy of Regional Expansion*

Andrea Goldstein and Pavida Pananond

1. Introduction

The international expansion of large companies from emerging markets is increasingly seen as a new defining feature of the global investment landscape. A number of big-ticket mergers and acquisitions, such as by Cemex and Tata Steel in Australia and the United Kingdom (M&As), respectively, have attracted considerable media interest, but the phenomenon is not limited to them and the implications for all stakeholders deserve a thorough analysis.

This chapter focuses on two South–East Asian countries, Singapore and Thailand, which rank high and are among the most important sources of OFDI from developing countries. In fact, as it pertains to a very successful and small city-state economy, Singapore holds the emerging economies' record for *per capita* outward foreign direct investment (OFDI) stock and flows. Some Singaporean multinational corporations (MNCs) are in the process of becoming major players in the global economy, while others have expanded their footprints regionally, mostly, though not exclusively, through M&As. Although numbers are more modest, Thailand nonetheless features as the third largest outward investor from South–East Asia

* The authors thank Joshua Felman, Rajiv Kumar, Ramkishen S. Rajan, Lai Si Tsui-Auch, and participants at the ICRIER workshop on Intra-Asian FDI Flows for comments and suggestions on earlier drafts. The usual caveats apply: in particular, the content of this chapter does not in any way represent the views of the OECD, its members, Thammasat University or the editors and publisher.

(UNCTAD, 2006) and is home to some large regional MNCs, particularly the Charoen Pokphand (CP) group which has long been one of the largest foreign investors in China.

At the same time, the characteristics of OFDI from Singapore and Thailand are rather different. While Singapore's OFDI has been led by the state holding company Temasek and other state-owned enterprises (so called GLCs, for government-linked companies[1]), Thai OFDI is driven by the private sector. Yet, their different nature must not obscure a crucial point — that understanding OFDI and corporate internationalization require a thorough analysis of the institutional context in which firms develop. In particular, that some GLCs' deals have stirred considerable controversy make it crucial to understand whether the same "economic nationalism" pressures that are seemingly gaining momentum in the OECD area (Goldstein, 2008), are also mounting in Asia.

We pair Singapore and Thailand in our analysis for two additional reasons. First, in 2004 Thailand was the fastest-growing ASEAN destination for Singapore's OFDI. Second, Temasek's 2006 acquisition of Thailand's Shin Corp, the holding company owned by then Thai Prime Minister, Thaksin Shinawatra, has proved to be the most controversial among Singaporean GLCs' investment in foreign countries.

We start by summarizing the main characteristics of Singapore OFDI and MNCs, i.e., motives, industrial and geographical distribution, and competitive advantages.[2] We point out that the existing literature has highlighted the limits of the regionalization strategy, although it has not addressed the increasing resistance to Singaporean MNCs — even if Temasek's ventures in some countries have met with resistance.[3] Then we explore the Thailand case to highlight some

[1] According to Singapore's Department of Statistics, GLCs are those in which Temasek Holdings or other statutory boards hold more than 20 percent of the voting shares. Some GLCs are managed by MND Holdings (also under the Ministry of Finance) and Sheng-Li Holding.
[2] In a companion paper we discuss in the greater depth how the internationalization of Singaporean state-owned enterprises fits into the literature on the international expansion of firms from developing economies (Goldstein and Pananond, 2008).
[3] In fact, to our knowledge Roberts and Dick (2005) is the only paper that analyzes GLCs' internationalization.

similarities, despite the much different scale of the two countries' OFDI and the fact that in Thailand, international expansion was led by the private sector. In the concluding section, we point out the potentials and pitfalls of the international expansion of Singaporean GLCs and Sino-Thai business groups and draw some implications on how these traits might have to change as they go global.

2. Hamlet Without the Prince? The Importance of Social Embeddedness in the Analysis of Asian Corporate Strategies

Studies of "Third World multinationals", sometimes referred to as "multinationals from developing countries",[4] have emerged as a separate stream of literature since the 1980s. Two different groups can be identified in the literature. While they are distinct in terms of timing and views on the nature of these MNCs' competitive advantage, both emphasize that developing countries' MNCs' competitive advantage lies in their ability to gradually accumulate technological skills from imported technology.

The first group argued that developing-country MNCs adapt the imported technology to their environment through downscaling techniques such as reducing operation scale, substituting machinery with human labor, and replacing imported inputs with cheaper local ones (see Wells, 1977, 1981, 1983; Lecraw, 1977, 1981; Kumar, 1982; and Lall, 1983a, 1983b). The second group believed that the competitive advantage of firms from developing countries is derived from these firms' ability to improve their technological capabilities through the learning-by-doing process (see Vernon-Wortzel and Wortzel, 1988; Cantwell and Tolentino, 1990; Tolentino, 1993; Lecraw, 1993, Ulgado *et al.*, 1994; Dunning *et al.*, 1997; van Hoesel, 1999). In sum, the literature on MNCs from developing countries

---

[4] Yeung (1994, p. 302–303) strongly criticized the term "Third World multinationals" as "imperialistic" and "not a theoretically fruitful way to conceptualize the nature of international business and production". Instead, the author suggested that a more unbiased term "developing country multinationals" be used instead.

has highlighted the technological capabilities accumulated through the process of learning as the key source of competitive advantages for developing-country MNCs.

Notwithstanding its valuable insights, this stream of literature is not without limitations. In fact, while the majority of scholars contend that the emerging MNCs can be "nested" within standard MNC theories (see UNCTAD, 2006), we argue that these multinationals have unique and distinctive characteristics that need to be pinpointed and explained. Moreover, research on Asian business demands a departure from theory that was developed in a US context, which tends to define rigor in terms of the use of quantitative methods, and limits the sorts of exploratory research that still may be most productive in helping us understand Asian business and management (Lynn, 2006).

The need of international business scholars to address the diversity of social, economic, and political institutions that affect MNCs' behavior has also recently been emphasized (see Rodriguez *et al.*, 2006, p. 734). Pananond (2001a, 2001b, 2002) contended that the existing literature offered a rather limited and deterministic interpretation of what constituted the competitive advantages of developing-country MNCs and of their development. The conventional approach of comparing MNCs from developing countries to their counterparts from developed economies led to deterministic implications that the former could catch up with the latter only through improving their technological skills. With such a strong hypothesis in mind, other explanations of alternative routes to the development of multinationals from developing countries were overlooked.

The "under-socialized" nature of the existing literature leads to a narrow interpretation of what constituted a firm's competitive advantages. Insofar as the prevailing literature interprets firms' behavior as the rational actions of atomized actors operating independent of social, historical or political pressure, standard theories failed to address how social relations and networks, as well as *sui generis* organizational structures such as state-ownership, could contribute to the competitive advantages of multinationals from many Asian developing countries (Pananond, 2001a, 2001b, 2002; Yeung, 1994, 1998). The internationalization process of four Thai MNCs, namely the Charoen Pokphand (CP) group, the Siam Cement group, the Dusit Thani group and the Jasmine group, was guided not only by their accumulated technological skills, but also by their networking capabilities, or the ability to draw from complementary resources of different partners and to turn them to the firm's benefits (Pananond, 2001a). While industry-specific technological skills were fundamental in creating their competitive advantages, networking capabilities served as an additional source of advantage that could be exploited across industries during these firms' growth and expansion.

Likewise, the role of the state cannot be ignored in the development of Singapore since independence. Its numerous GLCs are now going through a rapid phase of international expansion, deriving at least some sources of corporate competitiveness from close and preferential access to non-market resources. Insofar as these companies extend the political power of the Singaporean state, authorities and civil society in the host countries may perceive their internationalization as a threat to national sovereignty. This may, in turn, generate a higher level of political risk than that faced by their privately owned counterparts. While some of these political challenges may be disregarded and considered simply as economic nationalism on the part of the host countries, the international impacts of state entrepreneurship should be further debated. The case of Temasek's investment in Thailand is illustrative of the economic and political consequences that SOEs may face in their global quest.

3. Singapore Inc. Abroad

Singapore has used inward FDI as a key policy instrument to upgrade its international position. Insofar as this strategy has transformed the country's factor endowment, the government's stance toward OFDI has changed correspondingly (Blomqvist, 2002). Indeed, for more than three decades now, Singapore has also recorded significant OFDI flows. Singapore is the fourth largest outward investor from developing countries (UNCTAD, 2006), with S$174 billion as OFDI stock at the end of 2004 (Singapore Department of Statistics, 2006).[5]

3.1. *History*

Singapore's OFDI has gone through three stages of progressive engagement. Initially, some timid attempts were made to delocalize production of labor-intensive goods such as clothing to lower-wage countries that benefited from quota-free entry into major Western markets under the Multi-Fibre Agreement (MFA). OFDI was undertaken initially to counter labor scarcity and trade restrictions, in particular MFA quotas. This type of investment used host economies with less stringent quotas (Malaysia and Thailand initially, Mauritius later on) as an intermediate production point to third countries or the global market. In Mauritius, in particular, Singapore was the second largest investor in 1990–1998 (UNCTAD, 2001, p. 14).

In the second phase, authorities identified overseas investment and the development of offshore opportunities as a long-term solution to the nation's small scale and sluggish growth in demand and investment opportunities and drew a regionalization strategy comprising several programs (Pereira, 2005). In the 1980s, Singapore shifted away from traditional light industries into relatively more complex manufacturing activities, in particular electronic goods' assembly. In this second phase, OFDI aimed to reduce vulnerability and build a presence in other regional countries that could complement the small size of the domestic economy. The so-called industrial township projects characterized this phase of Singapore's regionalization.[6]

The third phase started after the 1997 Asian crisis when Singaporean MNCs began to use M&As in Asia and beyond to

---

[5] As of December 2004, 1US$ = S(Singapore)$ 1.64.

[6] Although ethnic Chinese multinationals and small- and medium-sized enterprises (SMEs) also contribute to Singapore's OFDI (Tsui-Auch, 2006), a significant, albeit decreasing, part of Singapore's OFDI corresponds to Singapore affiliates of foreign-controlled MNCs. The contribution of OFDI by foreign MNCs' affiliates decreased from 46 percent in 1996 to 39 percent in 2002 (UNCTAD, 2005).

Table 1: Destination of Singapore's outward FDI stock (percentage).

	1998	1999	2000	2001	2002	2003	2004
BVI	5.28	5.23	3.78	12.59	12.53	14.11	13.73
China	16.11	15.42	15.98	11.77	12.12	12.73	12.03
Malaysia	11.39	9.19	9.92	8.41	8.95	8.73	8.00
Indonesia	5.93	5.94	5.56	4.19	5.17	6.67	6.80
Bermuda	1.69	2.21	3.88	9.10	9.17	7.54	6.77
Hong Kong	10.14	11.22	8.66	8.60	8.04	7.22	6.65
Mauritius	4.26	3.73	5.00	2.83	3.64	3.85	5.29
US	4.05	4.53	6.29	5.49	5.54	5.80	5.19
Australia	2.04	2.01	2.64	1.89	2.23	2.99	4.93
UK	4.33	3.65	4.99	5.12	4.68	4.65	4.40
Others	34.78	36.88	33.30	30.03	27.93	25.70	26.20
Of which Thailand				3.23	3.11	3.02	3.86

Source: Singapore Department of Statistics (2006), *Singapore's Investment Abroad 2004.*

enhance their competitiveness. Most of these deals were made by GLCs in banking and other services (see below).

In terms of geography, four-fifths of Singapore's OFDI stock is in developing countries, with South, East and South–East Asia accounting for 48.9 percent of the total (Table 1) (Singapore Department of Statistics, 2006).[7] Within Asia, three ASEAN countries (Malaysia, Indonesia, and Thailand) accounted for the largest part of the rise in investment stocks in Asia (together approximately S\$38 million in 2004), while China came second at nearly S\$21 million. However, in terms of year-on-year growth, the fastest-growing region is Oceania (72 percent in 2004), followed by Europe (23.8 percent). Within Asia, the highest growth was in Thailand, where Singapore OFDI stock rose by an impressive 42.5 percent in 2004, much outpacing the 9.5 percent average growth in Asia. Investment in offshore financial centers is also becoming significant.

Sector-wide, financial services accounted for most of Singapore's OFDI stock in 2004, followed by manufacturing, commerce,

---

[7] In fact, the British Virgin Islands was the main destination in 2004 (7.3 percent of total stock), followed closely by China (6.4 percent).

Table 2: Composition of Singapore's outward FDI stock by activity abroad (percentage).

	1998	1999	2000	2001	2002	2003	2004
Manufacturing	23.39	24.67	25.40	20.11	20.88	21.68	20.30
Construction	1.19	0.86	0.79	0.51	0.48	0.48	0.45
Commerce	8.70	8.21	8.27	7.30	6.81	7.43	7.22
Transport	3.86	5.96	4.83	5.07	4.69	4.32	3.80
ICT	0.00	0.00	1.80	3.20	4.65	4.57	4.93
Finance	50.14	48.23	48.26	55.29	55.09	54.92	56.21
Real Estate	8.05	7.41	7.14	5.93	4.89	4.68	4.07
Business Services	3.24	3.12	1.95	1.35	1.29	0.72	1.76
Others	1.45	1.55	1.56	1.25	1.23	1.20	1.26

Source: Singapore Department of Statistics (2006), *Singapore's Investment Abroad 2004.*

information and communication, real estate, and transport and storage (Table 2). It should be noted that Singapore's OFDI in financial services overwhelmingly takes the form of investment holding companies in offshore financial centers in the Caribbean and Latin America (39.4 percent), as well as acquisitions of regional banks by Temasek-related banks such as DBS.

3.2. *Actors*

Established in 1974, Temasek plays center stage in the Singaporean economy and holds equity stakes of 20 percent or more in six out of the top ten MNCs (Table 3 and Table A.1). Temasek, which derives from the Javanese language "tan-ma-hsi", meaning "sea town", has stakes in 70 companies, including Singapore Telecommunications (SingTel), the DBS banking group, port operator PSA, Singapore International Airlines (SIA), shipping line Neptune Orient, logistics group SembLog, and Singapore Technologies (ST). This, in turn, is another diversified holding with interests in semiconductors, defence, property development, and hotels. With 2005 revenues of US$44 billion and net profit of US$5 billion on an asset base of US$126 billion, Temasek accounts for a quarter of stock market capitalization. As of October 2004, the slightly larger universe of GLCs accounted for

Table 3: Singaporean largest multinationals.

Company	Foreign assets S$ million		TNI index		Sector	Ownership as of 31 Mar 06 (Temasek)	Foreign countries of operation
	1999	2004	1999	2004			
SingTel	2078	18641	15.8	67.1	Telecoms	State (56%)	Australia, India, Bangladesh, ASEAN
Flextronics	n.a.	5862	n.a.	67.1	Electronics	Private (foreign)	Over 30 in four continents
Capitaland	n.a.	5231	n.a.	55.0	Real estate	State (42%)	Australia, China, Malaysia, Thailand
Asia Food and Properties	n.a.	3691	n.a.	90.4	Food and beverages	Private (domestic)[a]	Indonesia, China, Malaysia
Neptune Orient Lines	3870	3112	89.3	81.4	Transport	State (67%)	Over 140
City Developments	n.a.	2887	n.a.	58.3	Hotels	Private (domestic)[b]	18 in four continents
Singapore Airlines	1064	2423	33.6	25.3	Transport	State (57%)	UK, India, China, Philippines, 7 more

(Continued)

Table 3: (*Continued*)

Company	Foreign assets S$ million		TNI index		Sector	Ownership as of 31 Mar 06 (Temasek)[c]	Foreign countries of operation
	1999	2004	1999	2004			
Fraser & Neave	1232	1864	63.5	59.9	Food and beverages	Private (domestic)[c]	France, UK, Malaysia, Thailand
Keppel	2609	1340	19.1	37.9	Diversified	State (31%)	US, Mexico, Brazil, Benelux, 11 more
Sembcorp	n.a.	1315	n.a.	33.7	Utilities and marine	State (50%)	UK, China, Vietnam, UAE, Brazil, USA, Australia, India
Average	2170.6	4636.6	44.26	57.61			

Notes: [a] the Vijaja family owns 64% of shares; [b] Hong Leong Group; [c] following the acquisition of a 15% stake in December 2006, Temasek will emerge as the second largest shareholder after Overseas-Chinese Banking Corp and the Lee family which founded the bank. Fraser & Neave is 38 percent-owned by Asia Pacific Breweries.

Sources: UNCTAD (2001 and 2006), *World Investment Report* and company websites.

nearly 40 percent of total capitalization of the Singapore Exchange (SGX), while as of November 2005 the top six Singapore-listed GLCs accounted for nearly a quarter of total SGX capitalization (US Embassy, various years).

In its 2004 report, the first ever, Temasek revealed that it had spent US$5.9 billion on acquisitions in 35 countries in the previous year. In the 24 months to March 2006, Temasek invested abroad US$11 billion (Table 4). Over the next decade, Temasek has indicated its desire to reduce local-based assets to a third of its total portfolio from 44 percent in 2006. The significance of Temasek as Singapore's leading investor is evident. The percentage of Temasek's total foreign assets to Singapore's OFDI stock[8] rose from approximately 10.38 percent in 1999 to 18.45 percent in 2004.[9]

Temasek focuses on three areas of investments. At the global level, GLCs such as Singapore Airlines, NOL, PSA, and SembLog capitalize on Singapore's position as a major transport and logistics hub. Temasek's aim is to help develop these companies into leading international businesses. Keppel and ST Engineering are equally well-run and have a strong business outlook. Keppel and another GLC, SembMarine (SMM), control 75 percent of the global market for oil and gas rigs.[10] Indeed, the marine and offshore engineering segment accounts for 5 percent of Singapore's manufacturing output.

In Asia, the focus is on services sector such as banking, finance, telecoms, healthcare, education, and real estate. SingTel has spent about S$20 billion over 10 years expanding throughout Asia. It bought Optus, Australia's second-largest telecommunications company in terms of subscribers, in 2001 and also owns sizeable stakes

---

[8] Without the exact information on the total foreign assets of Singaporean firms, OFDI stock could be used as the closest proxy.

[9] Authors' calculation based on Singapore's Department of Statistics OFDI stock data and UNCTAD's (2001, 2006) data on Singaporean multinationals.

[10] In late 2005, SMM's subsidiary, PPL Shipyard, acquired Sabine Shipyard, located on the Gulf of Mexico. Initially, Sabine will be involved in repair and refurbishment of rigs and should later expand its operations to include rig construction. See "Cleaning Up After Katrina", *Business Week*, 5 December 2005.

Table 4:   Temasek's main acquisitions since 2005.

Company	Country	Date	Sector	Stake (price S$ million)
Mahindra & Mahindra	India	March 05	Motoring	4.7% (102)
Mplant (Malaysia Plantation)	Malaysia	March 05	Banking	14.73% (200)
TeleSystems	Russia	March 05	Telecoms	2.6% (491)
Pacific Airlines	Vietnam	July 05	Air transport	30% (83)
China Construction Bank	China	July 05	Banking	5.1% (2,300)
NDLC-IFIC	Pakistan	July 05	Banking	Raised stake to 72.6% (94)
Amtel Holland	Russia	July 05	Tire production	With a group of private equity investors (116)
Shringar Cinemas	India	July 05	Entertainment	14.9% (11)
Hopson Development Holdings Ltd	China	August 05	Property	8.33% (104)
Bank of China	China	August 05	Banking	5 (2,500)
CAO	China	December 05	Finance	4.65% (17)
Bumrungrad Hospital	Thailand	January 06	Health services	5.94% (46)
Shin Corp	Thailand	January 06	Telecoms	49.9% (3,100)
PT Chandra Asri	Indonesia	February 06	Petrochemicals	24.6% (1,134)
Tata Teleservices	India	March 06	BPO services	9.9% (553)
E.Sun	Taiwan	March 06	Finance	15% (652)
Standard Chartered	United Kingdom	March 06	Banking	11.55% (6,565)

Source: CLSA 2006 and authors' research.

around developing Asia.[11] CapitaLand is Asia's biggest mall operator and a leading regional property developer. It has won rights to build

---

[11] In particular, 21 percent of Thai Advanced Info Service; 31 percent of Bharti Tele-Ventures in India; 45 percent of Globe Telecom of the Philippines; 35 percent of Telkomsel in Indonesia; and a 45 percent stake in Pacific Bangladesh Telecom.

Table 5: Temasek's Pan-Asian banking footprint.

Institution	Country	Stake %	Mkt cap S$m	Stake S$m
China Construction Bank[a]	China	5	169979	8499
DBS	Singapore	28	24450	6846
Standard Chartered	United Kingdom	12	56839	6565
Bank of China[a]	China	5	Unlisted	2500
Bank Danamon	Indonesia	56	4241	2375
ICICI Bank	India	10	19816	1962
Hana	Korea	9	15336	1380
BII	Indonesia	35	1377	482
E.Sun	Taiwan	15	3061	459
Minsheng Bank	China	5	7648	382
Alliance Bank	Malaysia	15	1181	174
NDLC-IFIC Bank	Pakistan	73	Unlisted	140

Note: [a] The stakes are held by wholly owned Asia Financial Holdings.
Source: CLSA Asia-Pacific Markets.

70 percent of future Wal-Marts in China and plans to replicate the strategy throughout Asia.[12] In banking, in a short span of three years, Temasek has created a commendable pan-Asian franchise with stakes in a dozen banks, together valued at US$20 billion (Table 5). In March 2006, Temasek pulled off a major coup by acquiring 11.55 percent in Standard Chartered Bank from the estate of the late Khoo Teck Puat. The weight of China is expected to increase following Temasek's acquisition of 4.55 percent of Minsheng Banking, the country's largest private bank. Each time, Temasek did the buying, not its listed bank, DBS Group Holdings.[13] Currently these stakes are all stand-alones, with no synergy derived, due to local regulations in many of these countries that put a cap on foreign holding.[14]

---

[12] "Shopping Mall Maestro", *Business Week*, 3 October 2005.

[13] DBS, in which Temasek has a 28 percent stake, made a $5.7 billion bid for Hong Kong's Dao Heng Bank Group in 2001.

[14] Speculations of a merger between DBS and StanChart have been dismissed on the basis of a similar argument — that the Monetary Authority of Singapore (MAS) would like DBS, as also the other local banks UOB and OCBC, to retain their Singapore characteristics, which would be lost in case of such a merger.

Third, Temasek aims to invest in promising, knowledge-based companies in ASEAN with high growth potential, and which have brand, technology or distribution advantages. In India, in particular, Temasek and Standard Chartered Private Equity Fund formed the US$100 million Merlion–India Fund in August 2003, for investing in mid-to-late stage manufacturing and services companies. The fund excludes specifically investments in infrastructure, real estate, and trading.

Finally, it is important to highlight that Temasek maintains a strategic interest in more traditional sectors in neighboring countries. In Indonesia, a 38.4 percent stake in the largest listed oil and gas company (Medco Energi International) was acquired in 2004 and CDC Group palm plantation interests were taken over jointly with Cargill in 2005; in Malaysia, a 5 percent stake in Proton was bought in 2004.

3.3. *Drivers*

Establishing market presence overseas has been the most important driver (UNCTAD, 2005). Three specific motivations have been the perception that host countries (and China in particular) present important growth opportunities; the need that some Singapore MNCs with sufficient expertise and resources had to invest abroad to follow their regional and global customers; and the desire of large Singaporean MNCs to extend network coverage to key areas of their operations. Cost savings is not the most important reason for Singapore OFDI as production or labor costs account for a relatively low proportion of their total operational costs (UNCTAD, 2005). On the other hand, the importance of host markets as sources of cheaper and abundant resources, as well as potential markets was confirmed in Rajan and Pankargar (2000).

Since 1995, cross-border acquisitions have become the most significant entry mode of Singaporean MNCs (UNCTAD, 2005). Taking high equity stakes in foreign ventures is important in the hope of reaping future revenues and profits. In fact, Singaporean firms make these high stake decisions based on their previous experience in the particular host country, more than on other criteria such as their general international experience or the size of the subsidiary (Rajan and Pangarkar, 2000). As elsewhere in the region, Singapore's OFDI is sometimes driven by personal relations with the local partners or customers, as well as ethnicity and social connections.

The acquisitions so far were largely internally funded, as Temasek's dividend income from listed companies alone is estimated at US$2–2.5 billion annually (CLSA, 2006). In addition, it raised US$3.7 billion through diversification of stakes in SingTel, CapitaLand, SMRT, and CapitaCommercial Trust (CCT) over the past two years. Moreover, Temasek can borrow significant amounts, since it has raised only US$1.75 billion in bonds and enjoys AAA credit rating. Investors seem to prefer when acquisitions are done by a long-term investor such as Temasek, rather than by an operating company which has minority shareholders and shorter-term horizons.[15]

3.4. *Consequences*

Broadly speaking, Singaporean MNCs have benefited from investing abroad, especially when the host governments' attitudes were positive and the subsidiaries were of large size relative to the parent (Pangarkar and Lim, 2003). For instance, regional associates contributed 66 percent to SingTel's earnings in the third quarter of 2006, up from 36 percent a year earlier. Similarly, industrial township projects have succeeded in enlarging the industrial estate area for Singaporean investors and, to a more limited extent, in cementing bilateral ties between Singapore and lower-income ASEAN countries (Pereira, 2005; Yeoh and Wong, 2004).

Nonetheless, the GLCs' way of doing business, reliant on a combination of managerial skills and preferential high-level political access, has not always proven apt for transplants in other Asian countries. In the 1990s already, the *modus operandi* that served Temasek companies remarkably well in domestic ventures often proved inadequate in managing Chinese investments. On the one hand, China's political system

---

[15] "Singapore's Temasek takes lead in overseas drive", *Reuters*, 24 January 2006.

has proven very complex to navigate, especially when compared with great predictability of Singapore. On the other hand, Singapore has a contractual business culture in which deliverables, timelines, and the nature of risk sharing are fully specified. This has proved excessively formalistic in China's emerging business community (Kumar *et al.*, 2005).

More troubling have been the resistance, wariness and skepticism that Temasek's acquisitions have drawn in some cases (Table A.1), owing to its ownership structure.[16] Assets under Temasek management (S$129 billion in 2006) are still not very large in an Asian, let alone global, context. For Temasek officials and Singapore's leaders, Temasek is simply "an active investor and shareholder of successful companies" with pure business interests and no political favors nor privileges.[17] But Temasek, with the Singapore Ministry of Finance as its sole shareholder, cannot avoid being perceived as the main arm of the Singapore state in spearheading economic and business development.[18] Moreover, its private limited company status means that Temasek is not required to make public its accounts of operations. The insufficiency of information on decisions and operations sometimes renders Temasek into financial secrecy that could agitate local partners and authorities in host economies.

---

[16] In developed countries, the context has also proven very demanding, and Temasek's knowledge of new markets has been much weaker than managers probably thought. Under pressure to rapidly acquire size without additional competition, acquisitions have often been made at a considerable premium — for instance in the case of Optus, Australia's second telecom operator, SingTel paid 50 times earnings. Analysts have been disappointed by Optus's heavy reliance on revenue from mobile and traditional voice services and inability to raise earnings from broadband and pay TV services (Ovum, 2007).

[17] See the company website at www.temasekholdings.com.sg. The sign of GLCs' contribution to economic development is a matter of some debate (Tsui-Auch, 2006). Private businesses, both local and foreign, compete on a generally equal basis with GLCs, and in fact the electronics sector examples mentioned in the previous paragraph seem to suggest that GLCs, in addition to providing jobs, serve to maintain Singapore's global attractiveness in related industries. Still, in some cases the dominant role of GLCs in the domestic economy may have displaced or suppressed private entrepreneurship. There have been cases of GLCs entering into new lines of business or where government agencies have "corporatized" certain government functions.

[18] Temasek, in particular, has had a penchant for appointing former politicians, civil servants, and high-ranking military officials to positions as chairmen, directors, and senior managers in their first-tier subsidiaries (Low, 2001).

No previous international expansion of any state-related companies anywhere has had such a far-reaching impact as Temasek's acquisition of Thailand's Shin.[19] On 23 January 2006, Temasek announced that it was paying 49.25 baht, or US$1.37, per share to buy 49.6 percent of Shin through two newly established holding companies. Temasek's stake in Shin was raised to 96 percent after Temasek completed its tender offer process at the end of March 2006 (see Maa Nok and Dek Nokkrob, 2006b). Since Shin's shareholders were individuals (Thaksin Shinawatra's family members) who sold their shares through the stock market, the receipts from the deal were tax-free.[20]

Among the myriad of questions raised on the deal, the most important one involving Temasek was whether its acquisition of Shin through direct and indirect shareholding structure violated foreign equity limits.[21] Thailand's Foreign Business Act (1999) prevents foreign nationals from majority ownership in certain industries, including radio broadcasting, television broadcasting, and air transportation.[22] As the main holding company of the Shinawatra group, Shin controlled equity in AIS, ITV, Shin Satellite, and Air Asia, whose main businesses were mobile telephone services, television broadcasting, and low-cost air transport, respectively. Temasek's acquisition of Shin therefore made Temasek the major shareholder of those companies.

Although on paper Shin was still under Thai majority ownership, questions were also raised whether the convoluted nature of the deal

---

[19] The following paragraphs are based on Goldstein and Pananond (2007), where more details are provided.

[20] Although the sale of Shin Corp. to Temasek was exempted from tax because it was done by individual shareholders, many questions were raised about how these individuals obtained these shares. Investigations are being conducted on many aspects, including whether Thaksin's children should pay tax when they obtained these shares (see Maa Nok and Dek Nokkrob, 2006a; Charnchatreerat *et al.*, 2006).

[21] The Temasek–Shin deal stirred up a variety of legal and ethical questions. After the September military coup, Thailand's new government has set up a number of agencies and panels to investigate legal aspects of the deal. Key areas of investigations included foreign equity limits and tax-related issues of the transactions. As our focus in this chapter is on the role of Temasek, we put more emphasis on discussing the issues related to the company.

[22] See the full text of this Act at the Department of Business Development website, www.dbd. go.th.

was intended to circumvent the law. The practice of setting up companies with *prima facie* majority Thai ownership has been widely popular among foreign investors, since the interpretation of the law has placed more emphasis on ownership than on control. Nonetheless, the sensitive nature of the industries in which Shin operated, along with the identity of the buyer and the seller, made this deal stand out. That Thailand's strategic industries were sold to foreign firms already angered many Thais, and the fact that the acquiring firm was wholly owned by a foreign government further enraged their opposition.

Temasek is not a newcomer to Thailand and the events that unfolded after the coup, brought many setbacks for Temasek's presence in Thailand. On top of its direct investment in Thai firms such as Bamrungrad Hospital (6 percent), Temasek has also established its presence through several GLCs under its umbrella.[23] First, the Shin's share price has been falling since January, reportedly, resulting in paper losses at Temasek of almost US$680 million as of November 2006.[24] Other Shin companies have been suffering similar fate, with the latest blow being a ruling by the Supreme Administrative Court in December 2006 that ordered ITV to pay over 100 billion baht in fines for its breach of concession agreement. ITV lost control of its networks to the government in February 2007 after failing to comply (Wilson, 2007). In addition, the newly-established Assets Examination Committee has launched an investigation into whether cellular operator AIS benefited from "policy corruption" under the Thaksin government.[25] The results of these investigations, or even the process of launching them, will certainly bear negative impacts on Temasek's investment. Already, the appointment of Jimmy Phoon as new CIO in December 2006 was widely seen as a sanction on Ong, who has

---

[23] These include DBS Thai Danu Bank, which has been majority-owned by DBS Group since 1998, and TCC CapitaLand, a joint venture between Thailand's TCC Land and CapitaLand. Temasek's previous investment in the Shin group was conducted through SingTel's 19.26 percent stake in Advanced Info Services (AIS) — the mobile phone company that serves as the main breadwinner for the Shin group. SingTel was even initially rumored to be the buyer of AIS, as their common interests in expanding the mobile telephone market in Thailand could lead to business synergy (Charnchatreerat *et al.*, 2006).

[24] "Bangkok Insists Phone Deal Broke Law", *International Herald Tribune*, 16 November 2006.

[25] "Shin Corp Temasek Is Ready to Swallow Its Medicine", *The Nation*, 13 November 2006.

been appointed to the position of Chief Strategist.[26] However in September 2007, Mr. Phoon quit Temasek after an eight-year stint with the company. He announced that he would take up an advisory position with a local investment firm.[27]

Second, a number of investigations have been launched to scrutinize various aspects of the deal, including a police probe into Temasek's possible violations of foreign equity limits through the use of nominee companies and a probe into the trail of the money involved in the acquisition (Maa Nok and Dek Nokkrob, 2006b). An initial finding conducted by the Ministry of Commerce found that the nature of Kularb Kaew, one of the holding companies set up to acquire Shin, may have violated the Foreign Business Act, hence implying that Temasek could be found guilty of using nominees to disguise its holdings in Shin.[28] The targets of these investigations extended beyond Temasek and Thaksin's family members to cover a number of government officials who might have neglected their responsibilities in the supervision of those transactions.

Third, Temasek's every move in Thailand is likely to be under close scrutiny like no other foreign MNC has ever experienced. Moreover, with what has been perceived to be a stumbled start, Temasek will have a hard time finding local partners who are willing to be involved with it, especially in the Shin deal. According to a former finance minister, "everybody is afraid to get involved in this deal".[29]

As Yeung (2004) argued in his analysis of GLCs' investments in China, the Singapore's "unique business system in which the state plays a strong role in business and economy" is difficult to transplant. To Singapore's regional neighbors, Temasek is perceived as part of Singapore Inc., where political, bureaucratic and corporate worlds often seem inextricable (Tripathi, 2006). Different political, social and institutional relationships call for a reconfiguration of governance

---

[26] "Temasek Replaces Executive", *International Herald Tribune*, 7 December 2006.
[27] "Temasek's Chief of investment quits," *The Straits Time*, 21 September 2007.
[28] Although the Commerce Ministry's investigation was leaked to the media on 13 September 2006, it was never officially released. As of end-March 2007, the police investigation concerning the possible violation of the Foreign Business Act has not been finalized.
[29] *The Nation*, 13 November 2006.

mechanisms. Engaging local business is the obvious solution, and in Malaysia, for instance, Temasek has been cultivating business ties with the family of Najib Razak, the country's deputy Prime Minister.[30] But the choice of such partners must be sufficiently clever so as to avoid a worsening of the problems.[31] In Thailand, the spectacle of Thaksin's family members cashing out without having to pay a single baht for tax served as the last straw on top of a string of other corruption allegations against his administration. It ultimately contributed to the Thai coup of 19 September 2006.[32]

4. Thai Firms Abroad

While inward FDI in Thailand has been widely studied, not much is known about the activities, strategies, motives, and performances of Thai firms operating overseas. To provide some background, this section first presents the longitudinal industrial and geographical distribution of Thai OFDI flows, based on central bank statistics, and then examines the experience of the largest groups.

4.1. *History*

The Bank of Thailand (BOT) collects the most comprehensive set of statistics on OFDI, although it suffers from two flaws.[33] First, the

---

[30] "Temasek strengthens ties to Malaysia PM", *Financial Times*, 12 November 2004.

[31] As the discussant of this paper, Joshua Felman, commented on the basis of his experience in Indonesia, having a politically connected business partner — something that should, *prima facie*, be an asset to navigate emerging Asia — can turn out to be a costly liability when the regime changes.

[32] This is of course not to say that corruption, or the Shin deal, were the single most important factors behind the 19 September 2006 putsch in Bangkok, which "came at the end of a year of endlessly confusing turns, twists, advances, and reverses on the Thai political scene" (Montesano, 2006).

[33] See Ganjarerndee (2005) for a detailed presentation on the BOT OFDI collection. Although the Board of Investment (BOI) also collects OFDI information, the agency relies on information supplied by investing firms and the BOI-equivalent agencies in a limited set of other countries, notably ASEAN, Indochina, and China. The different format of data collection adopted in each country reduces the validity and reliability of the data. In addition, the BOI figures often refer to the planned total project value, without much indication for actual project investment. See Pananond (2001a).

BOT figures include only cash transfer through commercial banks, thus excluding outflows through other important means such as overseas loans and overseas savings.[34] Second, the BOT statistics on FDI outflows include only net capital flows for equity participation, but not parent companies' loans to overseas subsidiaries — a major component of direct investment figures.

Thai FDI outflows have gone through four different phases (see Figure 1): early development (1977–1988), rapid rise (1989–1997), post-crisis decline (1998–2000), and resurgence (2001–present). During the first phase, Thai FDI outflows were still very modest and concentrated in financial institutions in response to the strict control over foreign exchange transactions and capital movements (Vachratith, 1992). These controls drove domestic banks to set up

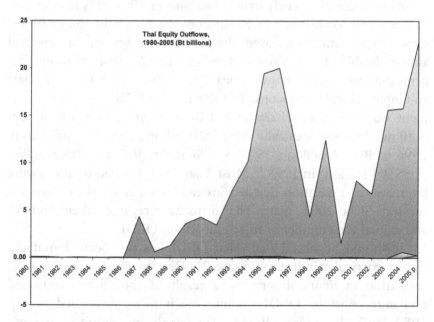

Figure 1: Total outflows of Thai FDI, 1980–2005.

Source: Bank of Thailand.

---

[34] After the crisis, the BOT has realized that their figures undervalue the actual amount of OFDI and is now in the process of launching direct surveys with investing firms.

overseas branches in Thailand's key trading partners (i.e., the United States) and leading international financial centers (i.e., Hong Kong and Singapore). These three countries absorbed more than 75 percent of total outflows during the first phase.

During the second phase, the OFDI stock grew more than 165 times, from US$13 million in 1980 to US$2.2 billion in 1995 (UNCTAD, 2003). The removal of exchange controls in 1990 and the creation of Bangkok International Banking Facilities in 1992 were key factors (Unger, 1998). Capital outflows shifted from investment in financial institutions to basic manufacturing industries, particularly food processing and textile. Although the geographical distribution of also broadened, with ASEAN absorbing the bulk of OFDI flows, Hong Kong and the United States remained among the most significant destinations (Table 6).

As the economic crisis struck Thailand in 1997, this rising trend took a sharp downturn. The flotation of the Thai baht and its subsequent depreciation increased the cost of foreign operations and almost doubled the amount of foreign-currency debts of most Thai firms that had been borrowing heavily to finance both their domestic and international expansions. The third stage of Thai outward investment was, therefore, characterized by a sharp decline. Investment outflows dropped drastically from Bt20 billion (US$789.3 million) in 1996 to Bt12.4 billion (US$395 million) in 1997 and Bt4.3 billion (US$104 million) in 1998.[35] Most Thai firms that had been enjoying international expansion decided instead to focus on their domestic survival. Since 2001, many Thai firms have regained their strength and gained the confidence to re-embark on OFDI.

It should be noted that Thai OFDI has not been dominated by any particular industry (Figure 2). Despite an initial heavy concentration in financial services, a result of the above-mentioned exchange controls, OFDI became much more diversified during 1989–1997 (Pananond, 2001a). Further diversification is apparent from post-crisis trends, for example in agriculture, the food and

---

[35] The average exchange rates (Bt: US$) for 1996, 1997, and 1998 were 25.34, 31.4, and 41.36, respectively (Economist Intelligence Unit, various years).

Table 6: Net flows of Thai OFDI classified by country (percentage).

	1970–1979	1980–1989	1990–1997	1998	1999	2000	2001	2002	2003	2004	2005	2006
Japan	0.0	4.1	0.3	-0.3	0.6	3.3	-0.4	2.1	1.6	0.3	0.7	0.2
United States	58.8	33.3	42.4	14.0	-2.8	-158.4	1.5	21.9	9.6	0.3	6.8	12.7
EU 15	0.0	0.2	3.3	21.2	8.0	-11.0	14.2	-16.4	7.3	-0.5	0.9	3.9
Germany	0.0	0.0	0.0	2.7	0.0	-0.2	13.6	-14.8	0.1	-0.4	-0.2	0.2
United Kingdom	0.0	0.1	0.5	-11.9	4.1	-8.6	1.5	-1.1	2.2	2.3	0.2	2.9
Ireland	0.0	0.0	0.0	22.0	3.3	0.0	0.0	0.0	0.0	0.0	0.0	0.0
ASEAN[b]	1.5	24.3	16.9	-15.8	68.1	54.2	58.3	36.0	45.8	44.8	79.6	55.6
Indonesia	0.0	7.7	5.0	-1.6	0.0	6.6	0.8	2.5	4.1	4.9	1.9	2.2
Malaysia	0.0	0.3	0.5	0.3	0.0	3.0	0.9	-0.8	0.8	0.4	3.8	-2.5
Philippines	0.0	0.0	0.0	7.7	1.5	0.0	-11.0	-2.0	7.4	7.9	2.2	0.6
Singapore	1.5	15.8	11.0	-38.7	62.3	14.8	27.4	32.3	5.3	3.7	42.8	28.2
Cambodia	0.0	0.0	0.0	1.3	0.9	3.2	1.0	-0.3	0.5	0.6	1.3	5.2
Laos	0.0	0.4	0.3	0.1	0.1	2.7	-8.1	0.3	0.4	0.3	-2.1	-0.5
Myanmar	0.0	0.0	0.0	1.8	0.9	1.9	40.1	-0.1	22.4	18.0	19.6	15.2
Vietnam	0.0	0.0	0.0	13.1	2.5	22.0	7.2	4.1	5.0	9.0	10.0	7.2

(*Continued*)

Table 6: *(Continued)*

	1970–1979	1980–1989	1990–1997	1998	1999	2000	2001	2002	2003	2004	2005	2006
Hong Kong	36.8	40.2	36.0	47.9	9.0	58.0	4.1	8.0	2.1	-5.8	5.9	4.3
Taiwan	0.0	0.1	0.0	0.0	2.2	19.3	1.8	0.5	-0.7	0.3	0.0	9.3
Korea, South	0.0	0.0	0.0	1.9	0.0	0.0	-0.9	0.6	0.3	0.4	0.0	-0.1
China	0.0	0.6	0.4	12.2	3.5	22.9	6.9	9.1	16.9	13.0	6.7	11.4
Canada	0.0	0.0	0.1	4.0	-0.6	0.2	0.0	0.2	0.1	0.3	0.4	1.7
Australia	0.0	0.1	0.0	1.3	0.1	1.1	0.1	1.0	1.0	0.8	0.4	2.4
Switzerland	0.0	0.0	0.0	0.0	0.0	0.0	0.0	0.1	3.4	5.6	-0.5	-0.6
Others	2.9	0.9	0.6	13.5	11.8	110.3	14.3	36.9	12.5	38.3	-0.3	-0.5
Total	100.0	100.0	100.0	100.0	100.0	100.0	100.0	100.0	100.0	100.0	100.0	100.0

[a] Figures exclude investment in the banking sector.
[b] Prior to 1999, ASEAN does not include Cambodia, Laos, Myanmar, and Vietnam.
Source: Bank of Thailand.

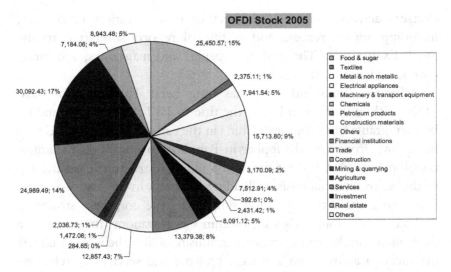

Figure 2:   Stock of Thai OFDI classified by sector (2005) (Absolute value in Bt million and corresponding percentage).

Source: Bank of Thailand.

sugar industries, and services, in particular trading, construction, mining, and quarrying.

4.2. *Actors*

Comprehensive firm-level data on international activities of Thai multinationals is not yet available. The popular practice of setting up holding companies to invest in various subsidiaries within the business groups enables large firms to reduce public exposure of their activities by placing them under the control of privately held holding companies. The reluctance of many Thai firms to provide information on their international activities remains a major obstacle in studying their behaviors.

At the same time, the number of powerful business groups in Thailand is relatively small, so it makes sense to concentrate on the largest ones, including Shin Corp of the Shinawatra family, Thai Beverage of Charoen Sirivadhanabhakdi and the Charoen Pokphand Group of Dhanin Chearavanont. Information on individual firms' overseas activities was pieced together from a variety of sources, including annual reports and additional reports submitted to the Stock Exchange of Thailand, newspapers and magazines, and direct correspondence with each firm.

Charoen Pokphand (CP) has long been Thailand's foremost MNC, although it recently lost the title to PTT.[36] Since its founding by immigrants from southern China in the early 1920s, the CP Group has grown from a seed supplier in Bangkok to one of Asia's largest conglomerates.[37] CP went through a major restructuring on the eve of the Asian financial crisis, offloading its shares in the Lotus convenience store chain to Tesco and simplifying the corporate structure. Still led by the founder's son, Dhanin Chearavanont, the group is a diversified conglomerate active in agribusiness (it is the world's largest producer of animal feed and tiger prawns) and services — telecommunications, logistics, and retailing — and had sales of US$15 billion in 2004. The rising number of free-trade agreements (FTAs) between Thailand and potential trading partners has prompted CP Trading Group Co Ltd to step up its overseas business expansion. CP will set up seed-manufacturing plants in India by forming a joint venture with government agencies, while another two plants in Turkey, where it is now the largest poultry producer, and Burma (Myanmar) will focus on size and capacity expansion.

Drawing on its Chinese ethnic origins, the CP Group was the first foreign investor to enter the Shenzen special economic zone in 1979. Thanakorn Seriburi, a long-time CP employee, has been supervising business development and investment in China since 1979. By 1997 Chia Tai, the CP Group's name in China, was the biggest foreign investor there with nearly 130 joint ventures ranging across a wide gamut of businesses in which it does not operate in Thailand, including

---

[36] See "Radicalism, Asian-style", *The Economist*, 22 March 2001; "Optimism in the Face of History", *Far Eastern Economic Review*, 26 August 2004; "China: Firms looking to Thailand trade", *The Nation*, 26 July 2004; "Economy of scale key to CP's success in China", *ibid.*, 3 March 2005; and Pananond (2001 and 2004).

[37] As Friedman *et al.* (2003) note, "CP Group is a large complicated conglomerate and the precise nature of transactions involving privately held affiliates is hard to know".

some such as motorcycle manufacturing (under the Dayang brand), TV production, and herbal remedies. CP Group also signed a memorandum of understanding with Krung Thai Bank, the country's largest state-owned bank, to co-invest in China's Business Development Bank. A subsidiary, CP Consumer Products, started importing Guizhou Tianan Pharmaceutical's Jin Tianan brand dietary products into Thailand. In 2003 it employed 70,000 people in China, where it generated almost a quarter of global sales.

Another leading Thai Conglomerate, Siam Cement (SCG), also has a diversified revenue base — consisting of cement, pulp and paper, petrochemicals, and building products — that aims at insulating returns. With foreign investors eager to leverage on its royal cachet, Siam Cement entered various joint ventures, making cars with Toyota, tires with Michelin, and television tubes with Mitsubishi Electric in the pre-crisis years. At its peak in 1996, SCG boasted 130 companies and total sales of more than US$6 billion. After the devaluation of the Thai baht, SCG found itself in desperate need of a makeover in the aftermath of the crisis. The Siam Cement group was one of the pioneering Thai multinationals that embarked on a rapid internationalization process in the early 1990s. Starting from its first overseas investment in the United States in 1991, the Siam Cement group announced its ten-year expansion plan in 1994 to become industrial leader in the Asia Pacific region. Such an ambitious plan led to an explosive international expansion. From 1993 to 1997, the group announced a total of 27 projects to be carried out in Indochina, China, Indonesia, and the Philippines. Such a major move put a strain on the group's financial resources. In addition, the group's preference for debt financing dealt a serious blow to the group's finances when the Thai baht was floated in 1997. At the end of September 1998, the group was faced with a total consolidated debt of US$5.2 billion, 23 percent of which was due within a year (Siam Cement Group, 1998).

To rebuild itself into a more flexible organization that could deal successfully in the increasingly competitive market, the group took a bold step in restructuring its overall operations. The restructuring resulted in the group focusing only on three core industries — cement, petrochemicals, and pulp and paper — and reducing its involvement in all the non-core sectors domestically and internationally.[38] To concentrate on debt management and organizational restructuring, overseas expansion was also halted during 1997–2001. Siam Cement's focused strategy has paid off as the group gradually regained its financial health. The group succeeded in reducing the proportion of its foreign debt from 90 percent of the total in 1997 to 2 percent in 2001, and was able to resume paying dividend in 2001, after a five-year break (Siam Cement Group Fact Book, 2003). A more focused strategy was also adopted in its international orientation, both industry-wise and destination-wise. Not only did the group been concentrating on its three core industries, it also directed most of its overseas activities to the ASEAN countries. It will invest Bt300 million in 2007 to establish two plants in Indonesia and another two in Vietnam, all of which will produce ready-mixed cement.[39] SCG Chemicals has plants in Indonesia, Iran, and China; SCG Paper Business produces packaging paper in the Philippines[40]; and SCG Building Materials Business has nine operations in Indonesia, the Philippines, Cambodia, Laos, and Vietnam.

Charoen Sirivadhanabhakdi, son of a fried-mussel-pancake street vendor in Bangkok, made his fortune with Thai Beverage, which operates Thailand's biggest brewery, Beer Thai, and the Sang Som

---

[38] Siam Cement underwent further corporate rationalization in 2001, resulting in six core businesses including: paper and packaging, petrochemicals, cement, construction materials; ceramic; and distribution.

[39] It presently exports about seven million tonnes per year. The main destinations are countries in South Asia such as Bangladesh and Sri Lanka, the South–East Asian region and the United States. It also exports 5 percent–10 percent cent to the Middle East. See "Siam Cement Industry aims to dominate Asean", *The Nation*, 18 December 2006.

[40] The financial and organizational restructure also allowed the group to strengthen its international expansions by channeling its resources to clearer targets. For example, the group's paper and packaging division announced its plans to enlarge its operations in Indonesia, Malaysia, and Vietnam, in order to increase its production capacity, and hence, its competitiveness in the South–East Asian region (*The Nation*, 18 November 2003). The post-crisis restructure of the paper and packaging division allowed the group to grow considerably through production upgrading and acquisition of other companies.

Group, Thailand's biggest distillery. Chang Beer is now the official sponsor of Liverpool's Everton soccer club.[41] Charoen also owns a portfolio of real estate projects through TCC CapitaLand — the joint venture with the Temasek-linked company CapitalLand. In May 2006, Thai Beverage raised S$1.37 billion in the Singapore Exchange's third biggest IPO ever. The company described the listing as necessary to access overseas markets through alliances, while also reaching the same standard as the prospective alliance partners.

Italian–Thai Development commands a leading position in the Thai civil and infrastructure market, where it built the Suvarnabhumi International Airport — the new airport in Bangkok. It is also active in the Philippines, Taiwan, Laos (Nan Theum II hydro-electric dam), Dubai (Palm Jumeirah Crescent Development), and India. In the latter, it has also successfully entered the civil infrastructure construction market following its acquisition of a majority shareholding in ITD Cementation India Limited (formerly Skanska Cementation India Limited) early in 2005. Ongoing and completed international projects have contributed approximately 24 percent to the company's revenues for 2005 and are projected to increase by a further 30 percent in 2006.

Among Thai state-owned enterprise (SOEs), Petroleum Authority of Thailand (PTT)'s upstream subsidiary PTT Exploration and Production has the broadest range of international operations. Thailand's power-generating capacity currently is overwhelmingly based on natural gas — more than 70 percent of the generation is gas-based — supplied mainly from Thai fields in the Gulf of Thailand operated mostly by Unocal of the United States. In 1990–1992 PTTEP signed concessions agreements for the Yetagun and Yadana fields in the Gulf of Martaban (operated by Petronas and Total, respectively) and some 25 percent of Thailand's total gas supply is now provided by Myanmar. PTTEP also operates projects in Vietnam, Indonesia, Cambodia, and Oman, and is also present as

---

[41] Chang Beer's involvement in Liverpool is rather different from Thaksin's purchase of Manchester City in July 2007. While Chang Beer's sponsorship was undertaken as a corporate agreement, Thaksin's takeover of Manchester City was a personal investment with no direct involvement of any Thai company.

238 Andrea Goldstein and Pavida Pananond

non-operator investor in some of these countries plus Algeria (see Pananond, 2007).

Finally, the Electricity Generating Authority of Thailand (EGAT) has been involved in hydroelectric power development in Laos along the Nam Theun River, a tributary of the Mekong, in the central region of the country. The project is structured as a BOOT (Build-Own-Operate-Transfer) arrangement and it will be implemented by Nam Theun 2 Power Company Limited (NTPC). NTPC's shareholders include EDFI, Italian–Thai Development Public Company Limited (ITD), Electricity Generating Public Company of Thailand (EGCO), and the Nam Theun 2 Power Investment Company (NTPI). EGAT signed a 25-year power purchase agreement with NTPC in 2002.

4.3. *Drivers*

The sudden surge of Thai OFDI in the 1990s reflected the opportunistic internationalization behavior of some Thai multinationals — the belief that they could operate businesses peripheral to their core competencies through partnership with those with experience and/or contacts — rather than previous accumulation of technological skills. Over a brief period, firms whose competitive advantages were largely based on networking capabilities were able to expand and seize opportunities in nearby economies characterized by weak market institutions.

Nonetheless, there were also some Thai MNCs that expanded abroad on the basis of their superior competitive advantage and accumulated experience. For instance, Siam Cement's decision to invest in ceramic tile and sanitary ware ventures in the Philippines reflected the group's confidence in its technological capabilities (see Pananond, 2001b).

The bulk of Thai OFDI was driven by resource-seeking and market-seeking purposes. Many firms that are involved in natural resource sectors, including PTTEP and EGAT, undertook their overseas missions to guarantee a steady stream of supplies for their production. Some of CP's agribusiness overseas investments in China were also motivated by access to new sources of supplies. Search for new market opportunities is a parallel driver. The threat of regional protectionism led many Thai firms to channel their investments to Europe and the United States in order to bypass trade barriers (Vachratith, 1992). The fear of losing their market after the United States cut its GSP privileges to Thailand prompted Siam Cement to establish its ceramic tile operations in the United States. More recently, Italian–Thai's strategy of seeking more international business opportunities responds to intense competition in the Thai construction industry which has decreased the profitability of the company's local operations.

4.4. *Consequences*

As we noted above, rapid international expansion, based largely on network relationships, led to Thai multinationals' imprudent and ill-advised decisions. Extensive borrowing and high debt-equity ratios to finance domestic and international expansions became disastrous after the baht was floated in July 1997. The difficult period that ensued both at home and in the region forced many firms to renounce overseas objectives and focus instead on domestic survival.

Thai President Foods and the Jasmine group are representative examples of Thai multinationals which were weak in both their technological and networking capabilities and were forced to considerably reduce their international activities. Chang Beer of the Thai Beverages Group, which owes part of its success at home to the capacity of influencing excise decisions on alcoholic beverages, may be a more recent similar example. So far it has yet to make an impression in overseas markets and rival Boon Rawd Brewery's Singha beer still represents "Thai beer" to the rest of the world.

Most other Thai MNCs appear to have learned that hasty expansion, either at home or abroad, without core competitive advantages can lead to futile results when the environment is no longer favorable. CP Group's overall performance, for instance, has been lackluster, especially in the retail sector where the Lotus Supercenter venture faces increasing competition. As a result it significantly altered its international strategy in the post-crisis years, shedding peripheral activities and focusing on its core industries, namely agribusiness, retailing (7-Eleven in particular), and telecommunications. Other Thai multinationals have also placed more emphasis on the development of industry-specific technological capabilities and have committed to transforming their personalized, relationship-based networks to more transparent and formal ties. Still, they seem unable to completely shake off their pre-crisis opportunistic behaviors. For example, some new projects launched by CP Group in the post-crisis years, including wine-making in Sichuan and Internet services provision in India and China, are driven by the opportunity to enter particular industries, despite the lack of synergies with the group's existing businesses in those countries.

5. Conclusion and Policy Implications

The chapter started with the ambition of contributing to a better understanding of the motivations and strategies of two peculiar classes of emerging economies' MNCs, namely Singaporean state-owned enterprises (including the holding company and its operative subsidiaries) and Thailand's diversified business groups. We argue that the international expansion of multinationals should be viewed in the context of their home countries' institutional conditions.

The tiny island-state of Singapore stands out in international competitiveness rankings thanks to an ad hoc mix of liberal trade and investment policies, result-oriented government-business interactions, and constant government intervention. This developmental state formula has delivered jobs, income, homes, education, security and welfare, while the rest of developing Asia, while certainly successful, still fights cronyism, corruption and nepotism. Some Singaporean companies have even managed to build strong core competencies and to successfully deploy them in international markets.

Nonetheless, the Temasek–Shin deal — coming on the heels of other polemic deals by GLCs — has revealed a number of potentials and pitfalls of the international expansion of state-related MNCs. GLCs serve as the commercial arm of the state to implement policies that aim to further integrate Singapore into the global economy. Close relationships with the home government can bring many benefits, including financial privileges and useful information on policy directions. Moreover, these firms typically operate in highly regulated sectors and have benefited from monopolistic or concessionary rights in their home base. To make matters worse, GLCs too often feel that they are accountable to nobody except their major shareholders — the home-country government.

It is, therefore, natural that, when it comes to international expansion, these firms tend to venture into the areas with which they were familiar. These sectors are most likely to be of strategic concerns to the host countries. Although the Singaporean government has claimed that GLCs are run on business principles and that the government has been relinquishing its control in GLCs, host country nationals and government could interpret the GLCs' international expansion as potential violations of their sovereignty.

It is inevitable for the operations of state-linked enterprises to bring about political risks that are not associated with regular private firms. The Singaporean experience must be seen in the broader context of a return to investment protectionism in many quarters. Since 2005, takeover attempts abroad by some state-owned enterprises from China and the United Arab Emirates have run into strong opposition, as have other operations by Russian companies that are perceived to be too close to the Kremlin (see Goldstein, 2007). These drawbacks of state-linked firms have been clear in the Temasek–Shin affair. It is a moot point whether the accusations levied at GLCs are fair or not — what is clear is that Singapore's foreign economic policy has to be more sensitive when GLCs cross borders and interacts in the political economy and social milieu in the region. Temasek and the GLCs need to be properly trained to navigate the political economy of emerging markets where political reforms are advancing in parallel with growing affluence, new political culture, democratization and impact of Internet on the society and polity.

In the case of Thailand, the central question is partly similar — are strategies that have been developed in response to a particular institutional context amenable to transfer to another? As long as the Asian business environment was characterized by market imperfections and weak intermediaries, the practice of relying on "generic" networking capabilities to offset technological weakness served Thai MNCs rather well. But when the competitive environment became less favorable, this type of strategy exposed its shortcomings. How Thai companies should act in the long run to enhance their overall competitive advantages is of course a separate theme.

In conclusion, this chapter argues that the term "third-world" MNCs does not refer to a homogeneous phenomenon. Corporate ownership is intimately linked to different institutional contexts and this impacts the type of competitive advantages that firms accumulate and the strategies they follow to develop (Van de Ven, 2004). In particular, a firm may derive its ownership advantages from intangible and non-business factors such as social and political networks. The importance of these resources is likely to be higher in economies that are still characterized by political and social nuances — a key feature among many developing countries. As emerging MNCs become more and more engaged in technology-related activities, and yet maintain specific idiosyncrasies, future studies could examine whether the complex and diverse reality of MNCs from emerging economies generate different patterns of internationalization.

Annex

Table A.1: Controversial Temasek deals in Asia and the Pacific.

Target company	Description
Ansett	SIA bought a 25 percent stake as a back-door entry to the Australian market in 1999. Mounting problems at Ansett, Air NZ's Australian 50% subsidary, forced the New Zealand government to intervene in 2001 and SIA to write off most of the investment.
Global Crossing	An earlier bid for Global Crossing, which controls nearly 100,000 miles of fiber optic submarine cables that connect

(*Continued*)

Table A.1: (*Continued*)

Target company	Description
	200 cities, by Hutchison Whampoa fell through when the Hong Kong-based company failed to meet US national security concerns. The deal between Global Crossing and ST Telemedia was initially opposed by the FBI, CIA and the Pentagon, all of which use Global Crossing's submarine network. ST Telemedia agreed to guarantee American law enforcement officials access the network for investigations. In addition, members of the company's board of directors must be US citizens who have obtained security clearances. The FCC found that the continued operations of Global Crossing will benefit competition by preventing discontinuance of service and providing customers choices among providers of telecommunications.
ICICI Bank	Under Reserve Bank of India (RBI) rules, the investment cap for foreign financial institutions or banks in Indian banks is 5 percent. The 2005 Comprehensive Economic Co-operation Agreement (CECA) set a 10 percent investment limit for Singapore firms in listed Indian companies. Temasek, through Allamanda Investments, holds a 7.37 percent stake in ICICI, India's largest private sector bank, and the Government of Singapore Investment Corporation (GIC) holds another 2.24 percent. In August 2006, RBI did not allow Temasek to increase its stake to 10 percent, considering that the combined Temasek-GIC stake in the bank would cross the 10 percent limit. In June 2007, at a time when ICICI is in the market for a major capital rise, the RBI agreed to a one-off arrangement under the CECA and to treat the two investment arms of the Singapore government as separate entities. Both the entities will have to approach the RBI for specific approval after they buy shares of the bank in the follow-on public offer.
Idea Cellular	ST Telemedia and Telekom Malaysia bid for 48 percent of the mobile phone operator in 2005. Indian authorities did not approve a joint bid arguing that SingTel, which is majority owned by Temasek, already holds a stake in Bharti Tele-Ventures and Indian rules do not allow the same company to hold two cellular licenses in the same region.

(*Continued*)

Table A.1: (*Continued*)

Target company	Description
Korea Exchange Bank	South Korean regulations forbid non-banking entities from owning more than 10 percent of a nationwide bank, in order to prevent conglomerates from controlling the banking sector. DBS was the only bank actively negotiating the purchase from Lone Star before walking away in June 2007, although it denied that the bid failed because of its parentage, insisting that it failed over a disagreement over price.
Philippines National Transmission Company (Transco)	On two occasions in 2003, SingPower was the only investor to submit a pre-qualification proposal for the concession. With two public biddings already declared failures, the Office of the Government Corporate Counsel issued an opinion to the PSALM board authorizing the government agency to initiate discussions with qualified and interested entities. By December 2003, a SingPower team conducted technical due diligence proceedings. The government, however, ended up conducting negotiations with three other groups. A consortium led by the Electricity Generating Authority of Thailand (Egat) submitted the highest bid of US$3.4 billion, but the government decided to scrap the negotiated sale process and revert to the traditional public bidding system.
Southern Bank	Temasek had to trim its stake in 2005, after it emerged that its total shareholding had breached the 5 percent mark, through indirect holdings through related companies. Temasek indirectly controls Malaysia's Alliance Bank and is therefore required to seek central bank approval before it can buy more than 5 percent of another Malaysian bank.
Telkomsel	SingTel has invested S$1.93bn (US$1.27bn) in Indonesia's largest mobile phone provider, making it the company's second largest overseas investment after Optus of Australia. Telkomsel was previously 77.7 percent owned by state-owned Telkom, with the remainder held by KPN Media — a subsidiary of Netherlands-based KPN International and Setdco, which controlled 17.3 percent and 5 percent,

(*Continued*)

Table A.1: (*Continued*)

Target company	Description
	respectively. KPN Media collapsed following the 1997 financial crisis and its stake was absorbed by the state. In 2001, a 22.3 percent stake was offered to SingTel via tender and a year later the operator upped its stake in Telkomsel to 35 percent. ST Telemedia owns a 42 percent majority shareholding in Indosat, Indonesia's second biggest mobile phone operator. Indonesia's Business Supervisory Competition Authority is currently assessing whether to investigate Temasek for alleged monopolistic practices in the mobile phone sector. Setdco CEO Setiawan Djody has urged the Singapore government to sell him the Telkomsel stake, arguing that this would be in the island state's best long-term interests.

Source: Goldstein and Pananond (2008).

References

Aykut, D and A Goldstein (2006). Developing country multinationals: South-South investment comes of age. Working Paper, No. 257, OECD Development Centre.

Blomqvist, HC (2002). Extending the second wing: The outward direct investment of Singapore. Working Paper, No. 3, University of Vaasa, Department of Economics.

Cantwell, J and PE Tolentino (1990). Technological accumulation and third world multinationals. Discussion Papers in International Investment and Business. No. 13, Reading, University of Reading.

Charnchatreerat, S, D Nakcharoen, N Pipat, W Akarasomcheep, T Eiamsamran and P Lertrattanawisut (2006). *Akara Deal Shin Corp Jed Muen Laan Suk Hun 'Kotranuwat' [Shin Corp's Bt70 Billion Super Giant Deal: Asset Concealment in a Familio-Global Scale]*. Bangkok: Matichon Books.

CLSA (2006). Temasek strikes again. *Singapore Market Outlook*, 28 March.

Dunning, JH (1993). *Multinational Enterprise and the Global Economy*. Wokingham: Addison-Wesley.

Dunning, JH, RV Hoesel, and R Narula (1997). Third world multinationals revisited: New developments and theoretical implications. Discussion Papers in International Investment and Management, Series B, No. 227, Reading, University of Reading.

Economist Intelligence Unit (various years). *Thailand: Country Report*.

Friedman, E, S Johnson, and T Mitton (2003). Propping and Tunnelling. NBER Working Papers No. 9949.

Ganjarerndee, P (2005). Thailand's balance of payments foreign direct investment statistics. presented at the UNCTAD Expert Meeting on Capacity Building in the Area of FDI, Geneva, 12–14 December.

Goldstein, A (2007). *Emerging Economies' Multinationals in the Global Economy*. Basingtoke: Palgrave.

Goldstein, A (2008). Who's afraid of emerging multinationals? In *The Rise of Transnational Corporations from Emerging Markets: Threat or Opportunity?*, K Sauvant (ed.), Cheltenham Glos: Edward Elgar.

Goldstein, A and P Pananond (2008). Singapore Inc. goes shopping abroad: Profits and pitfalls. *Journal of Contemporary Asia*, forthcoming.

Hiratsuka, D (2006). Outward FDI from and intraregional FDI in ASEAN: Trends and drivers. Discussion Papers No. 77, Institute of Developing Economies.

Kumar, K (1982). Third world multinationals: A growing force in international relations. *International Studies Quarterly*, 26, 397–424.

Kumar, S, S Siddique and Y Hedrick-Wong (2005). *Mind the Gaps: Singapore Business in China*. Singapore: Institute of Southeast Asian Studies.

Lall, S (1983a). The rise of multinationals from the third world. *Third World Quarterly*, 5(3), 618–626.

Lall, S (1983b). *The New Multinationals: The Spread of Third World Enterprises*. New York: John Wiley & Sons.

Lecraw, D (1977). Direct investment by firms from less developed countries. *Oxford Economic Papers*, 29(3), 442–457.

Lecraw, D (1981). Internationalization of firms from LDCs: Evidence from the Asean region'. In *Multinationals from Developing Countries*, K Kumar and MG Mcleod (eds.) Lexington, Massachusetts: D.C.Heath.

Lecraw, D (1993). Outward direct investment by Indonesian firms: Motivations and effects. *Journal of International Business Studies*, (Third Quarter), 589–600.

Low, L (2001). The Singapore developmental state in the new economy and polity. *The Pacific Review*, 14(3), 411–441.

Lynn, LH (2006). US research on Asian business: A flawed model. *Asian Business & Management*, 5(1), 37–51.

Maa Nok and Dek Nokkrob (2006a). *Shin: 25 Kam Tham Bueng Lang Deal Takeover Shin Corp [Shin: 25 Questions Behind the Shin Corp Takeover]*. Bangkok: OpenBooks.

Maa Nok, and Dek Nokkrob (2006b). *Shin Corp Kaab Rueng Ka Nang Ka Khao [Shin Corp Caught Red-Handed]*. Bangkok: OpenBooks.

Montesano, MJ (2006). Political contests in the advent of Bangkok's 19 September putsch. Presented at the *2006 Thailand Update Conference*, National Thai Studies Centre, Australian National University.

Ovum (2007). *SingTel-Optus*. January.

Pananond, P (2001a). *The Making of Thai Multinationals: The Internationalisation Process of Thai Firms.* Unpublished PhD Thesis, University of Reading, Reading.

Pananond, P (2001b). The making of Thai multinationals: A comparative study of Thailand's CP and Siam cement groups. *Journal of Asian Business,* 17(3), 41–70.

Pananond, P (2002). The international expansion of Thailand's Jasmine group: Built on shaky ground? In *Asean Business in Crisis,* M Bhopal and M Hitchcock (eds.), London: Frank Cass.

Pananond, P (2004). Thai multinationals after the Crisis: Trends and prospects. *ASEAN Economic Bulletin,* 21(1), 106–126.

Pananond, P (2006). Outward FDI from Thailand: Policy implications, *Presented at the Annual Seminar on Key Issues of FDI: Outward FDI from Asia,* ASEAN-UNCTAD, Chiang Mai, 10–11 April.

Pananond, P (2007). Emerging giants from ASEAN: The internationalization of Malaysia's petronas and Thailand's PTT. *Presented at the Annual Seminar on Key Issues of FDI: TNC Activities in Extractive Industries,* ASEAN-UNCTAD, Hanoi, 29–30 March.

Pananond, P and A Goldstein (2007). Enraging thy neighbours?: The potentials and pitfalls of Singapore's government-linked companies, *Proceedings of the Academy of International Business Annual Conference 2007.* London: King's College.

Pangarkar, N (2004). The Asian multinational corporation: Evolution, strategy, typology and challenges. In *Handbook of Asian Management,* K Leung and S White (eds.), pp. 155–206. Norwell, MA: Kluwer Academic.

Pangarkar, N and JR Lie (2004). The impact of market cycle on the performance of the Singapore acquirers. *Strategic Management Journal,* 25(12), 1209–1216.

Pangarkar, N and H Lim (2003). Performance of foreign direct investment from Singapore. *International Business Review,* 12(5), 601–624.

Peng, MW, KY Au, and DYL Wang (2001). Interlocking directorates as corporate governance in third world multinationals: Theory and evidence from Thailand. *Asia Pacific Journal of Management,* 18(5), 161–181.

Pereira, A (2005). Singapore's regionalization strategy. *Journal of the Asia Pacific Economy,* 10(3), 380–396.

Rodriguez, P, DS Siegel, A Hillman, and L Eden (2006). Three lenses on the multinational enterprise: Politics, corruption, and corporate social responsibility. *Journal of International Business Studies,* 37(6), 733–746.

Roberts, MJ and H Dick (2005). Developing international firm capabilities: Globalization strategies of Singapore's government-linked corporations. Working Paper, No. 7, Australian Centre for International Business.

Seng, TB (2002). Why it might be difficult for the government to withdraw from business, Retrieved from www.singapore-window.org/sw02/020210gl.htm (accessed 28 November 2006).

Shome, T (2006). State-guided entrepreneurship: A case study. Working Paper Series No. 4, Massey University, Department of Management and International Business.

Siam Cement Group (1998). *Annual Report*. Bangkok.

Siam Cement Group (2003). *Fact Book*. Bangkok.

Singapore Department of Statistics (various years). *Singapore's Investment Abroad*. Singapore: Ministry of Trade and Industry.

Temasek Holdings (2006). *Temasek Review*. Singapore.

Tolentino, PE (1993). *Technological Innovation and Third World Multinationals*. London and New York: Routledge.

Tripathi, S (2006). Temasek: The perils of being Singaporean. *Far Eastern Economic Review*, May, 48–55.

Tsui-Auch, LS (2006). Singaporean business group: The role of state and capital in Singapore Inc. In *Business Groups in East Asia Financial Crisis: Restructuring and New Growth*, S-J Chang (ed.), Oxford: Oxford University Press.

Ulgado, FM, CM Yu and AR Negandhi (1994). Multinational enterprises from Asian developing countries: Management and organisational characteristics. *International Business Review*, 3(2), 123–133.

U.S. Embassy (various years). *Singapore Investment Climate Report*.

UNCTAD (2001). *Investment Policy Review: Mauritius*, Geneva.

UNCTAD (2005). Case study on outward foreign direct investment by Singaporean firms: Enterprise competitiveness and development. Geneva: Trade and Development Board, Commission on Enterprise, Business Facilitation and Development.

UNCTAD (2006). *World Investment Report 2006: FDI from Developing and Transition Economies: Implications for Development*. New York: United Nations.

Unger, D (1998). *Building Social Capital in Thailand: Fibers, Finance and Infrastructure*. Cambridge: Cambridge University Press.

Vachratith, V (1992). Thai Investment Abroad. *Bangkok Bank Monthly Review*, 33, 10–21.

Van de Ven, H (2004). The context-specific nature of competence and corporate development. *Asia Pacific Journal of Management*, 21(1), 123–147.

Van Hoesel, R (1999). *New Multinational Enterprises from Korea and Taiwan: Beyond Export-led Growth*. London: Routledge.

Vernon-Wortzel, H and LH Wortzel (1988). Globalizing strategies for multinationals from developing countries. *Columbia Journal of World Business*, (Spring 1988), 27–35.

Wells, LT (1977). The internationalisation of firms from developing countries. In *Multinationals from Small Countries*, T Agmon and CP Kindleberger (eds.) Cambridge, Mass.: MIT Press.

Wells, LT (1981). Foreign investors from the Third world. In *Multinationals from Developing Countries*, K Kumar and MG McLeod (eds.) Lexington, Mass.: D.C.Heath.

Wells, LT (1983). *Third World Multinationals: The Rise of Foreign Investment from Developing Countries.* Cambridge, Mass.: MIT Press.

Wilson, D (2007). State-owned investment vehicles: Temasek lessons', *Bangkok Post,* 11 August.

Wong, PK and CY Ng (1997). Singapore's industrial policy to the year 2000. In *Industrial Policies in East Asia,* S Masuyama, D Vandenbrink and SY Chia (eds.), pp. 91–120, Singapore: ISEAS and Nomura Research Institute.

Yeoh, C and S Wong (2004). Selective state intervention and economic re-engineering: Lessons from Singapore's industrial parks in Indonesia and India. *Journal of Asian Business,* 20(2), 13–40.

Yeung, HWC (1994). Third world multinationals revisited: A research critique and future agenda. *Third World Quarterly,* 15(2), 297–317.

Yeung, HWC (1998) *Transnational Corporations and Business Networks.* London and New York: Routledge.

Yeung, HW (2004). Strategic governance and economic diplomacy in China: The political economy of government-linked companies from Singapore. *East Asia: An International Quarterly,* 21(1), 40–64.

Chapter 9

Outward FDI from Southeast Asia: The Malaysian Experience

Mohamed Ariff and Gregore Pio Lopez*

1. Introduction

The World Investment Report 2006 (UNCTAD, 2006)[1] noted that the stock of outward foreign direct investment (OFDI) from transition and developing economies in 2005 reached US$1.4 trillion, up from US$335 billion, 10 years ago. The report also stated that MNCs from Malaysia are extending their global reach (UNCTAD, 2006, p. 103). More impressive is that Malaysia's inward and outward flows are converging. Inward FDI increased from 23.4 percent of GDP to 36.5 percent while OFDI rose dramatically from 6 percent to 34 percent of GDP in 1990–2005.[2]

Malaysian companies have been investing abroad since the mid-1970s. However, Malaysian OFDI became significant in the early 1990s with the rapid liberalization of the global economy that came about with the end of the Cold War. Internationally, the completion of the GATT/WTO[3] Uruguay Round that began in 1986 and completed in 1994, regionally, the formation of the ASEAN[4] Free Trade Area (AFTA) in 1992 and domestically, the economic liberalization processes beginning in the mid-1980s were manifestations of the changing global economic order that encouraged OFDI.

---

* Comments by Arindam Banik at the ICRIER workshop are appreciated. The usual disclaimer applies.
[1] United Nations Conference on Trade and Development.
[2] UNCTAD FDI Key Statistics.
[3] General Agreement on Trade and Tariff/Word Trade Organization (GATT/WTO).
[4] Association of South–East Asian Nations (ASEAN).

This chapter examines the trends and patterns of Malaysian OFDI using the framework developed by Aykut and Ratha (2004) to identify its key determinants. The authors categorize the rationales for OFDI as push, pull, and strategic. These three rationales are then analyzed from a structural, cyclical, and institutional/policy point of view (Table 1).

The chapter relies on existing literature, publicly available data, and anecdotal evidence of Malaysian OFDI. OFDI in general, has not been comprehensively studied in Malaysia. There have only been two notable studies on Malaysian OFDI by Ragayah Mat Zin (1999) and Tham Siew Yean (2006). Ragayah had investigated factors such as business, production, management, and corporate strategy which influence Malaysian MNCs' decision to invest abroad, while Tham reviewed the trends, patterns, and policy issues of Malaysian OFDI. Both papers used a case study approach due to lack of secondary data on OFDI. Ragayah's key finding was that, "to expand and to find new markets for growth" was the main reason for Malaysian companies' investment abroad. In contrast, Tham's study had a myriad of findings on why Malaysian companies invest overseas.

The "Ugly Malaysian? South–South Investment Abused" provides a stylized view of corporate behavior of Malaysian MNCs abroad. As the title suggests, Malaysian OFDI has been described as being exploitative in nature. Most recently, in 2006, Bank Negara Malaysia (BNM) compiled a report on Malaysian OFDI for the period 1999–2005 describing trends, patterns, and determinants of Malaysian OFDI. There have also been a number of studies by various organizations that looked at OFDI from Malaysia as part of the ASEAN region such as Hiratsuka (2006) of the Institute of Developing Economies (IDE) and other organizations such as UNCTAD and ADB.[5]

While macro data on Malaysian OFDI is available, it is however not at the desired level of disaggregation.[6] Data collected by the

---

[5] United Nations Conference on Trade and Development and Asian Development Bank (UNCTAD).

[6] Aykut and Ratha (2004) highlight the challenges of estimating the South–South FDI.

Table 1: Factors affecting South–South FDI in the 1990s.

Rationale	Structural factors	Cyclical factors	Institutional factors
Push factors	Rising wealth in some emerging market economies increased supply of capital. Rising costs of labor and non-tradables encouraged relocation of production units to cheaper locations. Domestic deregulation to improve competition by breaking up monopolies prompted some large companies to branch into other countries. New technology and telecommunications improved information sharing and reduced transaction costs.	Low interest rates and low growth in industrial countries encouraged diversion of outflows from developing countries to other fast growing developing countries.	Capital account liberalization allowed resident companies to invest abroad. Growth of South–South trade through regional trading arrangements was often associated with investment agreements. Tariff and non-tariff barriers to trade encouraged the relocation of production units to other developing countries. Government policies encouraging the outflow of investment.

(Continued)

Table 1: (*Continued*)

Rationale	Structural factors	Cyclical factors	Institutional factors
Pull factors	Large and growing domestic markets.		Permitting foreign ownership of domestic companies encouraged FDI through mergers and acquisitions.
	Geographic proximity and ethnic and cultural ties.		Special tax and other incentives to attract FDI attracted more foreign investment.
	Supply of cheap labor.		
	Abundance in raw materials.		Preferential treatment of FDI over resident investment encouraged round tripping of resident capital.
			Export markets through preferential treatment.
Strategic reasons	Desire to procure critical inputs such as oil		Geopolitical considerations

Source: Aykut and Ratha (2004).

Department of Statistics (DOS)[7] provides the destination and OFDI type. BNM began publishing these data in 1993 through its Monthly Statistical Bulletin. UNCTAD[8] and the ASEAN Secretariat,[9] both maintain a database on FDI flows.

This chapter is organized as follows. Section 2 discusses the broad trends and patterns of Malaysian OFDI. Section 3 identifies the key determinants of OFDI using the Aykut and Ratha framework. Section 4 concludes the chapter.

2. Trends and Patterns in Outward Foreign Direct Investment (OFDI)

This section describes the trends and patterns of Malaysian OFDI by looking at the total amount in comparison with other Newly Industrialising Economies (NIEs) of Taiwan Province of China, Hong Kong, and Singapore, the destination and the sectors with the view of identifying patterns of Malaysian OFDI. Further, the ownership of companies engaging in the OFDI and the manner of these undertakings will also be described.

2.1. *Overall Performance*

Malaysia is well known as a destination for FDI and is now increasingly becoming a significant contributor to OFDI. Malaysia's contribution

---

[7] According to the IMF's Balance of Payments Manual, Fifth Edition, direct investment abroad is a form of direct investment, whereby companies invest abroad with the intention of obtaining a lasting interest (defined as holdings of at least 10 percent ownership) in an enterprise resident of another economy. In Malaysia, data on direct investment abroad (OFDI) in accordance to IMF definition are compiled and released on a quarterly basis by the Department of Statistics, Malaysia (DoS), the official compiler of Balance of Payments statistics. The data includes investment in the form of equity, reinvested earnings, and other capital (mainly loans). This data differs from the statistics compiled by Bank Negara Malaysia's Cash Balance of Payments (CBOP) Reporting System, which refer purely to outflow of funds in the form of equity and inter-company loans as well as for real estate acquisitions effected through the banking system, inter-company accounts, and overseas accounts. For the purpose of compiling balance of payments statistics, capital invested in or loans extended to subsidiaries abroad must be offset against the capital invested in or loans extended to Malaysia by subsidiaries abroad. At present, the CBOP System is not able to segregate this type of transaction (BNM, 2006).

[8] http://www.unctad.org/Templates/WebFlyer.asp?intItemID=3968&lang=1.

[9] http://www.aseansec.org/18177.htm.

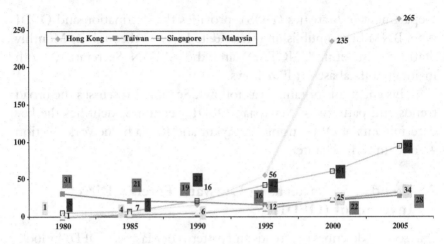

Figure 1: OFDI (Stock) as a percentage of GDP.
Source: UNCTAD FDI Key Data.

as a percentage of total FDI from South, East, and South–East Asia has increased from 1 percent in 1980 to 5 percent in 2005. It achieved an all time high of 7 percent in 1985. Valued in US dollar terms, Malaysia's OFDI stock has increased from US$197 million in 1980 to US$44.5 billion in 2005 (UNCTAD, 2006)[10] Although this does not match Hong Kong's enormous OFDI flows, it demonstrates a growing confidence of Malaysian firms to venture overseas. Hong Kong contributed 56 percent of total FDI in 2005, down from an all time high of 64 percent in 2000. Singapore and Taiwan, Province of China are the other significant performers in the region.

As a percentage of GDP (measured in current prices), the stock of OFDI from Malaysia has increased from 1 percent of GDP in 1980 to a remarkable 34 percent of GDP in 2005 (Figure 1). The performance has been one of steady increase with 12 percent recorded in 1995 and 25 percent in 2000. Hong Kong and Singapore are clearly in the lead with OFDI at 265 percent and 94 percent, respectively, of their GDP. Taiwan on the other hand has shown a decline in OFDI from 31 percent in 1980 to 16 percent in 1995 before rising to 28 percent in 2005.

---

[10] http://www.unctad.org/Templates/Page.asp?intItemID=3277&lang=1.

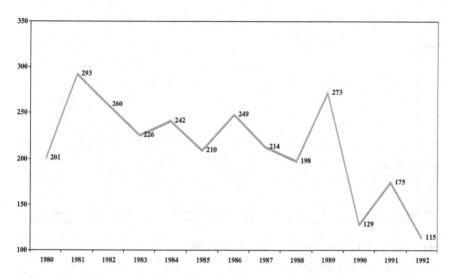

Figure 2: OFDI flows in US million (1980–1992).
Source: UNCTAD FDI Key Indices.

In terms of OFDI flows, for the period 1980–1992, annual flows did not exceed US$300 million (Figure 2). Except for 1981 and 1989, OFDI flows were trending downwards, reaching a low of US$115 million in 1992. OFDI during this period essentially involved Malaysian state-owned-enterprise purchasing equities of foreign corporations operating in Malaysia. This strategy was phased out in the mid-1980s and was replaced with state intervention through the private sector using Government Linked Companies (GLCs).[11]

This trend changed drastically in 1993 when OFDI flows jumped to "US$1063 million from the previous year" — a rise of more than 800 percent — signaling a change in strategy in response to the changing global and domestic scenario. This uptrend continued until the East Asian Financial Crisis in 1997 where it was reversed until 1998 after which it began to rise again. There was a drastic fall in 2001, where OFDI reached the lowest point since 1993 at US$267 million. It has however climbed to "US$2971 million in 2005" (Figure 3).

---

[11] Refer to Annex section for explanation on GLC.

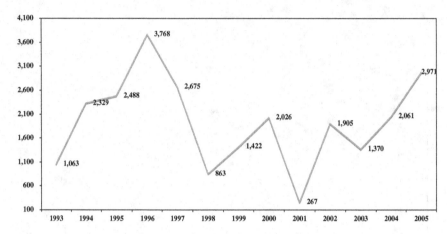

Figure 3:   OFDI flows in US million (1993–2005).
Source: UNCTAD FDI Key Indices.

This amount, however, is still lower than the historical high of US$3768 million recorded in 1995.

Malaysia was ranked highly overall as a source of OFDI. In UNCTAD's Outward Performance Index[12] Malaysia has remained among the top 35 OFDI countries except for the period 1990–1992 when it was ranked 42nd. Malaysia's best performance was for the period 1993–1995[13] when it was ranked eighth. This ranking correlates with Malaysia's overall performance in OFDI and economic growth (Figure 4).

2.2. *Performance of Malaysian Companies*

PETRONAS, ranked 59th, is Malaysia's only company in the world's top 100 non-financial MNCs, ranked by foreign asset in 2004 (Table 2). PETRONAS is the national oil company and enjoys monopoly oil and natural gas rights in Malaysia.[14] Malaysia also has six companies in the

---

[12] The Outward FDI Performance Index is calculated as the share of a country's outward FDI in world FDI as a ratio of its share in world GDP.

[13] http://www.unctad.org/Templates/WebFlyer.asp?intItemID=3241&lang=1.

[14] Refer to the Annex for an explanation on PETRONAS.

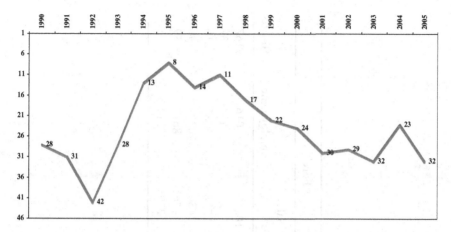

Figure 4: Malaysia's outward performance index ranking (1988–2005).
Source: UNCTAD FDI Key Indices.

top 100 non-financial MNCs from developing countries, ranked by foreign assets (UNCTAD, 2006). Interestingly, four of the six are GLCs. Malaysian International Shipping Corporation (MISC) is a subsidiary of PETRONAS, while Kumpulan Guthrie and Sime Darby are majority owned by Permodalan Nasional Berhad (PNB), a government-linked investment company (GLIC).[15]

These Malaysian companies were focused mainly in natural resources such as oil and gas, and forestry as well as capital-intensive industries such as transportation. The two private sector companies in the top 100, however, were diversified companies.

2.3. *Destination and Sector*

Malaysian OFDI is dispersed over more than 100 countries (BNM, 2006). The Labuan International Offshore Financial Centre (LIOFC) was the top location for Malaysian OFDI, followed by the United States and Singapore for the period 1993–2005. However, the flows to the LIOFC were far greater than those to the other locations. This

---

[15] Refer to the Annex for an explanation on GLICs.

Table 2:   Ranking in top 100 non-financial MNCs (by foreign assets) in 2004.

Corporation	Ranking	Industry	Foreign Assets (US mil.)	Foreign Sales (US mil.)	Foreign Employment	Foreign Affiliates
PETRONAS	2	Petroleum Exp./re	22647	10567	4016	167
YTL Corp. Berhad	32	Diversified	3359	571	1423	37
MISC Berhad	45	Transport	2625	1797	3785	16
Sime Darby Berhad	55	Diversified	1838	2636	6207	146
MUI Berhad	77	Diversified	1042	476	8612	39
Kumpulan Guthrie Berhad	86	Plantation	857	279	43514	1

Source: UNCTAD (2006).

may reflect the relative importance of the LIOFC as an investment center for Malaysian based companies. The BNM reported that:

> ...Investments in the finance, insurance and business services sub-sector reflected to a large extent activities of investment holding companies that were set up in IOFCs to centrally manage global investment operations... (BNM, 2006)

In the ASEAN region, only Singapore and Indonesia placed in the top ten destinations, while in the Asian region only Hong Kong and China were important destinations. Surprisingly, Mauritius was among the top 10 OFDI locations (Figure 5). Indeed, the cumulative investment for Mauritius was similar to that of Taiwan.

However, the main destinations of Malaysia's OFDI by category of countries for the period 1999–2005, have been to industrialized countries. Thirty-four percent of OFDI goes to this category of countries, namely to the United States the United Kingdom, Belgium, and the Netherlands — essentially the trading centers of the European Union. International Offshore Financial Centers such as the LIOFC and the Cayman Islands are also favored destinations with 26 percent

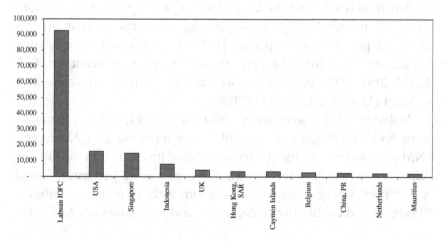

Figure 5: Top ten locations for OFDI (accumulated in RM million, 1993–2005).
Source: BNM Annual Report – various years.

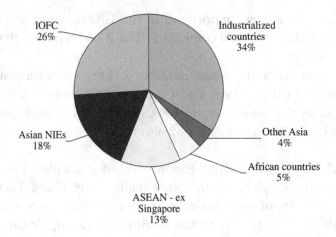

Figure 6: Malaysian direct investment abroad by region in percentage (1999–2005).

Source: BNM (2006).

of Malaysian OFDI heading to these shores. ASEAN[16] and NIEs investment collectively accounted for 31 percent of OFDI. Malaysia's OFDI to other parts of Asia (including China and India) and Africa did not amount to more than 9 percent cumulatively. Neither were the Americas (excluding the United States) an important destination.

OFDI to developing economies registered the highest growth rate at 25 percent for the period 1999–2005, with its share of total investment rising from 13 percent in 1999 to 31 percent in 2005 (BNM, 2006) (Figure 6). Malaysia was also a top ten source of FDI to Africa (UNCTAD, 2005a, 2005b).

Malaysian OFDI went mainly into the services, utilities, manufacturing and oil and gas sector — collectively amounting to 92 percent. BNM reported that within the services sector, investment in the finance, insurance, and business services was the largest at 43 percent, followed by transport, storage, and communications with 20 percent, utilities at 20 percent and distributive trade, hotels, and restaurants at 12 percent.

---

[16] ASEAN here refers to Brunei, Indonesia, Thailand, Philippines, Cambodia, Laos, Vietnam, and Myanmar. Singapore is included as NIE.

BNM further reported that investment in the transport, storage, and communications sub-sector was conducted mainly by companies in the telecommunications industry via acquisitions and joint ventures with foreign telecommunications companies. In the utilities (electricity, gas, and water) sub-sector, major acquisitions were regulated assets such as water services companies and power plants abroad. In the wholesale and retail trade, hotels and restaurants sub-sector, a significant portion of OFDI was in the distributive trade and hotel industries. The mining sector was dominated by PETRONAS, Malaysia's national oil company. Investment in agriculture was largely in palm oil plantations. Manufacturing investments abroad were concentrated in three main industries, namely fabricated metal products, machinery and equipment (48 percent); food, beverages, and tobacco (14 percent) and chemicals and petroleum-related industry (10 percent) (BNM, 2006).

2.4. Ownership and Outward Foreign Direct Investment Type[17]

The 2006 BNM report also provides an analysis on Malaysian OFDI by ownership and investment type. Ownership of Malaysian companies can be separated into three categories: (1) Government Linked Companies[18]; (2) RCCs — private companies in which residents have equity stake of more than 50 percent; and (3) NRCCs — private companies in which total non-resident shareholding is more than 50 percent.

2.4.1. Investment by Malaysian Controlled Companies (GLCs & RCCs)

BNM noted that investments from Malaysian GLCs and RCCs accounted for 61 percent of OFDI during 1999–2005 (Figure 7).

---

[17] This section utilizes a BNM report on OFDI due to lack of publicly available detailed data on this subject. For the complete report see: http://www.bnm.gov.my/files/publication/qb/2006/Q3/p6.pdf.

[18] For the purpose of the BNM report, BNM classifies GLCs as non-financial public enterprised in which the Government has an equity of more than 50% and with sales turnover of at least RM100 million. For a more detailed explanation of GLCs, RCCs, and NRCCs please refer to the Annex section. US$1 = RM3.5 (approximately).

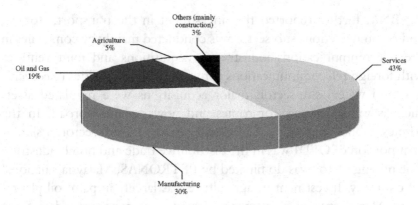

Figure 7:   Direct investment abroad by sector (1999–2005).
Source: BNM 2006.

The bulk of these investments were by companies in the services sector (48 percent), followed by mining (48 percent), agriculture and manufacturing (8 percent) each. GLCs were the dominant investors in the oil and gas, and the telecommunications industries, while the RCCs were the main driver for investment in the manufacturing, utilities, distributive trade, leisure, plantations, construction as well as banking and finance industries.

BNM noted that OFDI by Malaysian controlled companies (GLCs & RCCs) were undertaken mainly through acquisition of equity stakes and joint-ventures with foreign partners abroad. BNM further noted that 70 percent of these investment flows were for equity investments and real estate acquisitions. Investments by these Malaysian controlled companies were sourced mainly from internal funds (62 percent) and offshore borrowings (26 percent). BNM also noted that GLCs and RCCs conducted their investment mostly in developing economies with a significant amount channeled to the ASEAN and African regions as well as selected countries such as PR China, India, Sri Lanka, Pakistan, and some West African countries.

2.4.2. *Investment by Non Resident Controlled Companies (NRCCs)*

During the period 1999–2005, BNM reported that 39 percent of total gross outflows of OFDI were attributed to NRCCs. BNM noted that the share of NRCCs OFDI to total OFDI has declined from 35 percent in 1999 to 17 percent in 2005. The bulk of NRCCs investments outflows (91 percent) were in the form of extensions of inter-company loans to related companies abroad. NRCCs also preferred internally generated funds to finance their overseas investment. NRCCs in the manufacturing sector accounted for more than 60 percent of these investment flows. Within the manufacturing sector, 53 percent were in the manufacturing of semi-conductor and other electronic component industry and almost 20 percent to the manufacturing of radio, television sets, video recorder, and other equipment industry.

3. The Key Determinants of OFDI

There are many factors that have contributed toward both the pull and push for OFDI. Analyzing OFDI flows, there is a clear indication that the push and pull factors changed in the early 1990s demonstrated by the leap in Malaysian OFDI since 1993. The two phases, with the first from 1970 to 1990 and the second phase from 1991 onwards, demonstrate changes in the relevance of OFDI to the Malaysian economy.

3.1. *Push Factors*

The key push factors in the case of Malaysia has been rising wealth — both of individuals and corporations, high domestic savings, the rising cost of labor in Malaysia relative to its regional neighbors, the limits of domestic markets, domestic deregulation in strategic sectors such as health, education, telecommunications, and utilities, the promotion of OFDI by the government and of South–South trade, and trade liberalization in general, especially in the ASEAN region.

3.1.1. *Structural Factors*

A key determinant of OFDI had been the structural changes to the Malaysian economy due to Malaysia's impressive economic growth. Malaysia recorded an average growth rate of 6.5 percent in real gross domestic product (GDP) since Independence in 1957. GDP per capita in current prices grew by 7.0 percent per annum.[19] Concurrent with strong economic growth was full employment, which was achieved in 1991 at 4.3 percent. For the period 1992–1997, average unemployment rate was 3 percent and for the period 1999–2005 was 3.4 percent (ADB Statistics[20]). Gross domestic savings also increased from 28.8 percent of GDP in 1981 to 34.4 percent of GDP in 1990 and an impressive 43.3 percent of GDP in 2005. Similarly, gross national savings increased from 30.2 percent in 1990 to 38.5 percent in 2004 (ADB Statistics).

The development of the Malaysia Stock Exchange[21] further demonstrates the development of the private sector in Malaysia. The number of listed companies on the main board increased at an annual rate of 5.6 percent for the period 1981–2001. At the same time, the Composite Index (CI) grew at an average of 3.1 percent per annum. The CI reached a historic high of 1238 points in 1996 just before the East Asian Financial Crisis (Ibrahim, 2006, p. 75). The development of the stock market allowed companies to raise funds domestically at low cost and purchase assets in other economies.

3.1.2. *Cyclical Factors*

Malaysia had undergone a recession in the 1985 and 1998. The 1985 recession, particularly, had a direct impact in encouraging Malaysian OFDI. The property sector provides an illustrative example. Tham (2006) noted that the collapse of the property market in 1985 redirected OFDI toward business investment overseas from 1989 onwards. Motivated by the need to search for new revenue sources outside Malaysia, construction and property development companies have been making inroads abroad in countries such as the United Kingdom. Hong Kong, and China and in infrastructure concession and property

---

[19] See the 9th Malaysia Plan, Economic Planning Unit, p. 3
[20] Asian Development Bank (ADB) Statistics: http://www.adb.org/Statistics/ki.asp.
[21] Bursa Malaysia (Malaysia Stock Exchange) was formerly known as the Kuala Lumpur Stock Exchange.

development projects in developing countries in Asia and Africa particularly in India, South Africa, Mainland China, Cambodia, and Indonesia (BNM, 2006). Furthermore, in her seven-company study, Tham (2006) also noted that the saturation and competition in the services sector in the domestic market were the prime motives for companies to invest overseas.

3.1.3. *Institutional Factors*

As noted earlier, government policies in support of OFDI changed dramatically in favor of OFDI since 1991 in response to the structural bottlenecks, the recession of 1985 in Malaysia and then Prime Minister Mahathir's vision of South–South cooperation. Support for OFDI was further strengthened after the East Asian financial crisis and has become an official strategy of the government to ensure continued growth.

Government Policies   The early push factor that contributed to OFDI was the New Economic Policy (NEP), which promoted "Economic Nationalism" and "restructuring of the Malaysian economy". The objective of controlling and promoting the national economy prompted the first wave of Malaysian OFDI. The Malaysian government through state owned enterprise acquired British owned agency houses in Malaysia (Mat Zin 1999, Jomo, 2002) in the late 1970s and early 1980s. These agency houses such as Barlows, Boustead, Guthrie, Harrison & Crosfield and Sime Darby were involved in international trade, tin mining and plantation agriculture and had business interest in the South–East Asian region. The headquarters were in the home countries. The reverse takeovers were through state agencies such as PNB purchasing equity in the open market. An example of these prominent takeovers was the famous "Dawn Raid" on the London Stock Exchange (Martin, 2006).

Another significant event that had an indirect push on OFDI in the 1970s was the implementation of the Industrial Coordination Act (ICA), 1975. The ICA introduced a licensing requirement for manufacturing activity in Malaysia to "ensure the orderly development and growth of industries". Malaysian firms owned by non-Bumiputera had to offer 30 percent of their equity to Bumiputera interests. Foreign firms had to offer at least 70 percent to Malaysians, of which 30 percent had to go to Bumiputera individuals or agencies (Lee, 2002). This prompted capital flight from Malaysia by Malaysians of Chinese ethnic origin. Gomez and Jomo (1999) note the following:

> ...A number of prominent Chinese businessmen such as Robert Kuok, Lim Goh Tong, Tan Chin Nam and Khoo Kay Peng bypassed the state by diversifying their operations overseas...According to a Morgan Guaranty estimate, total capital flight during 1976 to 1985 amounted to USD12 billion (Gomez and Jomo, 1999, pp. 43–44)

However, OFDI during the period 1970–1990, as a percentage of GDP was not significant. Since 1991, the Malaysian government has increased the support for OFDI especially in the form of tax exemption, tax incentives and, special funds. Mat Zin (1999) noted the following:

> ...The Malaysian government introduced a package of incentives in 1991 in the form of tax abatement on income earned overseas and remitted back to Malaysia and tax deduction for pre-operating expenses. Beginning 1995, all income remitted by Malaysian companies investing overseas (except from banking, insurance and sea and air transport businesses) is fully exempted from income tax. (Mat Zin 1999, p. 470)

In 2003, an additional incentive was introduced for acquiring foreign owned companies abroad for high technology production within the country or to gain new exports for local products (MASSA News, 2005). Subsequent government policies promoting OFDI were focused on the agricultural sector. The National Agriculture Policy III (NAPIII)[22] formulated amidst the East Asian Financial Crisis in 1998, saw OFDI as a means of reducing Malaysia's significant trade deficit

---

[22] National Agriculture Policy III: 1998–2010.

in the agriculture sector. Furthermore, the government sought to ensure food security through OFDI.

The NAPIII noted the following:

> ...Reverse and offshore investments for strategic sourcing will be encouraged and judiciously pursued...Reverse investment in paddy production in low cost price producing countries will be encouraged...To meet the requirement for raw materials for the processing industries and increasing domestic demand for temperate fruits, reverse investments will be encouraged...Future production and expansion of oil palm cultivation will be in Sabah and Sarawak or through reverse investment in neighbouring countries, the South Pacific islands, Africa and Latin America. (Executive Summary, NAPIII)

OFDI then became a definite strategy in Malaysia's long term planning as seen in the Outline Perspective Plan III (OPP3),[23] implemented in 2001. The Outline Perspective Plan III notes:

> ...Efforts to promote reverse investments for food and plantation crops will continue to ensure supply of raw materials to industries while taking advantage of the cheaper production cost and the availability of resources overseas. (OPP3, p. 73)

The Malaysia–Singapore Third Country Business Development Fund, co-funded by the two countries, allows Malaysian and Singaporean enterprises to co-operate and jointly identify investment and business opportunities in "third countries" outside of Malaysia and Singapore. The fund's main objective is to encourage Malaysian and Singaporean enterprises to expand their business operations in the global arena. (MASSA, 2005)

The Malaysian Budget 2007 also outlined measures to help create Malaysian-owned MNCs. These included an increase in the paid-up capital of EXIM Bank by RM2 billion to enhance the bank's role

---

[23] OPP3 is a long term indicative plan for the period 2001–2010.

in providing financing for domestic companies investing abroad and the setting up of a RM100 million Overseas Investment Fund to finance start-up costs of domestic companies doing business overseas (BNM, 2006). In addition, BNM has set-up a RM1 billion fund to assist and stimulate local entrepreneurs especially Bumiputera entrepreneurs' to venture abroad (Tham, 2006, p. 10). The EXIM Bank also has the Overseas Project/Contract Financing Facility, which is available to Malaysian companies (investors/suppliers/contractors) undertaking projects overseas such as infrastructure, manufacturing, and other developmental projects.[24]

3.2. *Pull Factors*

The main pull factors that attracted Malaysian OFDI were the supply of cheap labor, the abundance of raw materials, large and growing domestic markets, geographic proximity, special tax and other incentives and the development of export markets through preferential treatment.

3.2.1. *Structural factors*

Beginning in the 1990s, there were signs that Malaysia was facing infrastructural bottlenecks and increasing shortage of labor — especially skilled labor. The rising costs of wages lead to overall cost of production (Tham, 2005). Facing these constraints, Malaysian based companies' sought to circumvent them through OFDI. Therefore, the key drivers in the case of Malaysia were (1) efficiency-seeking OFDI — taking advantage of low cost of factor prices in the host country and (2) market seeking OFDI — gaining better access to the markets of host countries and surrounding markets.

Hiratsuka (2006) argued, using the gravity model, that OFDI, as a percentage of trade, was highest in the ASEAN region, especially for Singapore, Thailand, and Indonesia. Hiratsuka's evidence supports the gravity model argument that geographical distance and markets

---

[24] http://www.exim.com.my/overseas.asp.

play a crucial role in determining OFDI. Hiratsuka also noted that Malaysian OFDI was also essentially efficiency- and market-seeking.

Efficiency-seeking OFDI   Economic liberalization through the WTO and AFTA process together with the emergence of new low cost economies in the region gave impetus for companies with high labor dependency to restructure and realign their operations to improve export competitiveness. Malaysian companies relocated to Laos, Cambodia, Indonesia, Vietnam, and China in search for lower factor prices. This was especially true for the manufacturing and textile sector. Malaysian OFDI in the manufacturing sector was essentially attracted by the opportunity to be low cost producers abroad. These companies employed the strategy of relocating their resource-intensive operations into low cost locations abroad to maintain competitiveness. Economies of scale such as large-scale plantations were also an important driver as Malaysian plantation companies invested especially in Indonesia to seek cheap abundant labor and land.

Market-seeking OFDI   Due to the limits of Malaysia's domestic markets, local firms have been driven to search for new markets. Mat Zin (1999, p. 479) noted that of the seven companies studied, seeking new markets or expanding existing ones were the main pull factors of five companies. Malaysia's largest export markets are the United States, the European Union, and followed by Japan (MITI, 2006b). Investments in industrialized countries were mostly done by NRCCs.

Malaysian companies have also managed to move up the value chain or develop integrated supply chain management through acquiring interest in or by forming joint ventures with foreign counterparts. These often involved acquiring physical assets such as manufacturing facilities, high technology and management expertise, brands and trademark rights to established products (BNM, 2006).

Proton, for example, acquired a British automobile company, which has acted as an R&D center and also import and distribution centers of cars and parts in the United Kingdom. Similarly, LKT, a semiconductor business equipment solution company and Pentmaster, a semiconductor manufacturing automation solution company, have set up service support centers and offices worldwide to support their customers and distributors (Hiratsuka, 2006).

Resource-seeking OFDI Malaysia's national oil company (PETRONAS) and plantation companies have been actively investing overseas in search of new resources (oil fields and plantation land) which have become scarce in Malaysia. Oil and gas is also a strategic resource. PETRONAS, underpinned by its vast knowledge and experience in domestic oil and gas exploration and extraction activities and the anticipation of higher global energy demand, had embarked on a strategy of global diversification (BNM, 2006). The similar advantages — experience and technical capabilities in plantation management and production — were key determinants of Malaysian plantation companies investing abroad, especially into Indonesia.

3.2.2. *Institutional Factors*

Developing countries such as Laos, Cambodia, Vietnam, and Indonesia in order to attract FDI have offered various kinds of incentives. Although, these incentives were not ranked highly by Malaysian companies (Mat Zin, 1999 and Tham, 2006) they were still important for attracting OFDI.

To date, Malaysia has concluded Investment Guarantee Agreements (IGAs) with 71 different countries including members of two groupings — ASEAN and the Organization of Islamic Countries (OIC). These IGAs adhere to the provisions of the Convention on the Settlement of Investment Disputes, which Malaysia acceded to in 1966. This convention is under the auspices of the International Bank for Reconstruction and Development. The IRBD also provides international conciliation or arbitration through the International Centre for Settlement of Investment Disputes.[25] Through these IGAs, Malaysian investors' rights are guaranteed. Malaysia is ranked second only to the People's Republic of China in the number

---

[25] http://www.mida.gov.my/beta/view.php?cat=3&scat=5&pg=118.

of IGAs signed among developing countries in Asia (See ADB Outlook, 2004).

3.3. Strategic Reasons

Geopolitical reasons have also been an important factor in promoting Malaysian OFDI especially to southern countries. Malaysia's "Prosper Thy Neighbor" foreign policy included technical cooperation and South–South investment. Malaysian foreign policy was also instrumental in Malaysia's national oil company OFDI.

South–South Co-operation   Malaysia has been promoting South–South co-operation actively especially during the Mahathir regime. As a member of the Non-Aligned Movement (NAM), the OIC, the Group of 15 and the Group of 77, Malaysia has advocated for South–South co-operation especially in the area of investment and technology. The close relationship between politics and business in Malaysia has also facilitated investments in developing countries as businesses reciprocate favors given by politicians (Jomo, 2002).

The key architect of South–South co-operation was the then Prime Minister, Dr. Mahathir Mohamad. The Malaysian South–South Association (MASSA) and the Malaysian South–South Corporation Berhad (MASSCORP) with a paid-up capital of US$14 million, demonstrates the importance of South–South co-operation to Malaysia. Some of Malaysia's active involvement during the Mahathir regime to promote south–south cooperation was as follows (8MP: 599–602):

- Group of 15 — The key activity promoted was the South Investment, Trade and Technology Data Exchange Centre (SITTDEC) which provided information services on trade, investment and technology transfer to member government, organizations and individuals;
- Asia–Africa Forum — Among the prominent activities organized were the First Africa–Asia Business Forum held in Kuala Lumpur in 1999 and the third Asia–Africa Forum in 2000; and

- Smart Partnership Dialogues — The Langkawi International Dialogue (LID) initiated by Malaysia based on the concept of collaboration on many levels between companies, public and private sectors and within public sectors has been held on an annual basis during the Mahathir regime.

ASEAN Free Trade Agreement The ASEAN Free Trade Area (AFTA) was established in January 1992 to eliminate tariff barriers among the member countries. The main objective is to integrate the ASEAN economies into a single production base and creating a regional market of 500 million people. Most of ASEAN is now a free trade area with the six major countries having reduced their tariff barriers for almost all products to no more than 5 percent. Furthermore, ASEAN is determined to reduce tariff levels to 0 percent by 2010 (ASEAN Secretariat). As AFTA is a preferential trade agreement, these privileges are only for companies located within ASEAN and where local content (materials used from ASEAN member countries) should be at least 40 percent.

The Framework Agreement on the ASEAN Investment Area (AIA) was then signed in 1998. The AIA aims to provide a more liberal and transparent investment environment by 1 January 2010. The AIA is part of the building block to contribute to the realization of ASEAN Vision 2020, which includes free flow of investments. These initiatives have promoted inter-ASEAN trade and investment with Malaysia being the second largest source of intra-ASEAN FDI.

World Trade Organization (WTO)   Malaysia acceded to the WTO in 1994. The Marrakesh Agreement made significant progress in three major areas (Mahani, 1994):

- Market liberalization, which could add approximately 1 percent of world real GDP and 10 percent to world trade upon full implementation of the Agreement;
- Strengthening of rules and institutional structures particularly the creation of the WTO which could decide on dispute and impairment of trade rules and principles; and
- Integration of new areas into the multilateral trading system such as agreement on services (GATS) and trade-related intellectual

property rights (TRIPs), trade-related investment measures (TRIMs), and the traditionally sensitive and contentious sectors (agriculture and textiles and clothing).

The three areas above had been both push and pull factors to Malaysian companies as they have forced the Malaysian government and corporations to comply with multilateral rules allowing foreign companies to penetrate Malaysian markets. At the same time, other members also had to comply with the multilateral rules allowing Malaysian companies to penetrate international markets.

Institutional Support   After the successful visit led by then Prime Minister Mahathir with the Malaysian business community to Chile, Brazil, and Argentina in 1991, two organizations were set-up to promote Malaysian OFDI — the MASSA and the MASSCORP. The idea of MASSA was conceived in response to concerns that Malaysia's export driven growth should not be solely dependent on the traditional markets of the United States, Japan, and the European Union. MASSA was a timely springboard for Malaysian companies to explore the relatively untapped potential of the South–South countries. The government has been supportive of the initiatives taken by MASSA and MASSCORP.[26]

The Malaysian Industrial Development Authority (MIDA), the Malaysian External Trade Development Corporation (MATRADE) and the Export-Import Bank of Malaysia Berhad (EXIM Bank) although focused on attracting FDI (MIDA) and developing overseas markets and exporting Malaysian products (MATRADE and EXIM Bank), have nevertheless supported Malaysia's OFDI through MIDA's Cross-border Investment Section, MATRADE's trade counselors located in 31 branch offices worldwide and the setting-up of funds under EXIM Bank for Bumiputera entrepreneurs to venture abroad (Tham, 2006, p. 10).

The government had also supported the setting-up of the South–South Information Gateway (SSIG),[27] an Internet portal that will

---

[26] Refer to the Annex for description of MASSA and MASSCORP.
[27] http://web5.bernama.com/ssig/about/index.php.

function as an exchange center and central depository for information, news and broadcast materials including the sharing of experience, knowledge, expertise, and skills.

4. Conclusion and Policy Implications

The main factors that have motivated Malaysian OFDI are similar to those that motivate FDI from developed countries. The selection of host locations by Malaysian companies is based on considerations such as production costs, supply chains, market size and access, investment incentives of host economies and access to resources. For Malaysia, location choice has also been motivated by additional factors such as brands and technology, strategic assets and decentralization of operations to diversify risks and improve returns.

Furthermore, Malaysia's historically liberal foreign exchange administrative rules, high domestic savings rates and strong economic growth that led to the rising wealth accumulation among domestic companies have also been key determinants for companies in Malaysia to invest abroad.

GLCs were the dominant players in the oil and gas and the telecommunications industries, while RCCs have been the main drivers for investment in the manufacturing, utilities, distributive trade, leisure, plantation, construction and banking and finance sector.

Malaysia's OFDI in general are sound business decisions and sustainable over a long period. The private sector has ventured into areas that they are competent in, having developed their capacity and capability domestically before venturing overseas. Nevertheless, there are also cases of Malaysian private OFDI suffering from wrong investment decisions. The heavy influence of the government in GLCs should be reduced over time to ensure OFDIs are more responsive to market conditions.

Malaysia is an open economy by any measure, with trade and FDI flows playing a pivotal role in the economy. Economic openness is a two-way street with both inflows and outflows. It is in this sense that OFDI represents an important cog in Malaysia's open economy. The emergence of Malaysia as a source of FDI for other countries, however, has serious macroeconomic implications for the Malaysian economy.

Understandably, much would depend on the macroeconomic circumstances. In the early 1990s, when Malaysia was running persistently large current account deficits, reverse investment was counterproductive. Usually, MNCs use their own foreign exchange earnings to make their overseas investments. In the Malaysian case, however, the companies investing abroad were not generating foreign exchange, but using foreign exchange generated by others. This would not have been a problem if there were sufficiently large current account surplus, which was not the case in the early 1990s.

Malaysian OFDI had worsened the country's balance of payments situation in the early 1990s. This was problematic as FDI inflows into the country were also drying up due to the massive diversion of foreign investment to China. To finance its balance of payments deficits, Malaysia had to resort to short-term capital inflows, which were volatile and footloose. Malaysia was sucked into the Asian financial crisis in July 1997 when foreign short-term capital fled from the country. The rest is history. Seen in this light, OFDI was one of the factors that had inadvertently contributed to the crisis. That said, one must hasten to add that this is not an argument against OFDI, but just that the timing was wrong.

The post-crisis situation is very different. Malaysia has been registering substantial current account surpluses, which has grown from 13.2 percent of GDP in 1998 to 16.7 percent of GDP in 2006. Malaysia's foreign exchange reserves have soared to US$87 billion, equivalent to 8 months of retained imports, more than 6 times short-term external debt. Malaysia now has far more reserves than it needs. It makes good sense to put surplus earnings to good use rather than to simply add to the ballooning reserves. Outward investment represents a good outlet.

What is more, investment opportunities at home are not all that bright. The fact that the country has been garnering Balance of Payment (BOP) surpluses year after year suggests that savings exceed investment. There is a glut of savings that need to find investment opportunities. As domestic investment opportunities have been lagging

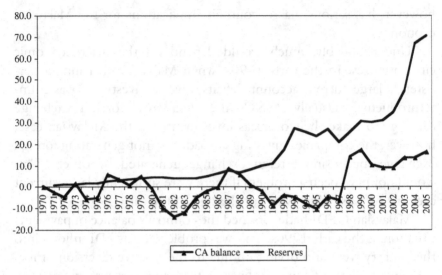

Figure 8:   Current account balance.

Source: Nambiar (2007).

behind savings, outward investments have become not only a better alternative but also a necessity.

Since trade and investment are inter-linked, OFDI appears to generate significant trade flows between the host and home countries. It is, therefore, of no surprise that Malaysia's major trading partners are also the major investment partners, either as sources of FDI inflows or as destinations for its own outward FDI.

Annex

G-15   The "G-15" is a selection of 15 GLCs held by the GLIC constituents of the Putrajaya Committee Group (PCG) and includes Maybank, Telekom Malaysia, Tenaga Nasional, Sime Darby, Commerce-Asset Holding, Golden Hope, MAS, Proton Holdings, Kumpulan Guthrie, Affin Holdings, UEM World, Boustead Holdings, BIMB Holdings, Malaysian Resources Corporation Berhad and Malaysian Building Society Berhad. The "G-15" accounts for about 65 percent of the market capitalization of listed GLCs.

GLC	Government Linked Companies (GLCs) are defined as companies that have a primary commercial objective and in which the Malaysian Government has a direct controlling stake. Controlling stake refers to the Government's ability (not just percentage ownership) to appoint Board of Directors members, senior management, make major decisions (e.g., contract awards, strategy, restructuring and financing, acquisitions and divestment etc.) for GLCs either directly or through GLICs. As of 26 July 2005, there were 57 GLCs with a total market capitalization of RM261 billion (approximately US$68.68 billion – US$1 = RM3.8 in 2005), 54 percent of Kuala Lumpur Composite Index (KLCI) and 36 percent of total Bursa Malaysia. www.pcg.gov.my/PDF/4.%20Section%20IV.pdf.
GLICs	GLICs are defined as Federal Government linked investment companies that allocate some or all of their investments to GLC investments. They are defined by the influence of the Federal Government in appointing/approving Board members and senior management, and having these individuals report directly to the Government, as well as in providing funds for operations and/or guaranteeing capital (and some income) placed by unit holders. This definition currently includes seven GLICs: Employee Provided Fund (EPF), Khazanah Nasional Bhd (Khazanah), Kumpulan Wang Amanah Pencen (KWAP), Lembaga Tabung Angkatan Tentera LTAT), Lembaga Tabung Haji (LTH), Menteri Kewangan Diperbadankan (Ministry of Finance Incorporated), and Permodalan Nasional Berhad (PNB)
Khazanah Nasional Berhad	Khazanah is the investment holding arm of the Government of Malaysia entrusted to hold and manage the commercial assets of the Government and to undertake strategic investments. Khazanah was incorporated under the Companies Act 1965 on 3 September 1993 as a public limited company. The Ministry of Finance owns the share capital of Khazanah, a body corporate incorporated pursuant to the Ministry of Finance (Incorporation) Act, 1957. Khazanah has an eight-member board comprising representatives from the public and private sectors. The Prime Minister of Malaysia is the Chairman of the Board. Khazanah has stakes in more than 50 companies with assets valued in excess of US$20 billion. Khazanah is also the state agency responsible for strategic cross-border investments. These companies are involved in various sectors such as power,

telecommunications, banking, automotive manufacture, airport management, infrastructure, property development, broadcasting, semiconductor, steel production, electronics, investment holding, research technology, and venture capital.

Some of the key listed companies in Khazanah's investment portfolio include Telekom Malaysia Berhad, Tenaga Nasional Berhad, CIMB Group, Proton Holdings Berhad, PLUS Expressway, UEM World Berhad, UEM Builders Berhad, PT Bank Lippo, and Time dotCom Berhad.

http://www.khazanah.com.my/.

PCG
The Putrajaya Committee on GLC High Performance (PCG) was formed in January 2005 to follow through and catalyze the GLC Transformation Programme. The Second Finance Minister chairs PCG, with participation from the heads of the GLICs, and representatives from the Ministry of Finance Incorporated and the Prime Minister's Office.

http://www.pcg.gov.my/index.asp.

PETRONAS
Petroliam Nasional Berhad (PETRONAS) was incorporated on 17th August 1974 under the Companies Act 1965. It is wholly owned by the Malaysian government and is vested with the entire ownership and control of the petroleum resources in Malaysia through an Act of Parliament — the Petroleum Development Act 1974. PETRONAS is a Non-Financial Public Enterprise and therefore does not report its financial standing. PETRONAS however has several of its subsidiaries listed on the Malaysian Stock Exchange (Bursa Malaysia) such as Petronas Gas Berhad and Malaysian International Shipping Corporation Berhad (MISC).

http://www.petronas.com.my/.

RCCs
Resident Controlled Companies are private companies in which residents have equity stake of more than 50 percent

NRCCs
Non Resident Controlled Companies are private companies in which total non-resident holding is more than 50 percent.

MASSCORP
The Malaysian South–South Corporation Berhad is a public limited company incorporated in 1992. MASSCORP is a consortium of 86 Malaysian shareholders who are corporate leaders in their respective fields of business. MASSCORP's mission is to promote bilateral trade and investment between Malaysia and South–South countries. MASSCORP also acts as a vehicle for trade promotions, export, investments and

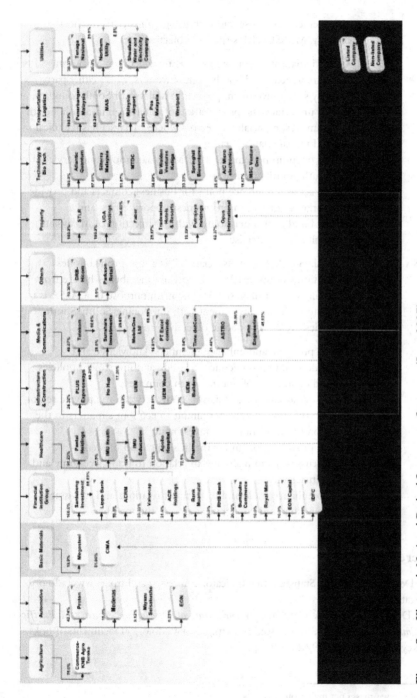

Figure 9: Khazanah Nasional Berhad Investment Structure (June 2007).

Source: Khazanah Nasional (www.khazanah.com.my).

management expertise and technology transfer to the host country. MASSCORP's specific objectives are

- To initiate and promote joint ventures between Malaysian entrepreneurs and South–South investors, where either party may set-up investment projects in Malaysia or South countries;
- To undertake the privatization of enterprises in South–South countries, especially in sectors where Malaysia has technical and managerial expertise;
- To open up new markets for Malaysian goods and services to South–South countries;
- To act as a reference point for business contacts and provide market information on business opportunities; and
- To build a stronger South with the injection of Malaysian capital and expertise.

MASSA　　Malaysia South–South Association[28] is a non-profit business association, set up in 1992, comprising members who are from the Malaysian business sector. The main purpose of MASSA is to promote trade and investment with developing South–South countries. MASSA's specific objectives are:

- To promote and enhance members' knowledge and understanding on economic, trade and investment policies and conditions of South–South countries;
- To act as an informal liaison body between the private sector and the government pertaining to economic matters in the promotion of trade and investment;
- To provide a forum for the dissemination of ideas, discussions and dialogues in relation to trade, economy and culture; and
- To enhance trade and investment relations and to foster friendship and cooperation among the members.

References

Asian Development Bank. Statistics, Key Indicators. Accessed at: http://www.adb.org/Statistics/ki.asp.

Asian Development Bank (1999). *Key Indicators of Developing Asian and Pacific Countries 1999*, Vol. 30. Accessed at: http://www.adb.org/Documents/Books/Key_Indicators/1999/default.asp.

---

[28] http://www.massa.net.my/about.htm.

Asian Development Bank (ADB) (2004). Outlook 2004. Accessed at: http://www.adb.org/Documents/books/ADO/2004/default.asp.

Asian Development Bank (2006). Key indicators 2006: Measuring policy effectiveness in health and education. Accessed at: http://www.adb.org/Documents/Books/Key_Indicators/2006/default.asp

Aykut, D and D Ratha, (2004). South–South FDI flows: How big are they? *Transnational Corporations*, 13(1), 149–177.

Bank Negara Malaysia (2005). Liberalisation of foreign exchange rules.

Bank Negara Malaysia (2006). *Quarterly Bulletin*, Third Quarter 2006. Accessed at: http://www.bnm.gov.my/files/publication/qb/2006/Q3/p6.pdf.

Battat, J and D Aykut (2005). *Southern Multinationals: A Growing Phenomenon.* mimeo (October 2005).

Boston Consulting Group (2006). *The New Global Challengers: How 100 Companies from Rapidly Developing Economies are Changing the World.* Boston Consulting Group.

Dervis, K (2005). Southern multinationals: A rising force in the world economy. *Cooperation South*, 72–80.

Economic Planning Unit (2006). Ninth Malaysia Plan 2006–2010. Economic Planning Unit, Prime Minister's Department, Putrajaya.

ESCAP/UNCTAD Joint Unit on Transnational Companies (1997). *Competitive Business Strategies of Asian Transnational Corporations.* Monograph No. 7, ST/ESCAP/1785 United Nations, New York.

Gammeltoft, P (2006). *Multinationals from the South: Outward FDI from the BRICs Countries.* Mimeo (September).

Giroud A and H Mirza (2006). Factors determining supply linkages between transnational corporations and local suppliers in ASEAN, *Transnational Corporations*, 15(3), 1–32.

Gomez, ET and KS Jomo (1999). *Malaysia's Political Economy: Politics, Patronage and Profits.* UK: Cambridge University Press.

Hiratsuka, D (2006). Outward FDI from ASEAN and intraregional FDI in ASEAN: Trends and drivers. Discussion Paper No. 77. Institute of Developing Economies, Japan.

Ibrahim, MH (2006). Stock prices and bank loan dynamics in a developing country: The case of Malaysia. *Journal of Applied Economics*, IX(001), 71–89.

Institute of Developing Economies, Japan and the Socio — Economic Research Institute, Malaysia (2004). *Trade, Investment & Economic Cooperation between China and Southeast Asia: The Case of Malaysia.* SERI, Penang.

Jomo, KS (ed) (2002). Ugly Malaysians? South–South Investments Abused. Durban, South Africa: Institute for Black Research.

Kumar, N (2006). Emerging multinationals: Trends, patterns and determinants of outward investment by India enterprises, RIS-DP# 117. India.

Lee, HA (2002). Industrial development and equity distribution in Malaysian manufacturing: Institutional perspectives. Paper No. 25, Centre on Regulation and Competition, University of Manchester. United Kingdom.

Malaysia South–South Association (2006). *MASSA News 2006*, 4th Quarter News Accessed at: www.massa.net.my/news/y6_q4_a6.htm.

Malaysia South–South Association (2005). *MASSA News 2005*, 2nd Quarter News Accessed at: www.massa.net.my/y5_q2.a1.htm.

Martin, S (2006). European plantation firms and Malaysia's new economic policy since 1970. Paper presented at the IEHA Congress, Session 94. Helsinki, Finland

Mat Zin, R (1999). Malaysian reverse investments: Trends and strategies. *Asia Pacific Journal of Management* 16, 3.

Ministry of International Trade and Industry, Malaysia (2006a). *Third Industrial Master Plan 2006–2010*. MITI.

Ministry of International Trade and Industry, Malaysia (2006b). *Industry, Investment, Trade and Productivity Performance, Fourth Quarter*, MITI.

Pradhan, JP, (2005). Outward Foreign Direct Investment from India: Recent Trends and Patterns. Working paper No. 153, Gujarat Institute of Development Research.

PriceWaterhouseCoopers (2005). Special feature: Malaysia goes abroad, Asia Pacific M&A bulletin, mid year 2005. PWC Hong Kong. Accessed at: www.pwchk.com/home/webmedia/1122530543139/m&abulletin_ap_jun2005_my_sp.pdf.

Sauvant, KP (2005). New sources of FDI: The BRICs. *The Journal of World Investment and Trade*, 6(5), 639–709.

Setapa, A (2004). Interfacing foreign capital with reverse investment. MIERScan, The Star, 22 Nov 2004. Accessed at: www.mier.org.my/mierscan/archives/pdf/drazmi22_11_2004.pdf.

Tham, SY (2005). Japan's response to globalization: Learning from Japanese direct investment. *Asia Pacific Trade and Investment Review*, 1(2).

Tham SY (2006). Outward foreign direct investment from Malaysia: Trends, patterns and policy issues. Paper presented at the ASEAN-UNCTAD seminar, "Key Issues of FDI: Outward FDI from Asia." Chiang Mai, 10 April 2006.

The World Bank Group (2005). Malaysia at a glance. World Bank. Accessed at: www.devdata.worldbank.org/AAG/mys_aag.pdf.

United Nations (2006). *World Investment Report 2006*, United Nations: New York and Geneva.

UNCTAD Key Data from WIR Annex Tables. Accessed at: http://www.unctad.org/Templates/Page.asp?intItemID=3277&lang=1.

UNCTAD (2005a). Internationalization of developing country enterprise through outward foreign direct investment, expert meeting on enhancing the productive capacity of developing country firms through internationalization, Geneva. TD/B/COM.3/EM.26, 5–7 December 2005.

UNCTAD (2005b). Policy issues related to investment and development: Emerging FDI from developing countries. Commission on investment, technology and related financial flows. 9th session. Geneva. TD/B/COM.2/64, 7–11 March 2005.

Chapter 10

Outward FDI Surge in the Midst of Weak Inward Investments: The Indonesian Experience*

Reza Y. Siregar and Anton H. Gunawan

1. Introduction

Addressing high rates of unemployment and poverty have been listed among the top priorities of the government of Indonesia. Given the new labor entrants into the economy annually, the government of Susilo Bambang Yudhoyono must achieve an annual GDP growth rate of between 6 percent and 7 percent over the next few years. In 2005 and 2006, the Indonesian economy grew only by 5.7 percent and 5.5 percent, respectively, driven largely by real consumption growth. However, to accelerate GDP growth, a strong surge in investment is vitally needed. Yet, despite the return of some stability and improvements in the general macroeconomic indicators[1] in the last couple of years, direct investment remained very low and continued to contribute very little to the overall economic growth of the country.

The flow of foreign direct investment (FDI) in the US$ 276 billion economy was less than US$ 5.5 billion in 2005 — around 2 percent of GDP, and this followed a six-year period in which foreigners sold off their Indonesian assets to the tune of almost of US$ 9 billion. During the rapid growth period of 1975–1996, the total growth of public and private investment contributed to around 36 percent of

* Comments by Chetan Ghate at the ICRIER workshop are appreciated. The usual disclaimer applies.
[1] Such as inflation, nominal exchange rate, key interest rates, balance of payment, and GDP growth rate.

the annual GDP growth rates in Indonesia. In 2002–2003, the contribution of investment to GDP growth was merely 1 percent (Van der Eng, 2004).

Compounding further the problem of weak inward direct investment, the country has at the same time experienced stronger outflows of direct investment. In 2004 and 2005, the flows of outward direct investment, reported by the World Investment Report (UNCTAD, 2006), averaged around 1.2 percent of the country's GDP.

While a number of studies have examined determinants of inward direct investment to Indonesia, we can only find one study that has looked at the forces behind outward investment from Indonesia (Lecraw, 1993). The objective of this chapter is to fill this gap by identifying a few of the possible push and pull factors behind the recent surge of the outward direct investment from the most populous country in South–East Asia. Various aspects of the investment climate in the domestic economy and the role of restructured domestic corporate sectors will be examined as domestic push factors in Sections 2–4. In Section 5, we look at the role of internalization strategy of the ethnic Chinese business firms in Indonesia. Section 6 offers some concluding remarks.

2. Basic Features and Stylized Facts

Inward direct investment has experienced boom and bust cycles in the past decade, starting with the rapid growth in mid-1990s to 1997, followed by a dramatic fall in 1999–2002, and a strong recovery starting 2003. In contrast, the stock of outward investment from Indonesia remained steady for most part of the last decade (Figure 1). The strong rush of outward direct investment only began in 2004, and by the end of 2005 the stock of outward investment from Indonesia was reported to be close to 90 percent higher than its level in 2003, and more than double its level in 1997. In sharp contrast, the stock of inward investment to Indonesia in 2005 was still less than 70 percent of its peak level in 1996 (Table 1).

The World Investment Report 2006 also listed Indonesia among the top 15 developing and transition economies in terms of the stocks

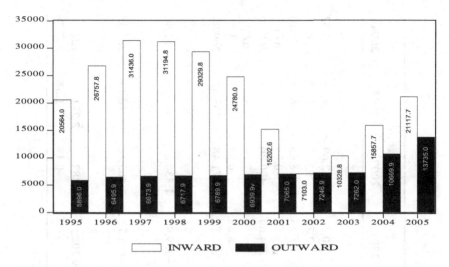

Figure 1: Stock of inward and outward direct investment (in millions of US dollar). *Source*: The United Nations Database.

of outward FDI in 2005. It was the first time that Indonesia was ranked in the top 15 during the past 25 years. Only seven other Asian economies were ranked higher than Indonesia as the sources of direct investment.[2] It is important to note, however, that in comparison to those high ranked economies, the outward investment from Indonesia is relatively small. For instance, Indonesia's outward investment in 2005 was only 12 percent and 3 percent of the investments from Singapore and Hong Kong, respectively.

Given its geographical location, attractive investment climate and dynamic economic growth rates, Singapore remains by far the favorite destination of Indonesian outward investment to ASEAN. On average, Singapore absorbed about US$300 million inflow of direct investment from Indonesia from 2001 to 2004, a relatively lower amount compared to the reported average flow from 1995 to 1997, but still close to 90 percent of total flows of outward direct investment from Indonesia to ASEAN economies. Malaysia also received a

---

[2] Those seven economies are Hong Kong, China, Singapore, Taiwan Province of China, People Republic of China, Malaysia, and Korea.

Table 1: The flows of outward and inward direct investment.

Country	Average 1995–1997	Average 1998–1999	2000	2001	2002	2003	2004
Outflows from Indonesia to Selected ASEAN (in millions of US$)							
Brunei	11.34	5.74	2.11	0.2	2.69	4.24	0.62
Malaysia	59.35	21.06	26.40	-2.75	62	2.73	4.43
Myanmar	2.3	2.9	7.51	3.48	3.43	5.63	2.10
Philippines	2.6	13.59	2.79	n/a	-0.01	0.01	n/a
Singapore	453.72	336.60	59.50	354.60	400.80	219.20	260.90
Thailand	9.6	1.95	4.26	n/a	2	4	n/a
Vietnam	13.67	2.51	7	5.06	0.57	n/a	1
Total *Outflows* to ASEAN (1)	552.64	384.71	109.57	361.72	471.48	235.81	269.05
Total Inflows from ASEAN (2) (in millions of US$)							
	358.23	-233.10	-232.55	-239.98	1,336.62	383.96	31.66
Total Net Inflows with ASEAN (2-1) (in millions of US$)							
	-194.41	-617.81	-342.12	-601.7	865.14	148.15	-237.39
Total Net Inflows with the World (in millions of US$ and in % of GDP)							
in millions of US$	4,374	-1,111	-4,700	-9,702	-8,282	3,211	2,121
% of GDP	11.6%	17.5%	12.3%	5.0%	-0.1%	1.3%	2.7%

Source: The ASEAN Secretariat Database and the United Nations Database.

significant share of direct investment from Indonesia during the pre-1997 crisis, but the size of flow declined continuously since 2000 (with the exception of 2002).

For outward direct investment from Indonesia to the rest of Asia, very limited official data or information was available when this study was conducted.[3] Based on the data of the foreign direct investment inflow to China, Hattari and Rajan (Chapter 3) found that the annual average flow of outward direct investment from Indonesia to China was around US$130 million between 2001 and 2005 or about 10 percent higher than the average from the previous 4 years period. Official data indicated that the total foreign direct investment to India from Indonesia up until 2004 was only about US$30 million (Kanwar, 2005). There have, however, been a number of official commitments of much-larger scale of investment projects by Indonesian firms in India after 2004.

Investments by Indonesian firms abroad have targeted a wide array of industries (Table 2). In Singapore, a fair share of the investments targeted the service industries, ranging from financial and insurance services to storage and transport facilities. A number of investment projects have also targeted the labor intensive industries, such as textile, garment and footwear in countries such as Cambodia, Vietnam, and China. The boom in the property sector in Asia has also attracted investment commitments from the Indonesian firms, including mega projects in various cities in India and China.

Given its size and importance in the local economy, the Indonesian ethnic-Chinese conglomerates have been the main drivers of the outward looking investment strategy (elaborated upon later). Together with the Ciputra Group, the Salim Group for instance has signed a memorandum of understanding in August 2006 to invest in various sectors in West Bengal in India, including major infrastructure projects (such as flyovers, bridges, port), townships, medical centers, and economic zones. The same joint-venture is involved in the development

---

[3] This problem is not particular to the case of Indonesia. Hattari and Rajan in Chapter 3 found data on the outflows of direct investment from source economies are incomplete for many countries in Asia.

Table 2: Selected destinations and targeted sectors of outward investment from Indonesia.

Country of Destination	Targeted Industries/Sectors
India	Cement; Real Estate; Infrastructure; Health-Care Facilities; Pulp and Paper.
Cambodia	Textile
China	Infrastructure; Textile; Real Estate; Agriculture & Food; Pulp & Paper; Consumer Products; Chemical
Malaysia	Oil; Real Estate; Pulp & Paper.
Singapore	Finance & Insurance; Health-Care Provider; Manufacturing; Oil Industry; Storage & Transport; Food Industry; Resort and Industrial Development (& Real Estate)
Sri Lanka	Textile
Thailand	Textile
Vietnam	Farming Equipment; Hotel; Mining; Real Estate; Textile

Source: The Business Times Singapore (11 September, 2006); AsiaNews.it (12 December, 2005); UBS Investment Research; various official web-sites of the relevant economies.

of a township project in Beijing, China. Another major Indonesian ethnic-Chinese conglomerate, the Sinar Mas Group, has expanded its business operations to China (Pulp and Paper; Agriculture and Food); Malaysia (Real Estate and Pulp & Paper); and to India (Pulp & Paper).

3. Empirics

To further understand factors contributing to the recent rise of outward direct investment from Indonesia, we conduct a number of panel regressions in this section. The first specification evaluates the roles of risk factors, namely economic risk, financial risk, and investment profile in explaining the flows of outward direct investment $\Delta(\text{OutFDI}_t)$ from the early 1990s to 2004. The second model looks at the balance sheet positions of the domestic corporate sector, and examines their roles in explaining the recent surge of outward investment. Finally, the full model will be tested to ensure the robustness of the results from the first two specifications.

3.1. *First Specification: The Risk Factors*

A number of key indicators of investment climate have consistently been identified by previous studies as determinants of investment in an economy.[4] Those factors can generally be grouped into three categories, viz.: (1) economic risk rating; (2) financial risk rating; and (3) investment profile.[5] Each rating is normalized to range from 100 (highest risk) to 0 (lowest risk).

The economic risk rating (ERR) evaluates the strength and weakness of the overall macroeconomics positions of an economy. Five factors influence economic risk rating, namely GDP per capita, real annual GDP growth, annual inflation rate, budget balance as a percentage of GDP, and current account balance as a percentage of GDP.[7]

The financial risk rating (FRR) examines the country's ability to finance its official, commercial, and trade debt obligations. To assess the financial risk of a country, a few key indicators are observed in the rating, such as foreign debt as a percentage of GDP, foreign debt service as a percentage of exports of goods and services (XGS), current account as a percentage of XGS, net liquidity (measured as months of import cover), and exchange rate stability.[7] As for the economic risk rating, each component is assigned its own weight, with the maximum weight given to current account factors, and the least weight for the net liquidity.

The third rating is the investment profile (IP). This rating assesses factors affecting the risk to investment in a country that are not covered by other ratings. Three key factors are assessed for the investment

---

[4] Refer to Bende–Nabende and Slater (2003), Ghura and Goodwin (2000), and Serven (2002).

[5] We adopted these three risk ratings from the International Country Risk Guide (ICRG) of the PRS group.

[6] Each factor is assigned a different weight. The current account has the highest maximum weight, while the GDP per head is given the lowest maximum weight.

[7] Estimated annual net liquidity expressed as months of cover and calculated as the official reserves of the individual countries, including their official gold reserves calculated at current free market prices, but excluding the use of IMF credits and the foreign liabilities of the monetary authorities (the International Country Risk Guide of the PRS group, http://www.countrydata.com).

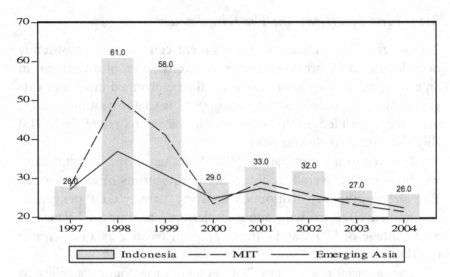

Figure 2:   Economic risk rating (ERR)

Source: The International Country Risk Guide of the PRS Group. Rating: 0 (lowest risk) — 100 (highest risk). MIT covers Malaysia, Indonesia, and Thailand; Emerging Asia includes the MIT, Philippines, Singapore, Korea, India, and Hong Kong.

profile, namely contract viability and the possibility of expropriation, profits repatriation, and payment delays.

Based on these three ratings, the MIT economies (Malaysia, Indonesia and Thailand) were found to be the countries most severely affected by the crisis in 1997 (Figure 2–4), with investment climates gravely deteriorated. The financial crisis of 1997 had transformed this group of countries, which had the most conducive investment climate in the South–East Asian region since mid-1980s, into the worst ones for at least two years after the crisis period (1998–1999).

Taking a closer look at the sub-components of the ERR, the sharp fall in the real GDP growth rates clearly was the major factor in increasing the level of investment risk. The ERR for the MIT economies was as low as 21.4 (out of 100 points) in 1996, and increased to its worst level in two decades at around 50.8 in 1998. For Indonesia, the problems in the macroeconomics indicators were more widely spread. The deteriorations of the ERR in 1998–1999 for Indonesia were the results of drastic worsening in all five components of the ERR, namely

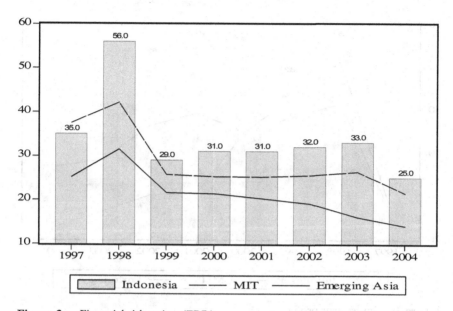

Figure 3: Financial risk rating (FRR).

Source: The International Country Risk Guide of the PRS Group. Rating: 0 (lowest risk) — 100 (highest risk). MIT covers Malaysia, Indonesia, and Thailand; Emerging Asia includes the MIT, Philippines, Singapore, Korea, India, and Hong Kong.

GDP growth rates, current account balance, budget, inflation, and GDP per capita level.[8]

In a similar manner as the ERR, the financial risk level (FRR) for the same group of Asian economies peaked in 1998. From the measures of countries' ability to finance the debt/obligation, the MIT countries shared a set of common problems. First, the rise in the exchange rate volatility was clearly a factor during the early stages of the 1997 financial crisis. Second, all three countries faced a severe decline in the international liquidity and a rapid accumulation of foreign debt. Indeed, debt service was a particularly important issue in Indonesia.

Since 2000, the three ratings have consistently indicated improvements in the overall investment climate and macroeconomics conditions in Indonesia. However, with the exception of the ERR, both the

---

[8] For the sake of brevity we do not report the breakdown of the three ratings. The sub-components are available upon request.

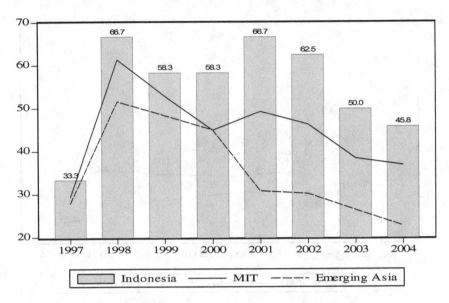

Figure 4:   Investment profile.

Source: The International Country Risk Guide of the PRS Group. Rating: 0 (lowest risk) — 100 (highest risk). MIT covers Malaysia, Indonesia, and Thailand; Emerging Asia includes the MIT, Philippines, Singapore, Korea, India, and Hong Kong.

financial risk rating and the investment profile rating in 2004/2005 were still relatively higher than the rates reported only a few years before the outbreak of the 1997 financial crises. Furthermore, a review of the three indicators across key major Asian economies shows that the investment environment in Indonesia remained among the most risky.

To confirm the contribution of investment climate in explaining the outflow of direct investment from Indonesia, we conducted an ordinary least squares autoregressive distributed lags (ARDL) panel regression for the case of the MIT economies during the period from 1990 to 2004.[9] We adopted a general to specific approach of Henry (1976)

---

[9] Data limitations prevent us from exclusively conducting a time-series test for Indonesia. The fixed-effect variable included is the individual country dummy. We tested both the least square random-effect and the fixed-effect models, and found the results to be in general consistent. However the test results for the random-effect testing are in general more robust, hence we opt to report the results in Table 3. The results for the fixed-effect testing can be made available upon request.

to derive the final test results. As shown in Equation (1), the lags of the changes in the investment climate variables are included to allow more time for the impact of the decline (or improvement) in those indicator on the outflows of the direct investment.[10]

$$
\Delta \log(\text{OutFDI}_{it}) = \alpha + \lambda \Delta \log(\text{OutFDI}_{i(t-1)})
$$
$$
+ \sum_{k=0}^{2} \beta_{t-k} \Delta \log(\text{ERR}_{i(t-k)})
$$
$$
+ \sum_{k=0}^{2} \delta_{t-k} \Delta \log(\text{FRR}_{i(t-k)})
$$
$$
+ \sum_{k=0}^{2} \gamma_{t-k} \Delta \log(\text{IP}_{i(t-k)}) + \varepsilon_{it} \qquad (1)
$$

where: $\Delta(\text{OutFDI}_{it})$ is the change of the outward direct investment from each of the MIT economies. $\Delta\log(\text{ERR}_{i(t-k)})$, $\Delta\log(\text{FRR}_{i(t-k)})$ and $\Delta\log(\text{IP}_{it-k})$ capture the rise and fall in the economic risk, the financial risk, and the investment profile indicators, respectively. All variables are in the log-forms, and hence the coefficient estimates (β, δ, γ) are the elasticities and (ε) is the independently distributed error term.[11]

Earlier studies, including Bende–Nabende and Slater (2003). Ghura and Goodwin (2000) and Serven (2002) have investigated a wide range of determinants of investment inflows. Based on their findings, we would expect an improvement in the investment profile and financial risk indicators should attract more investment locally, hence less outward investment — $\sum_{k=0}^{2}\delta_{t-k}$ and $\sum_{k=0}^{2}\gamma_{t-k}$ are expected to be positive. The return of a more conducive economic environment (or decline in economic risk), on one hand, should generate

---

[10] Given the limited degree of freedom, we only included up to two years lag for the initial general regression.

[11] All of these variables are found to be I(0) in the first differences. We tested for panel cointegration, but we did not find any cointegration relationship between the independent and the explanatory variables.

more investment for the domestic economy. However at the same time, improved confidence in the economy as a whole should also boost more confidence for the local corporate sectors to chase better returns abroad. Thus, $\sum_{k=0}^{2} \beta_{t-k}$ could either be positive or negative. We also include the adjustment variable, $\Delta\log(\text{OutFDI}_{i(t-1)})$, to capture the possibility that the level of outward direct investment at time (t) is going to be influenced by the past year level (t–1).

Consistent with the general findings of early studies, uncertainties regarding the investment climate were partly responsible for the outflows of direct investment from the MIT economies — with the R-square of around 0.41 (Table 3). Changes in the investment profile (IP) have the most immediate and significant impact on the outward investment, while the financial risk (FRR) had the least impact and took about two years to have some bearings on the outward investment of these economies. Interestingly, the test results also suggest that an improvement in the overall economic risk of these economies would actually lead to more capital outflows.

Table 3: Estimated coefficients.

Variable	Risk model	Balance sheet model	Full Model
Constant	0.121 (2.706***)	0.062 (2.131**)	0.079 (4.438***)
$(\Delta\text{OutFDI})_{t-1}$	0.248 (2.538***)		
$(\Delta\text{ERR})_t$	−0.375 (−2.327***)		
$(\Delta\text{FRR})_t$			−0.201 (−3.955***)
$(\Delta\text{FRR})_{t-2}$	0.278 (2.118***)		
$(\Delta\text{IP})_t$	0.567 (3.945***)		0.248 (3.381***)
$(\Delta\text{leverage})_t$		−0.912 (−2.716***)	
$(\Delta\text{leverage})_{t-1}$			−0.008 (−1.882*)
$(\Delta\text{leverage})_{t-2}$		−0.764 (−2.352***)	−0.011 (−3.188**)
$(\Delta\text{liquidity})_t$		0.176 (2.423***)	0.168 (4.029***)
$(\Delta\text{liquidity})_{t-1}$		0.109 (1.829*)	
Adjusted R-square	0.41	0.42	0.78
Durbin–Watson statistics	2.326	2.355	2.441
Prob (F-stat)	0.011	0.015	0.000

Note: *** significant at 1%; ** significant at 5%; and *significant at 10%.

3.2. Specification 2: The Balance Sheet

Another potential driver of the outward direct investment is the balance sheet position of the domestic firms. Weak corporate sectors had largely been blamed for the severity of the East Asian financial crisis in late 1990s. The restructuring of both corporate assets and liabilities have, therefore, been a priority for the most severely crisis-effected economies in Asia, including in Indonesia. Has the corporate restructuring process been successful in the crisis-affected economies? Three common measures of corporate sector vulnerability are considered in our study: (1) leverage rate to gauge solvency; (2) liquidity; and (3) profitability. Leverage is measured as the ratio of total liabilities to total assets. Interest coverage ratio captures the liquidity position. We use the Return to Equity (ROE) as a measure of profitability. Looking at these three indicators, the outcomes of the post-1997 balance sheet restructuring of the corporate sectors in key crisis-effected economies of the ASEAN-4 (Indonesia, Malaysia, Philippines, and Thailand) plus Korea have in general been mixed (Table 4).[12]

The devaluation of the local currencies in 1997 led to a spike in insolvency rates among the corporate sectors of the ASEAN-4 plus Korea and Indonesia. The firms in this region continued to be highly leveraged in recent years, even compared to the position of the corporate sectors in Emerging Asia in general. As experienced by other corporate sectors in the region, the corporate sector in Indonesia managed to reduce their leverage, albeit at a very modest rate. From 2002 to 2003, the rate increased again, but still lower than the pre-1997 levels.

The most encouraging trend has been with the ROE indicator. The corporate sectors of the crisis-affected economies have, in general, been enjoying strong annual profit since early 2000s, at rates higher than the average for the rest of the corporate sectors in emerging Asian economies. Based on the ROE ratios, the Indonesian firms were relatively more profitable than their counterparts in the region.

---

[12] Indicators of corporate vulnerabilities are adopted from the Corporate Vulnerability Utility (CVU) Database system of the International Monetary Fund. For cross-country comparisons, we apply market capitalization-weighted averages for all of the CVU indices. The CVU database only includes China, India, Indonesia, Korea, Malaysia, Philippines, Sri Lanka, Taiwan, and Thailand in the Emerging Asia group of economies.

Table 4:   Corporate sector vulnerability.

Period	Emerging Asia	ASEAN-4 & Korea	Indonesia
Leverage: (Ratio of total liabilities to total assets (in %))			
Average 1994–1996	44.46	50.65	45.91
Average 1997–1998	45.55	58.57	59.82
2001	43.62	52.50	59.86
2002	44.19	51.42	50.20
2003	44.39	49.74	49.59
2004	44.72	49.25	51.23
Profit (Return on equity (in %))			
Average 1994–1996	16.62	16.30	21.74
Average 1997–1998	13.42	8.34	4.26
2001	13.40	11.51	25.56
2002	15.04	16.57	40.23
2003	16.85	18.43	25.83
2004	20.94	22.61	28.17
Liquidity: (Interest coverage ratio (in %))			
Average 1994–1996	20.51	20.28	12.50
Average 1997–1998	19.79	13.35	16.84
2001	28.20	11.54	8.97
2002	27.56	17.57	7.88
2003	42.80	18.96	9.48
2004	37.03	26.08	13.15

Source: The corporate vulnerability utility database system of the International Monetary Fund.

The Interest Coverage Ratio (ICR) index confirmed a substantial improvement in the liquidity position of the firms. More importantly, the strong growth of the ICR rates of the corporate sectors in emerging markets in Asia during early to mid-2000s suggest that the region has indeed been facing excess liquidity and contributing to the global imbalances. In contrast to their counterparts in ASEAN and Korea, there had been more moderate improvement in the liquidity position of the corporate sector in Indonesia. It was only in 2004 that the firms in Indonesia were more liquid than they were during the pre-crisis.

The relevant set of questions we are interested in here is

(1) *Has the improvement in the overall balance sheet of the corporate sectors contributed to the rise in the outflow of direct investment, including from Indonesia?*
(2) *Has the return of strong profits and liquidity since the early 2000s contributed to a strong surge of outflows in recent years?*

To address these questions, an ordinary least squares ARDL panel regression is conducted for the case of the MIT economies (Malaysia, Indonesia, and Thailand) on the following equation.[13]

$$\Delta \log(\text{OutFDI}_{it}) = \alpha + \lambda \Delta \log(\text{OutFDI}_{i(t-1)})$$

$$+ \sum_{k=0}^{2} \beta_{t-k} \Delta \log(\text{Leverage}_{i(t-k)})$$

$$+ \sum_{k=0}^{2} \delta_{t-k} \Delta \log(\text{profit}_{i(t-k)})$$

$$+ \sum_{k=0}^{2} \gamma_{t-k} \Delta \log(\text{liquidity}_{i(t-k)}) + \varepsilon_{it} \qquad (2)$$

where: $\Delta\log(\text{OutFDI}_{it})$ is the change of the outward direct investment from each of the MIT economies. $\Delta\log(\text{leverage}_{(t-k)})$, $\Delta\log(\text{profit}_{i(t-k)})$ and $\Delta\log(\text{liquidity}_{(t-k)})$ capture the rise and fall in the leverage, the profitability and the liquidity positions, respectively.[14] All variables are in the log-forms, and hence the coefficient estimates (β, δ, γ) are

---

[13] As in the case of investment climate, data limitation prevents us from exclusively conducting a time-series test for Indonesia. The fixed-effect variable included is the individual country dummy. As for Equation (1), both the least square random-effect and the fixed-effect testing were carried out for Equation (2), and found the results to be in general consistent. Similar to the regression results on Equation (1), the test results for the random-effect testing are in general more robust, hence we opt to report the results in Table 3.

[14] All variables are $I(0)$ at the first difference. Quality data (with a sufficiently large number of firms captured by the survey) on the balance sheet for the countries included in the testing are only available since 1997 and 1998. Hence given the short period of observation, panel cointegration testing was not conducted.

the elasticities. The lags of the change in the balance sheet variables are included to allow more time for the impact of the deterioration (or improvement) in the corporate sector balance sheet on the outflows of the direct investment to be realized.[15] As with the previous regression, the general to specific approach of Henry (1976) is adopted to derive the final test results.

The improvements in the profitability and liquidity positions of the corporate sector are expected to induce more investment by the firms. Similarly, a lower leverage ratio, which implies lower debt burden, should free up more capital to be invested. Some of these investments may either be carried out abroad or locally. Thus, estimated coefficients (δ)and (γ)are expected to be positive, while (β) is expected to be negative, if the improvement in the balance sheet leads to more investment abroad. As for Equation (1), we include the adjustment variable, $\Delta\log(\text{OutFDI}_{i(t-1)})$, to capture the possibility that the level of outward direct investment at time (t) is going to be influenced by the past year level (t-1).

The test results suggest that the overall improvement in the balance sheet of the corporate sector has indeed partly been responsible for the rise of outward investment from these three economies (Table 3).[16] The adjusted R-square is over 40 percent. In particular, the decline in the leverage position and the rise in the liquidity appear to be significant determinant factors. The regression results suggest that the strong liquidity position, especially in 2004, and the relatively lower debt burden since 2002 contributed to the swelling of outward investment in 2004 and 2005 from Indonesia. Combining all test results for the risk and the balance sheet regressions with the stylized facts, one can also further argue that despite the investment opportunities in Indonesia, the poor investment climate and other less-conducive economic conditions discouraged the relatively liquid domestic firms from investing in the local economy.

---

[15] Given the limited degrees of freedom, we only included up to two years lag for the initial general regression.

[16] The role of $\Delta\log(\text{OutFDI}_{i(t-1)})$ is not found to be strongly significant for this regression.

3.3. *Full Model*

To ensure the robustness of our previous results we proceeded to test the full empirical model which incorporated both the risk factors and the balance sheet factors:

$$\Delta \log(\text{OutFDI}_{it}) = \alpha + \lambda\Delta \log(\text{OutFDI}_{i(t-1)})$$

$$+ \sum_{k=0}^{2} \beta_{t-k}\Delta \log(\text{ERR}_{i(t-k)})$$

$$+ \sum_{k=0}^{2} \delta_{t-k}\Delta \log(\text{FRR}_{i(t-k)})$$

$$+ \sum_{k=0}^{2} \gamma_{t-k}\Delta \log(\text{IP}_{i(t-k)})$$

$$+ \sum_{k=0}^{2} \vartheta_{t-k}\Delta \log(\text{Leverage}_{i(t-k)})$$

$$+ \sum_{k=0}^{2} \kappa_{t-k}\Delta \log(\text{profit}_{i(t-k)})$$

$$+ \sum_{k=0}^{2} \varpi_{t-k}\Delta \log(\text{profit}_{i(t-k)}) + \mu_{it} \qquad (3)$$

All variables have been described earlier, and are expected to have the similar signs for their coefficient estimates as discussed for Equations (1) and (2). The following key results are worth highlighting (Table 3):

(a) Consistent with the results from the Balance Sheet specification, we find the leverage and liquidity factors to be significant factors, but not the profit variable.

(b) Among the risk factors, we find investment profile ($\Delta(\text{IP}_{it})$) to be the most significant. The financial risk variable is also significant, but the coefficient sign seems to contradict our initial expectation.

(c) The adjusted R-square suggests that the movements of the right-hand side variables explained close to 80 percent of the flows of outward direct investment in this set of economies during the observed period.

Based on the empirical results from the three regressions, we can conclude that a combination of the risk factors and the balance sheet position have been significant determinants of OFDI from Indonesia.[17] The next section will identify more specifically a number of domestic and external factors that may have contributed to investment risk in Indonesia.

4. Sources of Investment Risks in Indonesia

4.1. *Corruption Abuses*

Considerable attention has been placed on the increasing cost of corruption and on its influence on both inward and outward direct investment of the country (for instance, see Hattari and Rajan in Chapter 3). A report done by University Indonesia suggested that bribes to the government bureaucracy raised business cost by at least 10 percent during the post-1997 crisis period.[18] The under-funding of the judicial branches of the government (from the police to the supreme court judges) and the decentralization measures which give more autonomy to local governments have been noted as factors contributing to the high rates of corruption in Indonesia during the post-1997 financial crisis period.

Although there is evidence of concrete efforts to eradicate corruption in Indonesia, the most recent annual report by the Political and Economic Risk Consultancy for 2007 reserves the dubious distinction of the most corrupt country in Asia to Indonesia. The ranking was based on the surveys done on expatriates working in each of

---

[17] One caveat should be added here. Given the small sample observations, the results have to be interpreted with care.

[18] "Indonesia: Investment Climate Statement 2003", the Embassy of the United States website (http://www.usembassyjakarta.org/econ/investment3.html).

the listed economies, namely China, Hong Kong, India, Indonesia, Japan, Korea, Malaysia, Philippines, Taiwan, Thailand, Singapore, and Vietnam.

Several findings from the survey are worth highlighting for the case of Indonesia:

- Corruption abuses in Indonesia have been found to be most rampant among this group of economies for ten consecutive years since 1997 (Figure 5).
- Corruption is rated as a major deterrent to place investment in Indonesia.
- In contrast to the case of Thailand, where the abuses were felt significantly more in the public sector, corruption appears to be pervasive in both sectors in Indonesia.
- Although there have been some improvements, the commitment of the government to fight corruption has been rated as

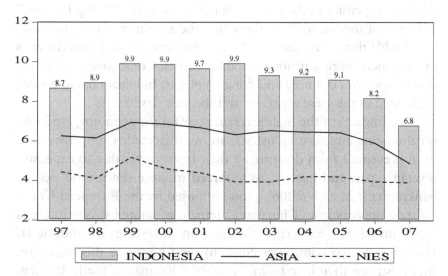

Figure 5: Corruption index.

Source: The Political Economic Risk Consultancy LTD. Asia economies include China, Hong Kong, India, Indonesia, Japan, Korea, Malaysia, Philippines, Singapore, Taiwan, Thailand, Vietnam. NIEs are Hong Kong, Korea, Singapore, and Taiwan. Rating (10) suggests the most severe incidences of corruption abuses.

"not serious". Similarly, the effectiveness of the judicial system to address corruption practices in the country is rated very low.

4.2. *Labor Law: Going Over Board?*

The post-President Suharto period (i.e., since mid-1998) has seen a number of revisions to the Manpower Act, including the 2003 Manpower Act giving workers many benefits and freedoms to organize. With the post-1997 revision, the current labor law has arguably swung from one in which workers being oppressed by the government to workers having too much power.

The Law No. 13 of 2003 Manpower Act has, in particular, been blamed for the rise in the labor cost in the country. One apparent source of the rising cost is the severance compensation. Under the 2003 Labor Act, employees were to be compensated not only when they were fired but also when they voluntarily quit the jobs. The cost of firing workers in Indonesia, estimated to be well over 100 weeks of wages, was among the most expensive in the world (Table 5). The 2007 "Doing Business" indicator of the World Bank show that the severance pay in Indonesia was double that of Thailand, and was significantly higher than the rates in many neighboring major economies in Asia. Consequently, from the cost perspectives of hiring and firing employer, Indonesia has in general been rated as the most expensive and the least flexible.

The impacts of the high severance pay on the economy, especially on the labor intensive industries, are multifaceted. Companies have been prevented from downsizing their labor forces due to expensive severance pay, and instead, were forced to close down (and declare bankruptcy). In early 2006, quotas imposed by the European Union on shoe imports from China and Vietnam generated strong interests from investors (especially foreign) in investing in Indonesia. However, "when companies come to see us and see this labor law, they postpone their investment" says the Chairman of the Indonesian Shoe Manufacturers' Association.[19]

---

[19] As quoted in: "Daily Policy Digest: Indonesia Labor Rule Takes Toll on Investment", National Center for Policy Analysis, December 8, 2006.

Table 5: Employment flexibility and hiring and firing costs. Selected Asian countries, 2007.

Country	Hiring		Firing			Rank
	Difficulty of Hiring Index (0–100)*	Cost of Hiring (% of salary)	Difficulty of Firing Index (0–100)*	Cost of Firing (weeks of wages)	Rigidity of Hours Index (0–100)*	
Indonesia	61	10	50	108	20	140
Cambodia	56	0	30	39	60	124
India	33	17	70	56	20	112
Philippines	56	9	20	91	40	118
Vietnam	0	17	70	87	40	104
Korea	11	18	30	91	60	110
China	11	44	40	91	20	78
Thailand	33	5	20	54	0	46
Malaysia	0	13	10	88	20	38
Singapore	0	13	0	4	0	3

Source: "Doing Business in 2007", the World Bank.
Note: * Index at 100 suggests most rigid or difficult and 0 captures most flexible.

The present government has taken the initiative to revise the 2003 Manpower Act as part of the investment-promotion package spelled out in a Presidential instruction issued in February 2006. In early-2006, the committee working on the revision of the Act proposed around 50 different changes to the 2003 law which would allow companies to hire contract-based workers and outsource permanent jobs and core businesses to other companies. The proposal was, however, withdrawn in the midst of heavy protest at the Presidential Palace in April 2006. Needless to say, the road to reforming the labor law will remain bumpy. By early 2007, there were about 188 labor unions in the country of which at least 68 were active and spread under four confederations. Compounding the already complex labor market condition in Indonesia, the fragmentation makes it even more difficult for the labor unions to agree on a common agenda for dialogue with both the government and the business community.

4.3. *Weak and Under-funded Infrastructure*

To achieve the targeted growth rate of 6 percent–7 percent per annum between 2005–2009, an estimate of $150 billion is needed to upgrade the nation-wide infrastructure in the country. Investment in infrastructure has, however, shrunk from 6 percent of GDP before the break of 1997 financial crisis to a paltry 2 percent in 2000, and only recovered to about 3 percent in 2004/2005 (Guerin (2006) and World Bank (2007)). At the current incremental-capital-output-ratios (ICORs) in Indonesia, investment has to grow by more than 12 percent for the GDP to expand by more than 6 percent in 2007. The investment growth for 2006 was less than 3 percent.

The lack of investment in infrastructure has partly been the impact of fiscal restraint and tight monetary policy implemented for a number of years during the post-1997 period. Largely due to the high cost of restructuring of the banking and corporate sector, the total central government debt outstanding rose to as high as 100 percent of GDP in 1999, and gradually declining to about

44 percent of GDP by June 2006.[20] The annual interest payment of this debt averaged about 18% of total annual central government expenditure from 2001 to 2005. In comparison, the average annual development spending of the central government during the same period was only about 14 percent of its annual expenditure (World Bank, 2007).

The lack of infrastructural investment has been compounded further by the decision of the provincial governments to put their development funds in the Bank Indonesia certificates (SBI), instead of pumping the funds into much-needed development projects. Due to efforts to mop up the excess liquidity caused by the injection of capital to troubled banks at the early stage of the 1997 financial crisis and the intervention to manage the volatility of the Indonesian rupiah, the 3-month SBI rates were hovering around 13.5 percent per annum during the period of 1999 to 2005 (Siregar and Rajaguru, 2005; Siregar, 2005). The relatively high return from what is considered to be a safe instrument has turned the SBI into a more attractive investment choice than investing in the real sector. Contributing further to the overall lack of liquidity, the commercial banks in Indonesia were reported to hold around 22 billion dollar worth of SBI in early 2007.

To attract investment into the country, the Investment Summits I and II were organized in Jakarta in January 2005 and November 2006, respectively. Unfortunately, achievements have, at best, been modest. During the first summit, 91 infrastructure projects worth a total of $145 billion were to be bid. By mid 2006, only three pipeline gas contracts, one power plan contract, and three toll road contracts were awarded. Many blamed the failure of the first summit on the inability of the government to follow through on the investment plans.[21]

---

[20] The regional governments in Indonesia had very small debt outstanding, less than 0.5 percent of the total government debt.

[21] Our discussions with various sources (including market players and government officials) suggest that too many "back-door" interventions by the high-ranking officials and/or their business associates have resulted in a low realized number of investment projects.

4.4. *High Starting-Up and Operating Cost*

With the challenges and shortcomings elaborated above, it is therefore not surprising that the cost of starting-up business in Indonesia
has been estimated to be the highest among major Asian economies
(Table 6). The high number of procedures (second only to China in
the Emerging Asia list considered here) is exposing potential investors
to not only delays in getting the required business permits (as
reflected by the length of time to get the permit), but also to rampant
corruption abuses discussed earlier. During his meeting with the
Vietnamese Business Delegation in early 2006, the coordinating
Minister of Economic Affairs and Industry of Indonesia admitted that
the investment regulation and taxation in Vietnam are more advanced
than those in Indonesia. The minister highlighted among others the
need to eliminate complicated investment rules, such as different
treatment for local and foreign investors and to reduce corporate tax.
More importantly, the list of contributing factors to the investment
climate discussed earlier has both the starting costs in Indonesia,
and the operation costs of already established firms in all sectors
of the economy. Business in Indonesia is close to 90 percent.

Table 6:   Starting business indicators, selected East Asian countries, 2007.

Country	Procedures (number)	Time (days)	Cost (% of income per capita)	Minimum capital (% of income per capita)	Rank
Indonesia	12	97	86.7	83.4	161
Cambodia	10	86	236.4	66.2	159
China	13	35	9.3	213.1	128
Korea	12	22	15.2	299.7	116
Philippines	11	48	18.7	1.8	108
Vietnam	11	50	44.5	0.0	97
India	11	35	73.7	0.0	88
Malaysia	9	30	19.7	0.0	71
Thailand	8	33	5.8	0.0	28
Singapore	6	6	0.8	0.0	11

Source: "Doing Business in 2007", the World Bank.

Only Cambodia reports a higher rate. Naturally, the worst-affected sectors are labor intensive, such as the textile, garment, and footwear industries.

Another factor contributing to the rise in the operating costs has also been the volatile and increasing price of crude oil in recent years. In its efforts to reform the budget, the Indonesian government has been attempting to undertake massive cuts in oil subsidies, especially since 2005, hence further exposing the local economy to the volatile world price of crude oil. A study done by the Citigroup has indicated that the Indonesian economy is among the most adversely exposed to the volatile global oil price. The study claims that if the price of crude oil were to reach US$100 per barrel, it would raise the domestic inflation rate by about 1.4 percent in Indonesia. At the same time, the economic cost of the high crude oil price is estimated to be 1 percent of its GDP (Table 7).

5. Internationalization Strategy of Ethnic Chinese Businesses

The role of Indonesian ethnic Chinese in the local economy is critical. In late 1990 and early 2000, the ethnic Chinese controlled over

Table 7: Asia emerging markets most exposed to an oil shock (oil Price = US$100) (rank by most adversely affected)

Impact on GDP (in %)		Impact on CPI Inflation (in %)	
Singapore	−1.4	India	2.1
Thailand	−1.3	Thailand	1.8
Philippines	−1.2	Philippines	1.7
China	−1.1	Indonesia	1.4
Indonesia	−0.9	Malaysia	1.4
Malaysia	−0.8	Singapore	1.4
Hong Kong	−0.7	Korea	0.7
India	−0.6	China	0.5
Korea	−0.3	Taiwan	0.5
Taiwan	−0.1	Hong Kong	0.1

Source: Global economic outlook and strategy, Citigroup, July 20, 2006.

80 percent of corporate assets and 160 of the 200 largest businesses in Indonesia (Yeung, 1999). As discussed earlier, this group of businesses is an important driver of the surge of outward direct investment from Indonesia. To understand what is behind the surge of outward investment from Indonesia, it is therefore imperative that we consider the development strategy of this key group of businesses in the country, particularly its internalization strategy.

A recent study by Yeung (1999) underlines four driving forces behind the internalization of ethnic Chinese businesses in South–East Asia:

(1) Tighter competition from global players domestically;
(2) Saturated home markets;
(3) Their home-based competitive advantages dissipate quickly through deregulation and;
(4) Their family successors are more outward looking in business practices and opportunity-seeking.

With the push for economic reforms aimed at attracting foreign investment to the local economy in most of the major South–East Asian economies since early 1980s, the monopolistic advantage and subsidies often enjoyed by the major ethnic-Chinese conglomerates dissipated. On the other hand, the rise of the South–East Asian economies, especially the export-oriented sectors, opened up new opportunities for the domestic firms to take advantage of the economic scale available in the International market. At the same time, there has been a gradual transition of management control to the younger generation of these largely family businesses. More and more of the new generation of business leaders looked to establish market shares abroad. The opening of China and the emergence of its special economic zones further facilitated the "regionalization" of the ethnic Chinese businesses. The Salim group of Indonesia, the Kuok brothers of Malaysia, and the Charoen Pokphand of Thailand were some of the leading ethnic Chinese conglomerates expanding their networks to different parts of Asia.

It is also important to note here that the violent anti-Chinese riots in Solo and Jakarta on the eve of the former President Suharto's fall in May 1998 had also been responsible for a sudden outflow of capital, owned by both ethnic and non-ethnic Chinese, from the local economy. Since then there has been continuous efforts by the government of Indonesia to improve the social and political environment for the Chinese Indonesians (Efferin and Pontjoharyo, 2006). These steps included the ratification of the United Nations Conventions on the Elimination of All Forms of Racial Discrimination (Wie, 2006). These efforts have, however, seen limited success in attracting back capital parked abroad by Indonesian citizens (including that of Chinese ethnics). A recent report published in a local magazine claims up to US$87 billion of Indonesian-owned assets/capital were still parked in Singapore in late 2006.[22] Without a significant improvement in the overall investment climate in Indonesia, it is doubtful that a substantial repatriation of this capital will take place.

6. Conclusion and Policy Implications

During the early to mid-1990s, the stock of inward direct investment continued to dwarf the stock of outward investment. In 1997, the stock of direct investment in Indonesia was close to 5 times that of outward investment. During the next decade, the landscape of the local economy has changed drastically. The economy has seen negative inward investment for five consecutive years (1998–2002), during which time the inward investment declined by more than 75 percent from its highest level in 1997. At the same time, there has been a steady flow of outward investments from Indonesia, contributing to net negative flows of inward investment during that five year span starting 1998.

This chapter has also shown that the outward investment of the Indonesian businesses has targeted sectors which have been badly in need of capital injections locally. The infrastructure sector in

---

[22] "Indonesian Rich People's Money Flourishing in Singapore", INFO Bank, December 2006, pp. 92–95.

Indonesia for instance is in a dire need of fresh capital to help support the overall target of GDP growth rates between 6 and 7 percent annually. Similarly, the more important than ever labor-intensive industries, such as textile, garment and footwear, have seen less and less fresh investment commitments and this has been compounded by the closures of major foreign firms.

This chapter has identified a list of key determinant factors of OFDI in Indonesia. Given the recent experiences of what could be considered as the lost decade for the Indonesian economy, the economic and social cost of failure to significantly eradicate corruption abuses, improve investment rules and regulations, reform labor law, and address infrastructure needs, will escalate exponentially in the near future. Addressing the challenges discussed earlier should also help position the local economy to compete and to benefit from the rapid development of the Asia region, pushed by the surges of the economies of China and India in the near future.

The chapter has also highlighted other factors contributing to the rise in outward investment from Indonesia. The internationalization strategy of the major ethnic-Chinese conglomerates has started as early as late 1980s and early 1990s. The capacity of the locally owned firms to compete in the global market should be positively recognized. Some promising progress has also been reported from the corporate sector restructuring in the country. Key performance indicators of the corporate sectors in the country suggest that the local firms are liquid and in a position to expand their productions abroad.

The present and future task for the government of Indonesia is, therefore, to ensure that the recent progress in the corporate sector and also the emergence of the Indonesian conglomerates as major regional corporations should not be a zero-sum game where the local economy is going to be left behind. It is imperative that the government of Indonesia strategically designs its macroeconomic policies to assist the local industries to move into higher value-added manufacturing chains of productions and service industries. With the rise of China and India, followed by the rapid emergence of the

Indo-Chinese economies, the old strategy of competing primarily based on labor cost and market size is unlikely to be effective.

References

Bende–Nabende, A and J Slater (2003). Private capital formation: Short-and long-run crowding-in (out) effects in ASEAN, 1971–1999. *Economics Bulletin*, 3(27), 1–16.

Efferin, S and W Pontjoharyo (2006). Chinese Indonesian business in the era of globalization : Ethnicity, culture and the rise of China. in *Southeast Asia's Chinese Businesses in an Era of Globalization: Coping with the Rise of China*, L Suryadinata (ed.), pp. 102–160, Institute of Southeast Asian Studies, Singapore.

Ghura, D and B Goodwin (2000). Determinants of private investment: Across-regional empirical investigation. *Applied Economics*, 32(14), 1819–1829.

Guerin, B (2006). Growth too slow for comfort in Indonesia. *Asia Times Online*, October 31.

Kanwar, OS (2005). An address at the 8th meeting of India–Indonesia joint business council (JBC) August 8, New Delhi.

Lecraw, DJ (1993). Outward direct investment by Indonesian firms: Motivation and effects. *Journal of International Business Studies*, 24(3), 589–600.

Mukherjee, A (2006). Commentary: Indonesia's labor pains. *People's Daily Online*, June 29.

Serven, L (2002). Real exchange rate uncertainty and private investment in developing countries. Policy Research Working Paper No. 2823, The World Bank.

Siregar, R (2005). Interest rate policy and its implication of the banking restructuring programs in Indonesia during the 1997 financial crisis: An empirical investigation. In *Institutional Change in Southeast Asia*, F Sjoholm and J Tongzon (eds.), pp. 72–90. Routledge Press.

Siregar, R and S Rajaguru (2005). Sources of variation between the inflation rates of Korea, Thailand and Indonesia during the post-1997 crisis. *Journal of Policy Modeling*, 27(7), 867–884.

UNCTAD (2006). *The World Investment Report*.

Van der Eng, P (2004). Business in Indonesia: Old problems and new challenges. In *Business in Indonesia: New Challenges, Old Problems*, MC Basri and P Van der Eng (eds.), pp. 1–20. Singapore: Institute of Southeast Asian Studies.

Wie, TK (2006). The Indonesian government's economic policies towards the ethnic Chinese: Beyond economic nationalism? In *Southeast Asia's Chinese Businesses in an Era of Globalization: Coping with the Rise of China*, L Suryadinata (ed.), pp. 76–101. Singapore: Institute of Southeast Asian Studies.

Wong, J (2006). China's economic rise and its implications for Southeast Asia: The big picture. In *Southeast Asia's Chinese Businesses in an Era of Globalization: Coping with the Rise of China*, L Suryadinata (ed.), pp. 14–37. Singapore: Institute of Southeast Asian Studies.

World Bank (2007). Spending for development: Making the most of Indonesia's new opportunities. *Indonesia Public Expenditure Review 2007*, Jakarta, Indonesia.

Yeung, HW-C (1999). The internationalization of ethnic Chinese business firms from Southeast Asia: Strategies, processes and competitive advantage. *International Journal of Urban and Regional Research*, 23(1), 103–127.

About the Editors

Rajan, Ramkishen S.

Ramkishen Rajan is an Associate Professor at the School of Public Policy, George Mason University (GMU), a position he has held since January 2006. Prior to that he was on the faculty of the School of Economics, University of Adelaide for five years. Prof. Rajan has also taught at the National University of Singapore and the Claremont McKenna College and has held visiting positions in various institutes in Asia. He specializes in international economic policy with particular reference to the emerging Asia-Pacific region. Prof. Rajan has been a consultant with the Asian Development Bank, the World Bank, the UN-ESCAP, and other institutions.

Kumar, Rajiv

Rajiv Kumar is the Director and Chief Executive of the Indian Council for Research on International Economic Relations (ICRIER), a New Delhi based economic policy think tank that was established in 1981. Dr Kumar has held this position since February 2006. From August 2004 to January 2006, he was Chief Economist with Confederation of Indian Industry (CII), and prior to that he worked with Asian Development Bank, Manila for over 10 years. He is a member of the National Security Advisory Board as well as a member of the Telecom Regulatory Authority of India since January 2007.

Virgill, Nicola

Nicola Virgill is a PhD candidate at the School of Public Policy, George Mason University. She received a Bachelor of Arts Degree in

Economics from Vassar College and a Master of Science Degree in Political Economy from the School of Oriental and African Studies (SOAS), University of London. Ms Virgill's research interests are economic development, trade policy, and entrepreneurship. Before coming to George Mason University, Ms Virgill was Deputy Manager in the Policy Unit of the Bank Supervision Department at The Central Bank of The Bahamas.

About the Contributors

Aminian, Nathalie

Nathalie Aminian is an Associate Professor of Economics, Faculty of International Affairs, University of Le Havre, France. She is a researcher at the Centre d'Etudes et de Recherches en Economie et Gestion Logistique (CERENE) and co-organizes an International Conference series in collaboration with Inha University, Inchon, Korea. Prof. Aminian previously served as Director of the Master Degree in International Business with a specialization in Foreign Trade and International Finance.

Ariff, Mohamed

Mohamed Ariff (Emeritus Professor) is the Executive Director of the Malaysian Institute of Economic Research (MIER). He has authored, co-authored and edited many books and monographs and numerous journal articles on issues relating to international trade, foreign direct investment, and regional economic integration.

Aykut, Dilek

Dilek Aykut is an Economist and Foreign Direct Investment (FDI) Specialist for the International Finance Team of the World Bank's Development Prospects Group, which produces the annual flagship publication Global Development Finance. Dr Aykut conducts research on FDI-related issues including trends, determinants, South–South FDI, and sectoral analysis.

Cheng, Shoaming

Shaoming Cheng is a Research Assistant Professor at the Regional Research Institute at West Virginia University. He received his PhD in Public Policy from George Mason University. His research focuses on firms' location strategy and the location of economic activities, the reasons why some places prosper and thrive while others decline, the ways in which local areas may capture the benefits of desired development strategies, and how entrepreneurship replaces traditional production assets in economic development.

Fung, K.C.

K.C. Fung is a Professor of Economics at University of California, Santa Cruz. He was previously a Senior Economist at the White House Council of Economic Advisers. Prof. Fung has been a consultant for the World Bank, the WTO, the USITC, and the ADBI as well as a senior research fellow at the BIS. He has taught at Stanford University, the University of Wisconsin–Madison, and the University of Hong Kong.

Goldstein, Andrea

Andrea Goldstein is a Senior Economist at the OECD Directorate for Financial and Enterprise Affairs, in charge of the Project on Freedom of Investment, National Security, and "Strategic" Industries. Andrea is involved in various research projects on multinationals from emerging, transition and developing countries, a topic on which he recently published *Multinational Companies from Emerging Economies — Composition, Conceptualization, and Direction in the Global Economy* (Palgrave, 2007).

Gunawan, Anton

Anton H. Gunawan is Country Economist for Citibank Indonesia, under the Asia Pacific Economic and Market Analysis Division. Prior to joining Citi Indonesia, he was with the Faculty of Economics,

University of Indonesia and was the Associate Director for Research at the Institute for Economic and Social Research at the University. Anton holds an MPhil in economics from Columbia University and MA in economics from University of Chicago.

Hattari, Rabin

Rabin Hattari is a consultant at The World Bank in the Finance, Urban, and Economics Department of the Sustainability Development Network. Prior to that he was employed at the International Monetary Fund (IMF) for five years, and also worked as an economic consultant for KPMG Consulting for two years. Mr Hattari specializes in International Economic Policy with particular reference to the developing Asia-Pacific region. He holds Economics degrees from the University of Georgia at Athens (B.Soc. Sci.), University of Indonesia (M.B.A.), and George Mason University (M.A.). He is completing his PhD in Economics at George Mason University.

Hiratsuka, Daisuke

Daisuke Hiratsuka is Director-General, Development Studies Center, Institute of Developing Economies in Japan. Dr Hiratsuka specializes in Economic Development and Regional Integration with particular reference to East Asia. He recently edited a volume on *East Asia's De Facto Economic Integration* (Palgrave, 2006).

Kumar, Nagesh

Nagesh Kumar is Director-General of Research and Information System for Developing countries (RIS) which is an autonomous research institution established with the financial support of the Government of India. He joined the faculty of RIS in 1985. During 1993–1998, Dr Kumar served on the faculty of the United Nations University — Institute for New Technologies (UNU/INTECH), Maastricht, the Netherlands. He has also been consultant to the World Bank, ADB, UNCTAD, UNIDO, UN-ESCAP, ILO and is the recipient of the

Exim Bank's first international trade research award and a GDN Research Medal. Dr Kumar has written extensively on international economic issues and regional economic integration in Asia.

Lin, Chelsea

Chelsea C. Lin is an Associate Professor of Economics at the National Dong Hwa University in Taiwan, since 2001. Prof. Lin's research focuses on areas of the international trade and the economies of East Asia, including the political economy of trade policies, the transition of the Japanese Keiretsu, and the foreign direct investment in China.

Lopez, Gregore Pio

Greg Lopez is Senior Research Officer at the Malaysian Institute of Economic Research (MIER). His research focuses on international trade and institutional economics. He is also a member of the Federation of Malaysian Manufactures Private Sector Task Force on Free Trade Agreements (FTAs).

Pavida Pananond

Pavida Pananond is an Associate Professor of International Business at Thammasat Business School, Thammasat University. Her research interests cover foreign direct investment and emerging multinationals from developing countries. Prof. Pananond's latest publications include "The Changing Dynamics of Thai Multinationals after the Asian Economic Crisis", *Journal of International Management* (November 2007), and "Explaining the Emergence of Thai Multinationals" in Henry Wai-chung Yeung (ed.), *Handbook of Research on Asian Business* (Edward Elgar, 2007).

Siregar, Reza

Reza Y. Siregar is a Senior Lecturer at the School of Economics, University of Adelaide in Australia, and an International Consultant

Economist at the International Monetary Fund, Singapore Regional Training Institute. He holds a PhD in Economics from the Department of Economics, Brown University.

Stough, Roger

Roger Stough holds the Northern Virginia Endowed Chair and Directs the Mason Enterprise Center as well as serving as Associate Dean for Research in the School of Public Policy at George Mason University. Prof. Stough has published over 20 books and numerous scholarly and professional papers in the areas of regional economics and policy, transport policy and entrepreneurship.

Index